10.95
/mo

CE

Sourcebook
in Criminalistics

Sourcebook
in Criminalistics

Carroll R. Hormachea
Virginia Commonwealth University
Richmond, Virginia

Reston Publishing Company, Inc., Reston, Virginia 22090
A Prentice-Hall Company

Library of Congress Cataloging in Publication Data

Hormachea, Carroll R.
  Sourcebook in criminalistics.

  Includes bibliographical references.
  1. Criminal investigation—Addresses, essays,
lectures.   I. Title.
HV8073.H735   364.12   73–9554
ISBN 0–87909–778–7

© 1974 by
Reston Publishing Company, Inc.
A Prentice-Hall Company
Box 547
Reston, Virginia 22090

10 9 8 7 6 5 4 3 2 1

Printed in the United States of America.

Foreword

With each passing year, the need for a closer cooperation between the police officer and the scientist becomes more apparent. As the complexities of the society increase, so too must the techniques of criminal investigation become more sophisticated, if they are to keep pace in solving crimes. The basics of police work remain the same but law enforcement personnel, in their quest for a more professional status, have become acutely aware of the need for the cooperation between themselves and the crime laboratory.

The modern police officer finds that the crime laboratory has become a significant part of the investigation team. Through this alliance, the officer can obtain technical evidence which is otherwise unobtainable. A case in point is the rise in narcotics-related crime. Crimes involving narcotics and dangerous drugs rely heavily on laboratory techniques to develop evidence.

Throughout my tenure as a police officer, later as Commander of Investigative Operations, and more recently as Chief of Police, I have been very much aware of the role of the laboratory in investigative work, both through the crime laboratory in our Bureau of Police as well as working in close contact with the Chief Medical Examiner's Office and the F.B.I. in solving crimes. Emphasizing the importance of the crime laboratory is the requirement that all members of the recruit class attend lectures by the Chief Medical Examiner, as well as attending an autopsy to learn the techniques of handling and preparing physical evidence.

The importance of the crime laboratory has been further underscored in Virginia by the establishment of the Bureau of Forensic Sciences. Through this agency, a statewide network of regional laboratories is being established to assist local police departments.

I feel that any person who wishes to enter the field of law enforcement should make himself familiar with the techniques of field investigation as well as ascertaining the capabilities of the crime laboratory in the development of evidence.

Through this book, I feel that Professor Hormachea has made a significant contribution to the police literature for the student of law enforcement as well as the practicing police officer.

Col. Frank. S. Duling
Chief, Bureau of Police
Richmond, Virginia

Preface

Investigation of crime and criminals, while basic to police work, is one of the more complex functions of the officer's duty. Methodically, using various investigatory techniques and equipment, he must attempt to piece together the evidence which will solve the crime and bring the guilty party to justice. One such approach is the application of scientific technology to crime detection or criminalistics.

Criminalistics utilizes the physical and natural sciences in the collection and evaluation of evidence. Such analyses of evidence are limited only by the training and imagination of the police scientist. During recent years there has been an increase in the use of laboratory techniques in crime detection.

The application of scientific techniques to the system of criminal justice is much broader than the evaluation of physical evidence. As scientific technology has progressed, the utilization of such innovations as the computer and electronics offers the system greater flexibility in combatting and solving crime.

This book is designed to offer the student an introduction to the field of criminalistics as well as to show the application of technological advances to crime prevention. The student is offered the opportunity to study the application of these various methods and techniques from members of the scientific and academic community, as well as from practicing criminalists.

The role of the computer as an aid to the criminal justice system is discussed. The advances in automated data processing offer a whole new world of ideas in fighting crime, as well as serving as an instrument for the prevention of crime.

Electronics has also opened new horizons for law enforcement and other elements of the justice system. Through the use of electronic technology, voice prints have been developed. Bugging, bomb detection, weapons detection, and even electronic photography have developed as real assets in the investigation process.

The *why* of scientific investigation is not to be overlooked, and the student is offered the rationale, as well as the techniques, for the gathering and preserving of evidence for the police laboratory.

Finally, the book deals with the future promise of science for the criminal justice system. The widespread use of the helicopter can be effective in the war on crime, patrolling and making would-be criminals painfully aware of their presence through sight and sound. Neutron Activation Analysis and its value in dealing with questioned documents and fibers also gives the student a promise of things to come.

Hopefully the student will find that this book will serve as a guide to the vast and fascinating field of criminalistics.

The author wishes to acknowledge the assistance of Messrs. Matthew Fox and David Ungerer of Reston Publishing Company and their staff for their cooperation and encouragement. Finally, a debt of gratitude to my wife, Marion, without whose encouragement and help this project would not have been.

Carroll R. Hormachea

Acknowledgments

"Forty Years of Distinguished Scientific Assistance to Law Enforcement." Reprinted by permission of Mr. L. Patrick Gray, Acting Director, Federal Bureau of Investigation, from the *FBI Law Enforcement Bulletin*, November 1972.

"The Investigative Process," by James W. Osterburg. Reprinted by permission from the *Journal of Criminal Law, Criminology and Police Science*, Vol. 59, No. 1. Published by the Northwestern University School of Law.

"What the Bones Tell—Today," by Dr. T. D. Stewart. Reprinted by permission of Mr. L. Patrick Gray, Acting Director, Federal Bureau of Investigation, from the *FBI Law Enforcement Bulletin*, February 1972.

"Landmarks and Hallmarks in Scientific Evidence," by Edwin Conrad. Reprinted by permission from the *Journal of Forensic Sciences*, October 1971. Published by Callaghan and Company, Chicago.

"Identification and the Forensic Pathologist," by G. T. Mann, M.D., and H. R. Wood, M.D. Reprinted by permission of the Chief Medical Examiner's Office of the Virginia Department of Health, Richmond.

"Physical Evidence Utilization in the Administration of Criminal Justice," by Brian Parker and Joseph Peterson. Reprinted from *Physical Evidence Utilization in the Administration of Criminal Justice*, by Brian Parker and Joseph Peterson. National Institute of Law Enforcement and Criminal Justice of the Law Enforcement Assistance Administration, Washington, D.C., 1972. pp. 14–23.

"Collection and Preservation of Scientific Evidence." Reprinted by permission of the Chief Medical Examiner's Office of the Virginia Department of Health, Richmond.

"The Location of Hidden Objects," by Barry J. Blain. Reprinted by permission from *The Police Journal*, June 1969. Published by the Police Journal of Chichester, Sussex, England.

"The Investigation of Deaths Due to Drowning," by W. M. Jennings, M.D. Reprinted by permission of the Chief Medical Examiner's Office of the Virginia Department of Health, Richmond.

"Statistical Features of Rape," by Arthur F. Schiff. Reprinted by permission from the *Journal of Forensic Sciences*, January 1969. Published by Callaghan and Company, Chicago.

"Breath Testers." Reprinted by permission from *The Police Chief*, August 1971. Published by the International Association of Chiefs of Police, Washington, D.C.

"The Kennedy Assassination: Hairs and Fibers." Reprinted from *The Report of the President's Commission on the Assassination of President John F. Kennedy*. U.S. Government Printing Office, Washington, D.C., 1964. pp. 586–592.

"Checlass," by E. H. W. Schroeder. Reprinted by permission from the *Journal of Forensic Sciences*, April 1971. Published by Callaghan and Company, Chicago.

"Disguised Handwriting," by E. F. Alford, Jr. Reprinted by permission from the *Journal of Forensic Sciences*, October 1970. Published by Callaghan and Company, Chicago.

"Tool Marks: An Aid in the Solution of Auto Larcenies," by Susan M. Komar. Reprinted by permission from the *Journal of Criminal Law, Criminology and Police Science*, Vol. 60, No. 1. Published by the Northwestern University School of Law.

"Fingerprinting: A Story of Science vs. Crime." Reprinted by permission of Mr. L. Patrick Gray, Acting Director, Federal Bureau of Investigation, from the *FBI Law Enforcement Bulletin*, July 1971.

"The Kennedy Assassination: Wound Ballistics Experiments." Reprinted from *The Report of the President's Commission on the Assassination of President John F. Kennedy.* U.S. Government Printing Office, Washington, D.C., 1964. pp. 580–586.

"The Role of Criminalistics in White-Collar Crimes," by Q. Y. Kwan, P. Rajeswaran, B. P. Parker, and M. Amir. Reprinted by permission from the *Journal of Criminal Law, Criminology and Police Science,* Vol. 62, No. 3. Published by the Northwestern University School of Law.

"A Simple Tool for Complex Problems," by Robert P. Shumate. Reprinted by permission from *The Police Yearbook,* 1968. Published by the International Association of Chiefs of Police, Washington, D.C.

"Criminal Justice Information Systems," from *Task Force Report: Science and Technology.* Prepared for the President's Commission on Law Enforcement and the Administration of Justice. Published by the U.S. Government Printing Office, Washington, D.C., 1967. pp. 68–79.

"NCIC—A Tribute to Cooperative Spirit." Reprinted by permission of Mr. L. Patrick Gray, Acting Director, Federal Bureau of Investigation, from the *FBI Law Enforcement Bulletin,* February 1972.

"Bank Surveillance Cameras." Reprinted by permission of Mr. L. Patrick Gray, Acting Director, Federal Bureau of Investigation, from the *FBI Law Enforcement Bulletin,* June 1971.

"Identification of Suspects by the Voiceprint Technique," by E. W. Nash and O. I. Tosi. Reprinted by permission from *The Police Chief,* December 1971. Published by the International Association of Chiefs of Police, Washington, D.C.

"Privacy of Voice Communication," by R. L. Carlson, J. M. Tellez, and W. L. Schreiber. Reprinted by permission from *The Police Chief,* August 1971. Published by the International Association of Chiefs of Police, Washington, D.C.

"Security Needs Science," by Jon Hawington. Reprinted by permission of the American Society for Industrial Security from *Industrial Security,* February 1972.

"A National Criminalistics Research Program," by Charles R. Kingston. Reprinted by permission from the *Journal of Forensic Sciences,* January 1971. Published by Callaghan and Company, Chicago.

"X-Ray Standards for Law Enforcement," by Charles N. Smith. Reprinted by permission from *The Police Chief,* May 1972. Published by the International Association of Chiefs of Police, Washington, D.C.

"Modern Methods Solve Crimes, Foil Crooks." Reprinted by permission from *Chemical and Engineering News,* October 20, 1969. Published by the American Chemical Society, Washington, D.C.

Contents

SECTION I

Elementary......
The Scientific Approach
to Crime Detection

"Elementary, My Dear . . . ." This famous phrase is recalled by mystery fans with great fascination as they picture the master detective of fiction making a pronouncement that he had solved the crime by identifying certain elements of physical evidence such as the criminal wearing built up shoes. Superior crime detection and science triumphed and the famous detective had solved another crime.

Investigation of crime is not usually so easy. The development of a sound case based on physical evidence is the result of diligent and patient work on the part of the detective assigned to the case as well as the support of other arms of the police service, including the police laboratory and the use of outside experts in the forensic science field.

This section serves to introduce the concept of scientific investigation and its application. Further, there must be an understanding that criminalistics is not just the application of chemistry or physics to evidence but the use of all of the physical sciences and many of the social sciences in the development of information. The charting of such information shows the need for well rounded education for the criminalist.

CHAPTER 1

Forty Years of Distinguished Scientific Assistance to Law Enforcement

A scheduled airliner crashed near the southeastern tip of North Carolina, taking the lives of all aboard. Experts from the Federal Bureau of Investigation's Laboratory, experienced in many areas of scientific examination, rushed to the scene to assist in determining the cause of the disaster.

Some of the first pieces of evidence to be examined were various articles of clothing from the body of one of the passengers found some 16 miles from the crash scene. These were soon followed by hundreds of other pieces of evidence which quickly set into motion the scientific personnel and equipment representing virtually every segment of an elaborate crime detection facility—the FBI Laboratory. Slowly the test tubes, microscopes, and spectrographs yielded from the debris found at the crash site the grim evidence that a bomb had been responsible for the fatal disaster to the aircraft, its crew, and passengers.

The final report compiled by the FBI Laboratory indicated that a dynamite explosion had taken place aboard the ill-fated flight. Triggered by means of a dry cell battery, the bomb had vented its carnage in the passenger compartment near the seat occupied by the victim whose body was found a considerable distance from the main crash scene.

Each day, in similar manner, the resources of the FBI Laboratory, which celebrated its 40th Anniversary November 24, 1972, are mobilized in the mounting struggle against crime.

The Formative Years

The 40-year history of the FBI Laboratory is one of growth and accomplishment. During the fall of 1932, a few file cabinets were removed from one room in the old Southern Railway Building, 13th and Pennsylvania Avenue, NW., Washington, D.C., in order to find available space for the crime laboratory of the FBI, then known as the Bureau of Investigation. One microscope was moved into the room, along with ultraviolet light equipment, a large drawing board, a helixometer, and some surplus bookshelves. A few tables were added to the equipment, and plans were made to bring in photographic instruments. A crime lab was in the making.

During the formation of its Laboratory, the FBI launched a program to locate businessmen, manufacturers, and scientists whose knowledge and experience might be useful in guiding the new facility through its infancy. With the future in mind an FBI Special Agent was enrolled in a course of study offered by the scientific crime detection laboratory of a large midwestern university.

The mere collecting and grouping together of scientific equipment, however, certainly did not constitute a complete laboratory for service to law enforcement. It needed qualified personnel. Training and selection of the Laboratory's staff were among the most important initial efforts. Then followed the slow but necessary task of educating law enforcement agencies throughout the country to the potential value of scientific examinations in criminal investigations.

Following the acquisition of some basic scientific instruments, the selection of properly trained personnel to operate them, and the notification of interested law enforcement agencies of its purpose and availability, the FBI Laboratory was officially established on November 24, 1932.

The FBI Laboratory facilities and experts are available without charge to all duly constituted Federal, State, county, and municipal law enforcement agencies of the United States and its territorial possessions. Examinations are made with the understanding that evidence is connected with an official criminal investigation.

During the first month of service, FBI Laboratory examiners handled 20 cases. In its first full year of operation, the volume increased to a total of 963 examinations. By the next year that figure was more than doubled. But this was only a thin shadow of the potential that loomed ahead for the FBI Laboratory. By the end of fiscal year 1972, total examinations had reached 495,000 for the preceding 12 months.

Specialization

While the new Laboratory gave assistance to law enforcement agencies of all sizes and from all regions of the Nation, the FBI received commensurate cooperation from them in return. In addition, manufacturers from throughout the country provided assistance in the form of reference collections or standards files. Typical are the Typewriter Standards File, the Automotive Paint File, and numerous other files for comparing known manufactured items with suspect samples. Just as the fingerprint examiner depends heavily on the comparison of a known print and a questioned print, so too does the Laboratory scientist, in many instances, depend on a comparison examination. The standards files are invaluable for this purpose.

The FBI Laboratory is staffed with specialists experienced in many scientific and technical fields. Specialization enhances the examination capability of the Laboratory, in that each unit limits its examinations to a relatively narrow field, thus making it possible for that specific department to research intensively in its discipline. This enables each unit to apply the most up-to-date equipment and knowledge to every aspect of its examinations.

A continuous program of adaptation and innovation is underway in the FBI Laboratory utilizing new developments in the examination of evidentiary materials. Many of the crimes investigated by local law enforcement agencies result in submissions of objects and samples found at the crime scenes to the FBI Laboratory for analysis and possible information of investigative value. Cases involving homicides and assaults on very young children place particularly heavy emphasis on the work of the crime laboratory because of the victim's frequent inability to offer effective testimony to the crime or make a positive identification of the assailant.

Document Section

Almost the entire spectrum of criminal violations is represented by evidence received in the Document Section. Examinations of handwriting, hand printing, typewriting, indented writing, obliterated writing, charred papers, shoe prints, and tire treads result in the appearances of document experts of the FBI Laboratory in all jurisdictional levels of courts throughout the United States and territories with ever-increasing frequency.

Recent testimony by a document examiner aided in conviction of a burglar and attempted rapist who, during the night of September 27, 1971, broke into the home of a Charles County, Md., woman who was alone and asleep in an upstairs bedroom. The intruder used matches from several paper matchbooks to light his way through the home, discarding the matches as they burned near the end.

The intruder proceeded to the upstairs bedroom where he attempted to rape the victim. He fled after the woman was successful in resisting the attack.

A short time later the suspect was arrested by local police. In his pockets were found several matchbooks which were submitted to the FBI Laboratory along with the match stems found at the crime scene. A Document Section expert identified two of the match stems found at the crime scene as having been torn from two of the books of matches found in the suspect's pockets.

The National Fraudulent Check File, Bank Robbery Note File, and Anonymous Letter File of the Document Section are familiar names to law enforcement agencies. These reference files serve as invaluable tools in associating unidentified evidence from throughout the country with particular suspects or crimes.

For example, during the period from 1965 to early January 1971, 168 questioned documents were submitted to the FBI Laboratory for examination in a case involving scurrilous, racist, and threatening letters which had been mailed to many prominent persons including a former Vice-President and three U.S. Senators. These letters, although anonymous and submitted from various parts of the country, were associated with each other, based on handwriting and hand printing, as a result of the Document Section's Anonymous Letter File.

Examination by the FBI Laboratory of one of the letters revealed a distinctive watermark. Another letter was found to contain the name "Morris" (fictitious) in indented writing.

Using information furnished by the FBI Laboratory concerning the watermark, the paper was traced by FBI Agents to a midwestern city siding and roofing contractor. A review of company records revealed the firm had an employee named Melvin James Morris (fictitious) who subsequently was identified by an FBI document examiner as the writer of the letters.

Morris was arrested, tried, and found guilty of violating the Federal Extortion Statute, thus ending a steady flow of threats which had spanned more than a 5-year period.

Physics and Chemistry Section

Because of the wide range of analytical techniques employed in the Physics and Chemistry Section, a correspondingly wide variety of evidence, much of it from crimes of violence, is handled in this Section.

Microscopy

Hair and fiber analysis is of special value where bodily contact is made with an object or another individual. While the examination of a human hair sample normally does not permit a certain person to be identified as the only possible source of the hair, a great number of comparable characteristics permits a strong probability to be established. It is also possible to eliminate a person as the source of a hair. Observation of hair characteristics will normally permit a determination to be made of the race of the person from whom the hair originated, as well as the part of the body from which it came. Hair studies may also reveal if the hair was forcibly removed or naturally fell from the body; if it was cut, crushed, or burned; if it was bleached or dyed; or if it was artificially waved. The nature and composition of clothing fibers exchanged during body contact in violent crimes against a person may be determined and compared with those of the clothing of a victim and suspect. Examinations are also made in this unit for invisible laundry marks and identifying characteristics of rope, string, tape, fabric patterns, and features related to woven material.

Serology

The body fluid most commonly associated with violent crimes is blood. The presence of blood on clothing, weapons, automobiles, home furnishings, in scrapings from fingernails, from surfaces at crime scenes, and on every conceivable object relating to a bodily injury may be relevant both in establishing a criminal act and in associating a suspect with the crime. In other instances, small stains of blood on objects may be determined to have come from nonhuman sources through analytical methods. These findings may thereafter be associated with another animal source, verifying a suspect's story and helping to clear the innocent. In still other situations, semen, saliva, and other body fluids are identified and sometimes classified as having originated from a person possessing a particular blood groups if the person from which the body fluid originated is a secretor. Recent developments in dried blood grouping techniques in the Serology Unit have enabled stains to be more specifically classified into additional blood grouping systems, thus narrowing down the possible sources from which they originated.

Mineralogy

The examination of soils and combinations of mineral substances requires utilization of instruments specially designed for petrographic work. Various particles of physical evidence found on the property of a suspect or on his person may be used to associate him with the scene of a crime based on the results of the Mineralogy Unit's analyses. These substances include soils, safe insulation, concrete, plaster, mortar, ceramics, glass, ore, and abrasives.

Chemistry—Toxicology

A number of different types of chemical examinations are conducted in the Chemistry—Toxicology Unit utilizing gas chromatography, infrared, and ultraviolet spectroscopy as well as chemical analyses to identify poisons, drugs, and other toxic materials as possible causes of a victim's death. Other materials, such as probable accelerants found at a scene of a fire or sabotage incident, are analyzed to determine if the act was in fact a criminal effort and to determine whether the materials contain any unusual substance that could provide a lead for investigators.

Firearms, Toolmarks, and Explosives

Probably best known of the examinations conducted in these areas is that of determining whether or not a questioned bullet was fired from a specific weapon. The firearms examiner may also be called upon to determine if firearms are operating properly or to conduct gunpowder and shot pattern tests. In other instances, examinations of a questioned bullet or cartridge case may assist in ascertaining the type of weapon used in a crime. Also possible, utilizing the basic principles of firearms examinations, is the identification of telltale marks left at crime scenes by punches, hammers, axes, pliers, screwdrivers, chisels, wrenches, and other objects. The explosives specialist is called upon to examine evidence recovered at the scene of explosions—a problem rendered the more difficult because of the inherently destructive nature of the crime.

Metallurgy

The popularity of motorcycles and the ease with which they may be illegally obtained and transported have resulted in a substantial increase in the number of altered serial numbers submitted for restoration to the FBI Laboratory. Obliterated numbers can also be restored on firearms, sewing machines, watches, outboard motors, slot machines, automobiles, tools, and other metallic items. Tests may show whether two or more pieces of metal are in any way related, the possible cause of metal separation, and if production specifications for the metals have been met.

Instrumental Analysis

Examiners in the Instrumental Analysis Unit conduct microscopic, microchemical, and instrumental analyses of a wide variety of physical evidence such as paints, plastics, metal, glass, rubber, and other minute specimens of materials too small for examination by other means. Spectrographs, spectrophotometers, chromatographs, and X-ray diffraction apparatus provide the Laboratory experts with the data necessary for the identification and quantitative analysis of trace evidence.

Neutron Activation

In neutron activation analysis a sample of unknown material is irradiated with neutrons (nuclear particles). Some of the irradiated atoms in the unknown material are thereby made radioactive and begin to disintegrate (radioactively) with the emission of gamma rays. The energy of these gamma rays is measured with a gamma ray spectrometer. These energy values are then used to identify the element in the original material. Quantitative measurement of the elements present can be made by comparing the radioactivity of the elements in the evidentiary material with the radioactivity of known amounts of these elements.

Cryptanalysis—Gambling—Translation Section

The President's declared war against the gambling interests of organized crime and the increased emphasis on antigambling enforcement by State and local authorities have dramatically increased the examinations conducted in the FBI Laboratory's Gambling Unit. Its personnel have a rich depth of experience in identifying, defining, and demonstrating the meaning and significance of wagering records and related materials used by bookmakers and numbers writers in the conduct of their illicit profession. Similar examinations are performed on recorded material obtained through court-authorized interception of telephone communications.

Attempts to thwart recognition of gamblers' records through the use of codes and ciphers are unmasked by FBI Laboratory cryptanalysts using electronic data-processing equipment. Through the joint efforts of gambling examiners, chemists, and document examiners, specialized papers used by bookmakers and numbers writers are identified or their sources established. The existence of gambling records also is frequently proved through the development of indented-writing impressions made on an underlying piece of paper and, in other instances, by the restoration of burned or multilated papers.

In casino and carnival games, the Laboratory cryptanalysis staff possesses the capacity and experience to mathematically define the odds favoring the game's operator. This includes detailed examinations of pinball machines, various types of slot machines, roulette wheels, and other gambling devices. Rigged equipment such as altered dice, marked cards, and electrically controlled dice tables can be exposed and their effects demonstrated.

The Organized Crime Control Act of 1970 caused some sports bookmakers in South Carolina to hire legal counsel in their search for loopholes in the new laws prohibiting certain gambling operations. The bookmakers were advised by their counsel to decentralize, thus—they thought—avoiding the prohibition of an enterprise involving five or more persons. Through a tangled web, layoff wagers were handled telephonically with seemingly fewer persons involved.

Into this gambling operation drifted a compulsive bettor with connections enabling him to place wagers with top New York bookmakers. The bettor was permitted by his New York sources to manipulate the handicap by one-half point, provided he furnished a minimum of $500 in wagers on each of the 13 professional football games each week. Lacking such resources, he began handling layoff wagers for local bookmakers. Soon he accepted these wagers at the established handicap and took advantage of the one-half point manipulation when forwarding the wagers to New York. This last tactic moved him from the ranks of a mere bettor to those of a layoff bookmaker using an interstate facility in violation of the law. His connections and those of others were traced, resulting in convictions against him and the bookmakers furnishing him layoff wagers.

It was an FBI Laboratory expert on gambling who explained the complexities of this bookmaking operation to the court and clearly refuted the defendant's denials of bookmaking activity.

The trial also established a precedent by holding that decentralized bookmakers, even though acting as independent businesses when dealing with the public, constituted a single enterprise when they exchanged layoff wagers with one another in violation of the law.

In addition to the assistance given gambling investigators in the breaking of bookmakers' codes and ciphers, the cryptanalytic staff can frequently recover the true meaning of encrypted messages in criminal matters. Many examinations of this type have very materially contributed to successful prosecutions in local investigations involving, for example, murders and narcotics.

Radio Engineering Section

In recent years, one of the fastest developing phases of law enforcement has been in the field of radio communications. Cities have grown to megalopolises, towns have become cities, and the need for larger radio systems and more sophisticated communications equipment has grown proportionately. The Radio Engineering Section of the FBI Laboratory is equipped with the most modern and up-to-date instruments, tools, and equipment and is staffed with specialists in this field. These specialists are primarily responsible for insuring that all of the field divisions are equipped with efficient, modern FM automobile two-way radio communications systems. This responsibility includes systems engineering, installation, evaluation of equipment, and maintenance procedures to be effected in each field division system.

Continual contact is maintained with the various commercial firms which manufacture radio communications equipment, as well as with military services and other civilian Government agencies. In this way, Laboratory engineers are kept abreast of the latest developments so that agents in the field may at all times be provided with the finest radio communications facilities in carrying out the Bureau's investigative responsibilities.

The expertise in radio and electronics required of the technical personnel assigned to the Radio Engineering Section is also used to advantage in responding to requests of other law enforcement agencies for examinations and testimony in matters involving electronic or mechanical devices. For instance, a recent marked increase in submissions by State and Federal officials of illegal electromechanical gambling devices has resulted in related testimony in State and Federal courts. Pinball machine gambling has often formed a financial base for organized crime-associated activities in States where the machines are in operation. Expert testimony has been found to be an essential element in establishing the nature of such machines in court.

Recent testimony was important in gambling cases in several Southern States involving over 4,000 machines valued at approximately $8 million. The successful conclusions of these cases to date have been in large part the result of long hours of preparation and excellent presentation in court by Laboratory experts assigned to the Radio Engineering Section.

The Impact

Impressive as they are, the hundreds of technical reports, the thousands of exhibits presented from the witness stands, the tens of thousands of words of expert testimony given, and the hundreds of thousands of scientific examinations conducted annually fall far short of measuring the full influence of the FBI Laboratory's contribution in the nationwide solution of crime. Of much greater importance is the growing realization that scientific crime detection is an essential tool in effective law enforcement performance. It is this impact on modern investigative procedures which is revitalizing present-day law enforcement efforts. It is a welcome and timely trend—in this 40th Anniversary Year of the FBI Laboratory—to be enjoyed not only by the entire law enforcement profession, but also by the people of our Nation who demand and deserve to have the best in crime detection.

CHAPTER 2

The Investigative Process

James W. Osterburg

The simplest view of criminal investigation is offered by suggesting that when answers to the questions—who, what, when, where, how, and why—are obtained the investigation is well launched, if not completed. A more sophisticated concept recognizes similarities between criminal investigation and the study of history. Both involve an inquiry into events of the past, a time differential being one of the greatest differences between them. An even more general concept views all methods of inquiry as having some elements in common; however, each discipline develops special investigative procedures which are particularly suited to it.

The few existing textbooks on the subject are barely suitable for use in an introductory college course on criminal investigation. Indeed the literature of the field in general is quite scant; almost all of the books written in recent times are included in the references (1–5).

Investigation as a Process for the Study of the Past

The general sources of information open to investigators concerned with a past event are: physical evidence, records and documents, and people. The disparity between the developed disciplines available to the historian as contrasted with the criminal investigator is significant. It suggests the need for a considerable increase in the support of much more academic study of criminal investigative methodology. Table 1 is perhaps the simplest means to illustrate the difference.

The contrast in sophistication of the theoretical and methodological aids available to the historian with those at the disposal of the detective suggests that considerable effort is needed to raise criminal investigation

TABLE 1

HISTORY AND CRIMINAL INVESTIGATION AS METHODS OF STUDY OF PAST EVENTS

SOURCE OF INFORMATION		ANCILLARY DISCIPLINES AVAILABLE TO ASSIST IN THE STUDY OF A PAST EVENT	
HISTORY	CRIMINAL INVESTIGATION	HISTORY	CRIMINAL INVESTIGATION
Physical Evidence			
1. Fossils	1. Impressions (Tool, Tire, shoe)	1. Paleontology	1. Criminalistics
2. Bones	2. Narcotics	2. Geology	2. Chemistry
3. Material Remains of Man	3. Paint	3. Zoology	3. Physics
	4. Bullets	4. Physical Anthropology	4. Immunology
	5. Blood	5. Archaeology	5. Botany
	6. Flora		
Records and Documents			
1. Memoirs	1. Fraudulent Checks	1. Art History	1. Criminalistics
2. Letters	2. Threatening Notes	2. Linguistics	2. Questioned Document Expertise
3. Official Documents	3. Kidnap Letters	3. Information Theory–Storage and Retrieval	3. Photography
4. Manuscripts	4. Miscellaneous Documents		
5. Books			
6. Paintings			
People			
1. Folklore Tales	1. Victim	1. Cultural Anthropology	1. Techniques rather than disciplines are available. Questioning Surveillance Informants
2. Cultural Survivals	2. Eyewitnesses	2. Ethnology	
	3. Suspects		
	4. Others related to victim, suspects, and crime scene		

from the level of a crude craft to that of a professional discipline. The reasons why this has not occurred sooner are legion, but the most important is that practitioners themselves have never demanded that the necessary resources be made available. An ostensibly ever-rising crime rate, the United States Supreme Court, and a Presidential Crime Commission have brought this problem into perspective. The First National Symposium on Law Enforcement Science and Technology held in March 1967 at the Illinois Institute of Technology in Chicago was a partial response to the now recognized need for a general improvement in law enforcement practice.

Before proceeding with a description of the various aspects of criminal investigation, some mention must be made of constitutional restrictions which, in the United States, are imposed on the process. These limitations restrict the use of certain procedures and hence make the process operate at less than peak efficiency. In a democracy, this is a price that must be paid because other values—such as man's inherent dignity—are given higher priority. Mention will be made later in this paper on the effects of certain decisions on the particular phase of the process under consideration. This will be done to indicate the effects of legal requirements especially on the application of science to the criminal investigative process.

Physical Evidence

There are two distinct aspects to physical evidence: crime scene search, and the examination of the evidence in a crime laboratory. The literature of Criminalistics (6–13) is much more advanced than the general literature of criminal investigation.

Crime Scene Search. The crime scene search is the starting point of most investigations. This search is usually the responsibility of the detective assigned to the case; however, large departments may have supplementary specialists available. The search involves (a) the recognition, collection, and preservation of physical evidence; (b) the determination of the modus operandi of the criminal.

Modus operandi files are maintained by many police departments to record the unusual facts or peculiarities associated with the commission of a crime. For example, the detective notes that a criminal has entered a building in some uncommon manner. If several such burglaries are investigated they may be grouped together through recognition of the "M.O." Thus, various clues from associated crimes might be pooled to identify the criminal or to provide information for planning surveillance strategy and tactics in order to apprehend him during some future attempt at a similar crime. While this aspect of crime scene search must be mentioned, it has produced a somewhat limited return under present operating conditions.

Role of the Crime Laboratory. The examination of the crime scene for physical evidence is usually one of the first steps in the investigative process. To be successful the detective must have an understanding of the crime laboratory and its limitations; he must be taught to recognize not only common types of crime scene evidence but also that which is not obvious; he must, in addition, be very familiar with the requirements of the scientist, as well as those of the lawyer, in the collection and preservation of clue materials.

Physical evidence—blood, paint chips, tool impressions, bullets, finger-prints, heroin, alcoholic beverages, and so on—is examined in a crime laboratory. This discussion of the role of the laboratory is given from the viewpoint of the field detective and not from that of the laboratory expert. The last two examples of physical evidence—heroin and alcoholic beverages—are typical of substances submitted for analysis. A few con-firmatory tests are often all that are required to establish the nature of the substance. Classical "wet" chemistry or instrumental analyses suffice to answer promptly the general form of inquiry, viz., "This white powder is alleged to contain heroin. It is requested that the powder be analyzed." In most cases the allegation is correct, and analysis is quite simple. The other extreme is the problem of identification of a general unknown. Fortunately, this latter problem does not arise too often and may never be solved if the quantity of evidence is limited in amount.

One of the basic tasks of the crime laboratory is the identification of substances. Quite frequently this is contraband, or materials otherwise regulated by law. A chemist's testimony is required to establish that a necessary "element" (as ethyl alcohol or heroin) is present in order to comply with the definition of the particular crime. When all of the elements of the crime are established, the commission of a crime has been established. The laboratory has shown only that a crime has been committed but not that a particular person has committed it. Personal observations of a police officer or an eyewitness provide the evidence necessary to identify the perpetrator.

When the crime laboratory, through the examination of physical evidence, establishes a connection between the crime scene or victim and the criminal, it has achieved another of its major purposes. The term *associative evidence* is applied to those physical traces which, through laboratory examination and evaluation, are shown to be in one-to-one correspondence.

The development of associative evidence is accomplished most often by a comparison of crime scene evidence with test evidence related to the criminal. Thus, a crime bullet is shown to have been fired by a sus-pect's gun by comparison with a bullet deliberately fired through the suspected gun. Similarly a crime scene impression is related to a tool, tire, or shoe by making a comparison exemplar with the suspected im-plement.

The formidable obstacle to obtaining comparison standards imposed by the Mapp (14) and the Miranda decisions (15) will only be alluded to here as a problem. This is worthy in itself of a dialogue between scientists, civil libertarians, and lawyers. Indeed, the fundamental divi-sion between the needs of science for known standards and the limita-tions unwittingly placed upon their collection must be reconciled if science is to make any great contribution to the administration of justice.

Some mention must be made of the fact that a laboratory finding can be most useful during interrogation. One of the necessary conditions in obtaining a confession is the realization by the suspect that evidence is available against him. Clue materials which may be examined in his presence are particularly valuable, especially if the result is visible—as the development of a fingerprint, a color change in a chemical test, or a photograph showing any associative evidence developed in the case.

Another exceedingly important role the laboratory plays in the investigative process is the exoneration of the innocent through the examination and evaluation of physical evidence. The measure of personal and institutional satisfaction is unbounded when a possible miscarriage of justice is prevented.

Records as a Source of Information

The use of records in law enforcement is treated largely from the administrative point of view in the scant literature of the field with almost no consideration given to their use as an investigative aid. What has been written is largely useless for the obvious application of computer technology to this problem. Some creative, exploratory thinking in this area has been undertaken by the staff of the New York State Intelligence and Information System.

To be of greatest value to the investigative process, records must be thought of as stored information which is there to be retrieved by the imaginative investigator. Thus, whether files are maintained expressly for criminal investigative purposes or exist as a necessary concomitant to good business practice, stored information may serve in the following ways:

To follow-up or provide new leads.

To identify the perpetrator.

To trace and locate a suspect or criminal.

To recover stolen or lost property.

Follow-up or Provide New Leads. The laundry and dry cleaner mark file and the fraudulent check file, if properly maintained, are examples of law enforcement information useful for follow-up purposes. The state automobile license plate file is an example of a governmental file maintained for one purpose but nevertheless useful for follow-up; however, this file could be more useful for police purposes if, for example, the color of the car was required to be provided on the registration form. This is an example of how some files presently operated in various other agencies of government could be made more useful for law enforcement and at almost no cost.

The many directories compiled by the telephone companies, both for public and intracompany usage, are especially helpful for follow-up purposes.

The pawn broker file is a good example to illustrate how new leads are provided. In addition to a handwriting specimen, i.e., a signature on the pawn slip, a personal description of the person who pledged a stolen article may sometimes be obtained. At times the behavior of the individual seeking to pawn an item is so suspicious, or the item is recognized as probably stolen, that the shop owner surreptitiously telephones the local police, meanwhile detaining the customer on some pretext. The city directory, although a private publication and therefore not available for every city, is a source of additional information on the residential and business community. Quite often this directory is used in connection with partial information obtained verbally from some other person who was contacted during the investigation.

Identify the Perpetrator. The criminal photograph file (or the rogues' gallery as it is sometimes called) and the modus operandi file are probably as successful as any files maintained for identification purposes. The two files are often in the same quarters and supplement each other. The latent fingerprint file enjoys every limited success in the identification of criminals on the basis of fingerprints alone. When computer technology addresses itself to the problem of fingerprint identity instead of fingerprint classification, a breakthrough of major importance may occur. The problem is formidable and may require that the storage of single fingerprints in a computer be accomplished first.

Trace and Locate a Suspect or Criminal. When the identity of a criminal is known but he (or a suspect) is absent from his usual places of abode, work, and recreation, the investigator is faced with a problem of tracing and locating that person. The basis of this effort is the knowledge that people are gregarious and that they tend to flee to places familiar to them. Thus, the police in those areas can be alerted to be on the lookout; the transfer of any school records of a child may be used to trace the parent; relatives or friends may be placed under surveillance —these are some measures that may be taken to trace and locate a person after flight. Since in general most people require some continuity in their business pursuits (and in the use of public utilities), business records are often quite useful for tracing purposes. In especially important cases, wanted circulars and posters may be distributed.

Although this is a discussion of the use of records in tracing missing persons, mention was made of surveillance and the use of posters. This illustrates some of the difficulties in describing investigation as a process. It would certainly be misleading merely to describe the use of records for this purpose. The mere mention of each technique at the appropriate place later in the discussion might result in some lack of appreciation that several approaches to the solution of the problem are in the process simultaneously. There are many other places in this treatment of investigative procedure where similar comments would be in order; however, having made the point once, we shall pass over it in the future for the sake of economy.

Recover Stolen or Lost Property.   The major problem in accomplishing this objective is to make certain that the complainant's description of the property coincides with its description when it comes under police cognizance either directly or through a pawn shop. Through carefully structured forms this problem is readily solved. Computers are also obviously useful. Their large memory and the considered selection of property discriminants makes possible the operation of a system over a much wider area than was heretofore possible. Thus traveling a hundred miles or crossing a state line to pawn a stolen article will not preclude the possibility of detection if the law enforcement computer systems are interfaced.

Data Surveillance.   It is perhaps as appropriate at this point as anywhere in the paper to comment on some concern already being shown over the intrusion of privacy by computers. Westin has made a most succinct statement of both sides in this issue (16):

> . . . if society were to follow the technological and social-engineering possibilities, it is entirely possible that basic information about each major aspect of the individual's life will be collected in various functional master memory systems. His complete educational record from preschool nursery to post-graduate courses could be in the educational master file, including the results of all intelligence, aptitude, and personality tests taken during his lifetime. The individual's complete employment record would form another master computer dossier containing every job held, the rate of pay, efficiency ratings, employer evaluations, personality tests, recommendations, outside interests, family relation to work, and more, all available on instant printout when the individual is being considered for new employment. The master credit file could contain all the information needed to do a thorough financial analysis of the individual, including such items as his income, fixed expenditures, pattern of past discretionary spending, savings, investment, and predicted expenses based on personal

and family history, and predicted promotion levels. Other central dossiers might deal with health, civic activity, and criminal records. Every person could have a personal identification number, and computer scanning of a cardholder's fingerprint or voiceprint would serve to control assumption of another's identity number. These computer transaction systems and central record files of the future could bring enormous benefits to mankind—in the form of planning, efficiency, and social control. Unless the issue of privacy is in the forefront of the planning and administration of such future computer systems, however, the possibilities of data surveillance over the individual in 1984 could be chilling. . . .

A few thoughtful spokesmen, including some within the computer community, have begun to raise questions about safeguarding privacy and liberty in the age of the electronic dossier. But, so far, these voices have been a small cautionary note in the larger rousing chorus of computer designers and users who are pressing for integrated, freely circulating information systems. Serious as the problem of physical surveillance devices is in the 1960's and promises to be in the 1970's, it may be dwarfed completely by the surveillance of individual and group life that unlimited use of electronic data systems could bring to American life in the next decade.

While this may seem a departure from a description of the investigative process, it is necessary for many suggestions will undoubtedly be made at this conference concerning the use of computers to improve investigative efficiency. It is wise to recognize that there are values other than effectiveness that must be considered. Political scientists, lawyers, and civil libertarians must be brought into the dialogue promptly.

People as a Source of Information

The victim of a crime or an eyewitness to it are obvious sources of information; less obvious but nonetheless valuable at times are informants (17) and relatives or associates of suspects. Of course considerable effort is involved in obtaining information from informants. They need to be cultivated constantly if any dividends are to result. Surveillance of a suspect or his associates is another source of information; however surveillance of any degree of sophistication requires a commitment of resources in men and vehicles that only the larger and better equipped departments can afford.

Questioning.   A distinction is made between interviewing and interrogation. While both have much in common, the essential difference is perhaps best suggested by the words: antipathy, uncooperativeness, hostility.

Thus victims and eyewitnesses are interviewed; suspects and criminals are interrogated. The Miranda decision rendered by the United States Supreme Court (18) has established a set of guidelines governing the questioning of persons under detention when the aim is obtaining incriminating information. Predictions concerning the impact of these rules range from "disaster" by the police to "forced innovative improvement" in the entire investigative process by civil libertarians.

Information from people ranges from confessions, through clues of value for follow-up purposes, to details of no value to the investigator. In the post-Miranda era confessions are likely to be fewer in number and more skill and specialization will be required to obtain them. It remains to be seen whether or not follow-up clues are affected by Miranda through application of the "fruit of the poisonous tree doctrine." For example, can a weapon mentioned in an illegal confession be used as evidence in its own right if the source through which it was located was the confession? Presumably the Court will rule on this in the future. Of course follow-up clues provided through interviewing are unaffected by Miranda.

Investigative behavior involving a follow-up clue may result in:

Checking or hunting through a record file.

Talking with other people.

Searching for physical evidence.

Additional follow-up continues until all leads are exhausted and no more are forthcoming or the perpetrator's identity has been established. The "mix" of physical evidence, records, and questioning that spells success obviously differs from case to case.

Personal Descriptions. The victim or eyewitness to a crime is often able to describe the criminal. The problem of transferring this information to other law enforcement personnel or to the public at large has been attempted in three ways: portrait parle or a printed verbal description of the physical characteristics and clothing of the criminal, use of a police artist to capture the likeness, and use of a mechanical device to combine a limited choice of salient features—forehead, hairline, eyebrows, eyes, nose, mouth, chin, ears, and so on.

The police artist makes possible an almost infinite variety of feature nuances to capture the Gestalt image; mechanical recording is more limited in reproducing the likeness but more rapid transmission of image data is possible. The use of electronic data processing to retrieve images of possible suspects from a file is an obvious application of computer technology to investigation. A significant expenditure of funds to build such a file, the need for more research and development, and the training of users of the file to acquire the proper imput information are some of the obstacles to current widespread use of this technique.

Surveillance. Surveillance, referred to earlier in this paper, may be described as the unobtrusive observation of a person, place, or thing. A "person" is usually a suspect or a relative or friend of a suspect; however, any individual is a potential subject of a surveillance if there are reasonable grounds to believe that discreet observance of his activity might provide significant information.

Examples of "places" include liquor stores, supermarkets, banks, drug stores, or other places where transactions are largely in cash, or where contraband such as narcotics is available. Residences and places of business hardly need mention. Indeed *any* place may become sufficiently interesting to place it under surveillance.

"Things" which are worth watching secretly include: automobiles, the ransom dropped at a designated spot, and the fruits or instruments of a crime which were hidden immediately after its commission. In the latter situation, their discovery is made through other investigative procedure without the knowledge of the perpetrator.

Surveillance has a dual function in police work. One facet serves the investigative role; the other fulfills the preventive function. The objectives of surveillance, expressed concisely, are:

To locate a suspect.

To obtain detailed information concerning the nature and scope of a suspect's activities.

To prevent the commission of a crime.

There is a temptation to discuss surveillance as though it is an independent investigative technique. It is, of course, seldom so. For example, information acquired through legitimate wiretapping or interviewing often supplements and confirms facts developed through surveillance. Investigative techniques complement each other. The successful detective is the one who knows how to season his efforts with the proper amount of each.

Activities of a Suspect. An investigator needs details of the nature and scope of a suspect's activities for the following reasons:

To obtain evidence necessary to establish probable cause for a search warrant or arrest.

To identify the associates of a suspect and to infer from their observed behavior, as a group, any criminal intentions or plans they may have.

To obtain information for the interrogation of a suspect.

Behavior of Suspect and Associates. There may come a point in an investigation where it seems unlikely that a sufficient amount of evidence will be produced to establish guilt of a suspect beyond a reasonable doubt; however, by using his judgment and perhaps information from other sources, the investigator may have substantial grounds for believing the person is engaged in criminal activity. Under these circumstances the suspect may be placed under surveillance. If an efficient, professional criminal is involved, considerable manpower and equipment are required. While with some luck there may be a quick, satisfactory outcome, it is more likely that weeks or even months will be required before results are achieved.

Information for Interrogation. Horowitz (19) has analyzed the conditions necessary to obtain a confession. Of these there are two which may be assisted by information obtained through surveillance. The necessary, but by themselves insufficient, conditions referred to require the suspect to believe that:

Evidence against him is available;

Forces inimical to his interest are being employed with maximum effort.

The detailed, personal facts that a thorough surveillance puts at the disposal of an investigator can be devastating if used adroitly during an interrogation. Revealing, at an auspicious moment, some inconsequential detail about a person's behavior can lead him to believe his life is an open book to the police. After a few such clever uses of information, and if the other necessary conditions outlined by Horowitz have been met, an admission or confession may result. For an innocent person, of course, the internal pressure of guilt knowledge is not coupled with the other requisites for confession, and so none is likely to be obtained. Confirmation of the confession by checking details admitted to by the subject must be followed through diligently.

The decision to invest significant surveillance resources and the stage in the process where such a decision is made are dependent upon many factors: other priority needs, availability of a surveillance team, and other investigative developments as the case progresses. The economist's concept of "tradeoff" is applicable in arriving at a decision whether to continue the surveillance or not.

Technology has produced sophisticated electronic equipment that is useful for surveillance purposes. If such devices are not to be outlawed completely it behooves the law enforcement fraternity to pay heed to the clear message transmitted in the Westin paper (20). Certainly some safeguards are necessary. A colloquy with those concerned with the invasion of privacy would be profitable. Until this discord is solved it will be hazardous to build the investigative process on the assumption that this source of information will be legally available for long in the future. The problem should be met head on rather than by covert usage and an "ostrich head-in-the-sand" approach.

Motives. Crimes may be divided into two classes from the standpoint of motive. Crimes such as robbery, rape, and burglary have "universal" motives which are of little value in furthering the investigation. Other crimes may have "particularized motives," for example, homicide, arson, and assault. In these crimes, when the motive is discovered, the relationship between victim and criminal may be deduced. The high clearance rate for homicide is based, at least in part, on this logic. Experience is helpful in ferreting out the particular motive for a crime. In some crimes a determination of who has benefited from its commission is suggestive as to motive; in others it is through adroit interviewing that the motive may be learned.

Criminal Investigation—Art or Science

It is convenient to view investigation as part of a continuum with the left-hand limit representing the "art" aspects and the right-hand limit the "science" aspects of the process. Also some people are better endowed naturally with the attributes of a "good" detective.[1]

Intelligence

Curiosity and imagination

Keen observation and retentive memory

Knowledge of life and people

Technical "know-how"

Perseverance

Freedom from bias and prejudice

Honesty and courage

Sensitivity, discretion, and tact

[1] As developed in class discussion with police officers and regular academic students.

Physical fitness and neat appearance

Report writing ability.

Others less gifted may nevertheless become acceptable investigators if the elements of investigation are reduced to procedures and principles that are teachable. The rapidity and efficiency of this accomplishment will determine our future ability to educate and train investigators.

At the present time we are at an undefined point somewhere along the continuum and, hopefully, we are moving toward the science end of the spectrum. However, criminal investigation is not yet a process that can be characterized in steps or by precepts which, when followed, will unerringly lead to a solution of a crime. It can be perhaps better compared to cooking—the ingredients are the same for all chefs; but what they do to and with them, how they add and blend the items, how much heat (or energy) they apply—these are the factors which make the difference between a routine and an exceptional outcome, success or failure.

REFERENCES

1. O'HARA, C. E., *Fundamentals of Criminal Investigation*, Thomas, 1956.

2. DIENSTEIN, W., *Technics for the Crime Investigator*, Thomas, 1952.

3. SODERMAN, H. and O'CONNELL, J. J., *Modern Criminal Investigation*, 5th ed., rev. by C. E. O'Hara, Funk & Wagnalls, 1962.

4. FITZGERALD, M. J., *Handbook of Criminal Investigation*, Greenberg, 1951.

5. GROSS, H., and JACKSON, R. L., *Criminal Investigation*, 5th ed., Sweet & Maxwell, Ltd., 1962.

6. KIRK, P. L., *Crime Investigation*, Interscience, 1953.

7. NICKOLLS, L. C., *The Scientific Investigation of Crime*, Butterworth, 1956.

8. O'HARA, C. E., and OSTERBURG, J. W., *An Introduction to Criminalistics*, Macmillan, 1949.

9. SVENSSON, A., and WENDEL, O., *Techniques of Crime Scene Investigation*, 2nd rev. Amer. ed., Ed. J. D. Nicol, Elsevier, 1965.

10. TURNER, R. F., *Forensic Science and Laboratory Technics*, Thomas, 1949.

11. GLAISTER, J., *Medical Jurisprudence and Toxicology*, 9th ed., Williams & Wilkins, 1950.

12. GONZOLES, T. A., VANCE, M., HELPERN, M., and UMBERGER, C. J., *Legal Medicine, Pathology and Toxicology*, 2nd ed., Appleton-Century-Crofts, 1954.

13. GRADWOHL, R. B. H., *Legal Medicine*, Mosby, 1954.

14. Mapp v. Ohio, 376 U.S. 643 (1961).

15. Miranda v. Arizona, 384 U.S. 436 (1966).

16. WESTIN, A. F., *Science, Privacy, and Freedom: Issues and Proposals for the 1970's.* Part I—The Current Impact of Surveillance on Privacy, *Columbia Law Rev., 66,* 1003 (1966). At p. 1013–1014.

17. HARNEY, M. and CROSS, J. C., *The Informer in Law Enforcement,* Thomas, 1960.

18. MIRANDA, *loc. cit.*

19. HOROWITZ, M., Psychology of Confession, *J. Crim. Law, Criminal., and Pol. Sci., 47,* 197 (1956).

20. WESTIN, *op. cit.*

CHAPTER 3

What the Bones Tell–Today

Dr. T. D. Stewart

The beginning of a period of progress is sometimes difficult to pinpoint exactly, but in this case undoubtedly it falls within the years 1948–1949. At that time the Memorial Division of the Office of the Quartermaster General, U.S. Army, was engaged in identifying the war dead from the Pacific "theater." The operation centered in a special laboratory in Hawaii and the anthropological direction there, during these particular years, was in the hands of Dr. Mildred Trotter, on leave from Washington University Medical School, St. Louis, Mo., where she was professor of gross anatomy.

Dr. Trotter was aware of the unsatisfactory state of bone identification and especially the anthropologists' dissatisfaction with their available means for estimating stature from the lengths of the long limb bones. As I explained the situation in this Bulletin in 1951, ". . . we do not know the degree of reliability [of a stature estimate] in any particular case. Also, the formulas and tables [upon which we rely for the estimate itself] are still based upon a series of 100 French cadavers measured in 1888. This is a shorter population than now exists in America. Research under way should provide a better basis for stature estimation."

Better Estimates of Stature

The "research under way" was that undertaken by Dr. Trotter during her stay in Hawaii. She accumulated long-limb-bone measurements on 1,115 white and 85 Negro males between the ages of 17 and 49. By correlating the measurements of selected individuals with the statures of the same individuals taken in life, she was able to construct superior formulas for estimating maximum stature from either a single long-bone length or from a combination of long-bone lengths, together with the respective errors of estimate and a correction for ages beyond 30 years. Dr. Trotter reported on this work in 1952 jointly with Goldine C. Gleser, a statistician.

Trotter and Gleser augmented their report with data on the Terry Skeletal Collection derived from dissecting-room cadavers in Washington University Medical School. This sample consisted of 255 white and 360 Negro males, 63 white and 177 Negro females. It was used primarily for deriving corresponding formulas for estimating the stature of females.

Following the Korean war the Memorial Division used the Trotter and Gleser formulas exclusively in estimating statures of the war dead and with satisfactory results. Yet there was a suspicion that the Army population of this war was different from that of the preceding war and hence that a review of the relationship between long-bone lengths and stature was in order. Accordingly, since the importance of improving identification methods had been demonstrated, the Army gave Dr. Trotter a contract to undertake the new study.

This time her initial sample consisted of 4,672 white, 577 Negro, 92 Mongoloid, 112 Mexican, and 64 Puerto Rican males between the ages of 17 and 46. She found that, whereas at the time of World War II there appeared to be no significant increase in the statures of American males after the age of 18, by the time of the Korean war American males were continuing to grow to at least the age of 21 and possibly to 23. However, the resulting formulas for estimating maximum stature in whites and Negroes proved to be little different from those developed from the World War II sample. On the other hand, the resulting formulas for the Mongoloids, Mexicans, and Puerto Ricans offered a means of estimating the statures of these American minority groups with more assurance of reliability than theretofore. All this data was reported by Trotter and Gleser in 1958.

It is now possible also to estimate stature from certain long-limb-bone fragments. Using samples of male and female whites and Negroes from the Terry collection (now in the National Museum of Natural History), Gentry Steele developed formulas using defined segments of the femur, tibia, and humerus. As published (1970), each formula has an error of estimate. The method is applicable, of course, only when fragments of one or more of these three bones include one or more of the defined segments.

New Formulas

I cannot stress too much the importance of the errors of estimate provided with each of the new formulas used in estimating stature. It is recommended that a formula with the lowest possible error of estimate be picked according to the bones available. If, say, the error for the selected formula is ± 1.83 cm., and the stature estimate turns out to be 170.0 cm., then the chance that the individual in question was between 168.2 and 171.8 cm. tall (170.0 ± 1.83) is 68 percent. But what about the remaining third of the population—those who depart most from the mean? To be on the safe side, it is better to double the error of estimate. In that case, using the same example, the chance that the individual in question was between 166.3 and 173.7 cm. tall (170.0 ± 3.66) is 95 percent. When I think of some of the stature estimates I made prior to 1952, I am shocked at how little allowance I made for the range of error.

Better Estimates of Age

In 1951 the most widely used data on skeletal aging were those presented by Krogman in a 1939 issue of this publication. They had been derived mainly from dissecting-room populations in which old individuals predominate. Moreover, some of them had been assembled through studies on separate bones and thus fail to give a picture of the variability of an individual's aging process as a whole. An opportunity to refine the existing data came in 1954 when the Army's Memorial Division picked the writer to analyze the age changes in the remains of American soldiers killed in Korea. The results of this work, based on 375 skeletons ranging in age from 17 to 50 years, were published in 1957 by Thomas W. McKern and the writer.

Figure 1 compares the time ranges during which certain epiphyses unite, both as stated by Krogman in 1939 and by Stewart in 1963. Since none of the war dead were below the age of 17, certain early uniting epiphyses (for example, that at the distal end of the humerus) were never found ununited in the military series. In these instances (indicated in the figure by question marks), the age of beginning union is derived from Flecker's X-ray study on the living. The point is that, according to the evidence of the American war dead, uniting epiphyses tell an individual's age at death within ranges of from 4 to 7 years, rather than the previously accepted ranges of from 2 to 3 years.

A New Scheme Offered

The Korean war dead also yielded information on age changes other than epiphyseal union. Suture closure was shown to be unreliable for purposes of age estimation, as Singer (1953) had claimed. On the other hand, a new scheme was offered for evaluating the metamorphic phases of the articular surfaces of the pubic symphysis that yields both an age

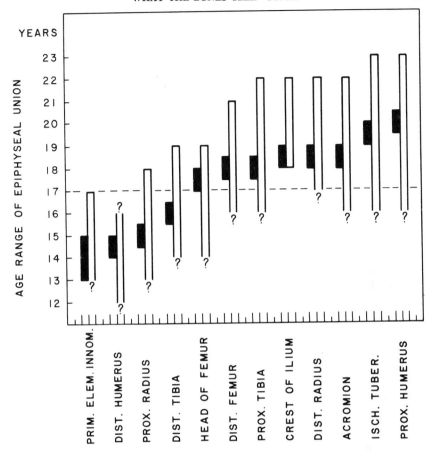

Figure 1. This diagram illustrates the gain in appreciation of the age ranges of epiphyseal union in males. The solid bars are the ranges given by Krogman in 1939; the open bars are those for the Korean War dead (McKern and Stewart, 1957). Both united and ununited epiphyses were observed at all ages represented in these ranges (from Stewart, 1963).

estimate and an error of estimate. Because of the age limitation of the military series, however, the estimation of age from the pubic symphysis by this new scheme decreases in reliability rapidly after the age of 30. This being the case, it is helpful to know that the Korean war study enables one to rate a large pattern of skeletal age changes. Additionally, the writer has shown (1958) that around 35–40 years of age arthritic lipping makes its presence manifest in males with increasing frequency in certain joints, especially in the vertebral column.

Tooth Structure and Age

Aside from these war-connected developments, the main advances in the area of aging during the last 20 years relate to the teeth. The well-known ages of tooth eruption have been supplemented by extensive X-ray documentation on the rate of root calcification. By this means considerable refinement of the age estimate in both sexes is possible between the ages of 2 and 15 (Garn et al., 1958). At much older ages—say, from 30 years onward—tooth structure gives better estimates of age than do the gross bones (Gustafson, 1950; Miles, 1963). Yet, in these advanced years the microscopic structures of teeth and bones probably yield equally good results (often within ± 5 years) when the examiners have been properly trained and have gained extensive experience (Kerley, 1965).

Better Estimates of Sex

Anyone working with human bones over the past 20 years should be better able now than at the beginning of the period to estimate correctly the sex of unknown remains. Besides, having learned more about the significance of certain bony characters (Fig. 2, for example), such a person now has a variety of metrical techniques to aid him. One of the simplest of these—the ischium-pubis index—is the ratio between the ischium and pubis lengths as measured from the point in the hipbone socket (acetabulum) where these two bones meet and fuse. This ratio differentiates adult males from adult females in around 90 percent of cases when due attention is paid to race (Washburn, 1948). By adding measurements of other bones and applying rather sophisticated statistical procedures—discriminant function or multivariate analysis—the estimate is said to be improved to around 95 percent, depending on the parts available (Giles, 1970). Note, however, that all of this applies only to the post-adolescent skeleton. Prior to the development of the secondary sex characters, there is, with one exception, still no sure way of distinguishing between male and female skeletons. The exception relates to the fetal period, the only subadult period for which documented skeletal material is available. R. J. Boucher's method (1955) for distinguishing the sexes at this period, based on the shape of the sciatic notch in the pelvis, enabled her to get correct results in 85 percent of 107 British whites, in 84 percent of American Negroes, but in only 68 percent of American whites. How well the method will work in inexperienced hands is open to question.

Figure 2 deserves special attention because it shows pathological changes on the inner or dorsal aspects of two adult female pubic sym-

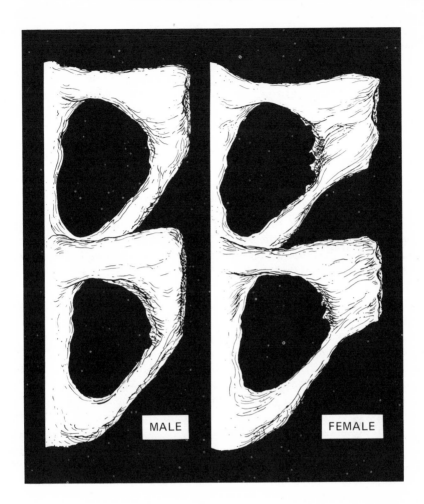

Figure 2. Comparison of the left pubic bones of two adult males (top: U.S. National Museum No. 332,539; bottom, 279,583) and two adult females (top: U.S. National Museum No. 332,548; bottom, 279,585), as viewed from behind. In each case the articular surface of the pubic symphysis presents to the right. Bordering this surface in each of the females is a row of pits representing scars of parturition. Note that the area where the pits occur is more nearly square in the females than in the males and that as a result the profile of the lower border is concave, whereas in the males it is straight or convex. This extension of the pubic bone is part of the adjustment of the female pelvis for childbearing and therefore a good indicator of sex.

physes. In 1957 the writer called attention to the fact that these changes occur almost exclusively in females, beginning in the age period of child-bearing. From all indications they are the result of damage—hemorrhage, ligamentous tears, etc.–during parturition. Depending on the extent of the damage, the dorsal margin of the articular surface eventually may become undermined and more or less irregular in outline. Before this observation was reported, such irregularities were often mistakenly interpreted as a sign of old age. Now we know that the scars of parturition reinforce the other signs of the female sex and must be discounted in age estimates (Stewart, 1970). Obviously, evidence that a female decedent has borne one or more 'children is in itself an important identification feature.

Better Estimates of Race

The only important recent breakthrough in the identification of race has come about through the application of sophisticated statistical procedures to skull dimensions. The methods used are essentially the same as those mentioned for the identification of sex. In both instances the discriminating ability of the dimensions has been determined. The highly trained eye can see the difference, but the untrained eye would do well to turn to the computer.

One area where the metrical approach to the estimation of race has special application is crossbreed populations. The American Negroes fall into this category. By determining the most racial-discriminating measurements of West African and European crania, W. W. Howells of Harvard University has provided (1970) a means for showing how closely a skull suspected of belonging to an American Negro approaches one or the other group represented in the mixture.

More could be done along this line by extending the method to other skeletal parts. The writer pointed the way in 1962 when he showed that Negro femora tend to have much less forward bowing of the shaft and often less forward torsion of the upper end than those either of whites or of American Indians (cf. Fig. 3). These features by themselves are never surely diagnostic of race, but are useful as supportive evidence.

General

Estimates of size, age, sex, and race do not provide positive identification of the remains of an individual; they merely assign him to a general class. Only physical characteristics unique to the individual and matchable to records made in life tell for certain who the individual is. From the standpoint of the skeleton, dental records and body X-rays are most likely to be useful for this purpose. In one case studied by the writer—a 35-year-old white male of average height and slender build (indicated by his belt) —there seemed to be no easy way to locate the dentist who had ben re-

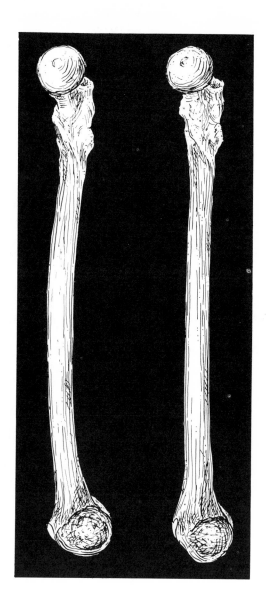

Figure 3. Negroes tend to have straighter bones than Whites. In these two adult male femora, note that the shaft of the left one (Terry Collection No. 1026, White) is bowed to the left (forward) much more than that of the right one (U.S. National Museum No. 255,591, Negro). The often greater forward torsion of the femoral head and neck in Whites does not appear in the example seen here.

sponsible for the numerous restorations in the teeth. The case was solved, however, when a newspaper published an artist's effort to produce a likeness based on the skull and a reader reported its resemblance to a missing acquaintance. The missing person's dentist verified the identification from his records.

In another case—a young white girl—attention was called to a white spot (aplasia) on an upper front tooth, a conspicuous feature which the relatives and friends of a missing girl remembered.

Bone injuries severe enough to suggest that the individual may have been hospitalized can lead sometimes to existing X-rays and thereby to positive identification. For example, among the remains of American soldiers killed in Korea that I examined was one with an old healed fracture of an armbone which proved to be the key to the identification, but not until considerable time and effort had been expended in locating an X-ray. With one exception, the records derived from the skeleton agreed with the assembled records of the indicated individual made in life. The discrepancy had to do with the fracture: there was no suggestion of the indicated individual's having broken his arm. Even the parents of the indicated individual denied that their son had ever had such an injury. Yet the agreement between the two sets of records was so close otherwise that the authorities persisted in their search and finally located the indicated individual's college roommate. The latter related how his friend had gone out for football practice one spring, had broken his arm, and had stayed on for summer school to prevent his parents from learning about the injury. The college dispensary produced the X-ray that confirmed the identification.

REFERENCES

BOUCHER, B. J., *Sex Differences in the Foetal Sciatic Notch,* Journal of Forensic Medicine, vol. 2, pp. 51–54, 1955.

FLECKER, H., *Time of Appearance and Fusion of Ossification Centers as Observed by Roentgenographic Methods,* American Journal of Roentgenology and Radium Therapy, vol. 47, pp. 87–159, 1942.

GARN, S. M., LEWIS, A. B., KOSKI, KALEVI, and POLACHECK, D. L., *The Sex Difference in Tooth Calcification,* Journal of Dental Research, vol. 36, pp. 561–567, 1958.

GILES, EUGENE, *Discriminant Function Sexing of the Human Skeleton,* pp. 99–109 in Personal Identification in Mass Disasters, edited by T. D. Stewart, Washington, D.C., 1970.

GUSTAFSON, G., *Age Determinations on Teeth,* Journal of the American Dental Association, vol. 41, pp. 45–54, 1950.

HOWELLS, W. W., *Multivariate Analysis for the Identification of Race from Crania*, pp. 111–121 in Personal Identification in Mass Disasters, edited by T. D. Stewart, Washington, D.C., 1970.

KERLEY, ELLIS R., *The Microscopic Determination of Age in Human Bone*, American Journal of Physical Anthropology, vol. 23, pp. 149–163, 1965.

KROGMAN, WILTON M., *A Guide to the Identification of Human Skeletal Material*, FBI Law Enforcement Bulletin, vol. 8, No. 8, pp. 3–31, 1939.

MC KERN, THOMAS W., and STEWART, T. D., *Skeletal Age Changes in Young American Males, Analyzed from the Standpoint of Age Identification*, Technical Report EP–45, Environmental Protection Research Division, Quartermaster Research and Development Center, U.S. Army, Natick, Mass, 1957.

MILES, A. E. W., *Dentition in the Estimation of Age*, Journal of Dental Research, vol. 42 (1, part 2), pp. 255–263, 1963.

SINGER, RONALD, *Estimation of Age from Cranial Suture Closure. A Report on Its Unreliability*, Journal of Forensic Medicine, vol. 1, pp. 52–59, 1953.

STEELE, GENTRY D., *Estimation of Stature from Fragments of Long Limb Bones*, pp. 85–97 in Personal Identification in Mass Disasters, edited by T. D. Stewart, Washington, D.C., 1970.

STEWART, T. D., *What the Bones Tell*, FBI Law Enforcement Bulletin, vol. 20, No. 2, pp. 2–5, 19, 1951.

STEWART, T. D., *Distortion of the Pubic Symphyseal Surface in Females and Its Effect on Age Determination*, American Journal of Physical Anthropology, vol. 15, pp. 9–18, 1957.

STEWART, T. D., *The Rate of Development of Vertebral Osteoarthritis in American Whites and Its Significance in Skeletal Age Identification*, The Leech, Johannesburg, vol. 28, Nos. 3–5, pp. 144–151, 1958.

STEWART, T. D., *Bear Paw Remains Closely Resemble Human Bones*, FBI Law Enforcement Bulletin, vol. 28, No. 11, pp. 18–21, 1959.

STEWART, T. D., *Sternal Ribs are Aid in Identifying Animal Remains*, FBI Law Enforcement Bulletin, vol. 30, No. 7, pp. 9–11, 1961.

STEWART, T. D., *Anterior Femoral Curvature: Its Utility for Race Identification*, Human Biology, vol. 34, pp. 49–62, 1962.

STEWART, T. D., *New Developments in Evaluating Evidence from the Skeleton*, Journal of Dental Research, vol. 42 (1, part 2), pp. 264–273, 1963.

STEWART, T. D., *Identification of the Scars of Parturition in the Skeletal Remains of Females*, pp. 127–135 in Personal Identification in Mass Disasters, edited by T. D. Stewart, Washington, D.C., 1970.

TROTTER, MILDRED, and GLESER, GOLDINE C., *Estimation of Stature from Long Bones of American Whites and Negroes*, American Journal of Physical Anthropology, vol. 10, pp. 463–514, 1952.

TROTTER, MILDRED, and GLESER, GOLDINE C., *A Reevaluation of Estimations of Stature Based on Measurements of Stature Taken During Life and of Long Bones After Death*, American Journal of Physical Anthropology, vol. 16, pp. 79–123, 1958.

WASHBURN, S. L., *Sex Differences in the Pubic Bone*, American Journal of Physical Anthropology, vol. 6, pp. 199–207, 1948.

CHAPTER 4

Landmarks and Hallmarks in Scientific Evidence

Edwin Conrad, J.D., M.A.

Introduction

In the field of scientific evidence we should be concerned about landmarks and hallmarks of justice. A landmark is a reference point in a stage of development. While it may be a landmark as such, it may in turn represent progression or regression. The term "hallmark," on the other hand, connotes the element of quality or progress in man's quest for truth. When dealing with the cases involving scientific evidence, one should determine whether one is dealing with a landmark, a stage of development, or with a hallmark, a true state of progress and achievement. In this paper the philosophical aspects of scientific evidence shall be stressed and specific scientific techniques shall be left for subsequent examination and discussion.

The Quest of Diogenes

The ghost of Diogenes, with lantern in hand and searching for the honest man, is still stalking across these lands. Times have changed but the quest for truth still goes on. The lantern of Diogenes has been replaced in many cases by modern scientific techniques of crime detection, but Pontius Pilate's question to Jesus some 2,000 years ago, "What is truth?" is still reverberating through the corridors of halls of justice. The forensic scientist has made great forward progress in his search for truth, but it may be that the answer to the question may never be really attained until it is possible to probe and read the innermost recesses of man's mind.

During studies by the author two principles of proof have emerged which may be succinctly stated as follows: (1) truth is like an iceberg—most of it is submerged, (2) truth is a sleeping dog—let it *lie!*

The Myth of Frye

In 1923 the United States Court of Appeals in the celebrated case of Frye v. United States (1) set up the polestar guiding the forensic scientist:

> Just when a scientific principle or discovery crosses the line between the experimental and demonstrable stages is difficult to define. Somewhere in this twilight zone the evidential force of the principle must be recognized, and while the courts will go a long way in admitting expert testimony deduced from a well-recognized scientific principle or discovery, the thing from which the deduction is made must be sufficiently established to have gained general acceptance in the particular field in which it belongs (2).

Lawyers and scientists have blindly accepted the validity of this principle of scientific proof and the courts have solemnly repeated this test several thousands of times since. While the case had some validity in rendering the results of lie detector tests inadmissible, yet, the quoted rule was antiquated on the day of its pronouncement. Does one realize that in 1923 no scientist, under the principle of the Frye case, could possibly testify that an atom could be split, even though his own studies and experiments had indicated otherwise? Could Fermi and Bahr have testified as to atomic fission on January 26, 1939, in any courtroom, this being the time of the famous Washington conference on the same subject? Could Copernicus in the 16th century have testified that the planets revolved about the sun?

On July 19, 1969, could Dr. Werner von Braun testify in a court of this land as an expert that man would implant his footprints on the lunar sands? The artificial and already obsolete principle established by the Frye case, requiring general scientific acceptance of the instrumentality of proof in the particular field in which it belongs, stood unchallenged since 1923, despite the fact that it has been in direct contradiction to the very liberal rule as to the admissibility of expert testimony. However, late in 1958, the Appellate Department, Superior Court, Alameda County, California, softened the requirements set forth in the Frye case. In holding admissible the results of the Nalline test to prove a state of drug addiction, this court observed:

> No experts were called by defendants and the expert testimony stands uncontradicted in the record with this exception. Each of the People's experts did admit on cross-examination *that the medical pro-*

fession generally is unfamiliar with the use of Nalline and, therefore, it cannot be truthfully said that the Nalline test has met with general acceptance by the medical profession as a whole, general acceptance being at present limited to those who deal in the narcotic problem. (Italics supplied.)

Should this factor render the testimony inadmissible? We believe not. All of the medical testimony points to the reliability of the test. It has been generally accepted by those who would be expected to be familiar with its use. In this age of specialization, more should not be required (3).

The California viewpoint is based upon the realities of this day of specialization. Frye has been fractured. It is considered that Frye is a landmark and Williams (3) a hallmark of justice.

The Coppolino Criterion

In Frye and Williams we observe the development of a system of scientific evidence but the picture was not yet complete. The missing link was supplied by a Florida appellate court in the now famous case of Coppolino v. State (4), a symphony in the study of scientific evidence. The case involved the use of complex, lengthy, and impressive scientific and medical testimony, both by the prosecution and the defense, as to the cause of death of an alleged murder victim, Carmela Coppolino, who was alive and well on August 28, 1965. On August 29, 1965, she was dead. The body was exhumed four months later.

The pathologist for the prosecution testified that the deceased was in good health at the time of her death and at the conclusion of her autopsy after the exhumation of the body he was not able to determine the cause of death, although he found no natural cause. He did find a needle injection track in the left buttock. Following the autopsy, he turned over certain portions of the body tissue to a toxicologist for examination.

According to Judge Mann, in a concurring opinion, he found that a general toxicological investigation disclosed no possible cause of death. A puncture wound in the left buttock like that which a needle would make and a track of a needle disclosed by examination of the subcutaneous fat, suggested death by something injected into her body. He likewise found that the accused was an anesthesiologist and had used succinylcholine chloride, which in sufficient quantity will cause cessation of breathing (5).

There is both prosecution and defense evidence in the case that it was believed impossible by medical scientists to demonstrate the presence of succinylcholine chloride or its component parts in the body.

The tests of the toxicoloogist for the prosecution to detect a component part of such drug were new, devised by him specifically to detect the presence of a component part of the drug in the body of the deceased. The toxicologist, after the death of the victim and following the autopsy, discovered the means of identifying a component part of the drug (succinylcholine chloride) in the human body—something deemed impossible by the medical and scientific specialists in the field. Accordingly, the toxicologist testified to a reasonable scientific certainty that the decedent received a toxic amount of succinylcholine chloride. Upon being recalled, the pathologist for the prosecution, basing his opinion on his own negative autopsy and upon the positive findings of the toxicologist, concluded to a reasonable medical certainty that the decedent died from an overdose of said drug. The District Court of Appeals of Florida, Second District, admitted such evidence, over objections that the testimony of the toxicologist was still in an experimental stage and did not meet the scientific reliability standard of Frye. A new hallmark principle of scientific evidence has now been recognized by the Florida case and may be stated in the words of Judge Mann:

> The tests by which the medical examiner sought to determine whether death was caused by succinylcholine chloride were novel and devised specifically for this case. This does not render the evidence inadmissible. Society need not tolerate homicide until there develops a body of medical literature about some particular lethal agent (6).

Summary

From 1923 until 1958 the cause of scientific evidence was placed in the rigid straitjacket of Frye, which required a scientific test to be generally accepted in the particular field in which it belonged. In 1958 Williams recognized the specialized nature of science and accepted scientific evidence known only by a few specialists in the field. The Coppolino criterion of 1969 states that new and novel tests in the scientific field do not necessarily render them invalid, if they are authenticated by their discoverer; society need not tolerate a homicide until science develops a body of literature about some particular lethal agent. This is indeed giving the scientist more faith in courts which are willing to bolster sound scientific methodology not dictated by scientific public opinion polls.[1]

---

[1] As a matter of historical interest it should be stated that the pathologist for the prosecution was Dr. Milton Helpern, Chief Medical Examiner of New York City. The toxicologist for the prosecution was Dr. C. J. Umberger, Office of the Medical Examiner, New York City.

REFERENCES

1. 293 F 1013, 54 App DC 46, 34 ALR 145 (1923).

2. Ibid., 293 F 1014.

3. People v. Williams, 164 Cal App2d Supp 848, 331 P2d 251, at pp. 253–254 (1958).

4. Coppolino v. State (Fla App), 223 So2d (1968), appeals dismissed (Fla), 234 So2d 120 (1969), 399 US 927 (1970).

5. Ibid., pp. 74–75.

6. Ibid., p. 75.

The Scene of the Crime:
The Officer's View

Preserve the crime scene! This admonition states the responsibility of the officer on the scene of a crime. This responsibility is second only to the preservation of life and order. Curiosity seekers and other well meaning spectators must not be allowed to disturb the scene. This cardinal rule of investigation cannot be overemphasized because of the importance of finding evidence in the proper context with reference to the crime.

The crime scene is unique, offering physical evidence directly connected with the crime. It is unique in that all physical aspects can never be exactly duplicated. Once an object is moved it can never be replaced in quite the same manner. Seasoned investigators stress this point over and over to rookie officers to forestall overzealous behavior as they assist in investigations.

Evidence takes many forms and the investigator must be alert not to overlook seemingly insignificant objects which might shed some light on the crime and the identity of the criminal. He must be meticulous in measuring distances between objects of evidence and their relation to the central focus of the investigation. He must conduct a thorough search of the area, seeking evidence. This search demands that the officer understand the scene since he is looking for things which do not belong or objects which are out of place.

After carefully handling and gathering evidence, the investigator must prepare the material for the crime laboratory which

43

will seek to establish the relationship of the object to the crime. Through the scientific analysis of evidence, the guess-work is taken out of the investigation and the proof in many cases can be indisputable.

This section also deals with the crime scene and the gathering of evidence. Also included is a summary on forms of material evidence and why they are important to the investigation. Through the use of such information, the officer can develop an appreciation for the value of physical evidence and can promote a closer cooperation with the crime lab and others concerned with the evaluation of scientific evidence.

The importance of photographic skills cannot be overlooked. The investigator must seek to photograph the crime scene from every perspective in order that the evidence presented cannot be questioned as to its relation to the crime.

The investigator must handle all evidence with great care. All evidence must be securely packaged for delivery to the crime lab, in order that its value is not lost.

Identification of the victim is another responsibility of the investigator. In the case of homicide, this is often done in cooperation with the medical examiner or the coroner at the autopsy. Such is usually the case where death has occurred some time previously.

Searching the crime scene and other relevant premises is of great importance to the investigation and often the weapons or other tools used in the crime have been buried or thrown in open fields.

Throughout, it should be stressed that a good investigation can only be the result of cooperation on the part of the officer at the scene, the investigators, and the criminalist and others consulted. This is especially true in working with scientific personnel outside the police community in the development and subsequent evaluation of evidence.

Incident investigation is not limited to crimes, but also can be initiated by industrial security personnel responsible for the security of various corporations. The same principles would apply and security personnel, who usually have law enforcement backgrounds, utilize these principles.

CHAPTER 5

Identification and the Forensic Pathologist

Geoffrey T. Mann, M.D.
Hobart R. Wood, M.D.

The identification of persons by sight alone leads to endless mistakes in ordinary life without any particular inconvenience. In connection with criminal identification, serious results may occur.

The human eye and photography are notoriously unreliable even in the identification of recently dead persons. Even greater difficulties are encountered with mutilated, decomposed, or fragmentary remains.

In 1927, a "body" who had been identified by photograph turned up at her own funeral protesting against her interment.

In 1953, the photo of a man, wanted for information in connection with a murder, was televised. Dozens of people said they had seen him —often simultaneously—hundreds of miles apart. Actually, the man was lying dead in a cellar at that time.

Early attempts to establish a reliable method of identification were made by Bertillon in 1880. The system named after him employed detailed descriptions of the features and measurements of height, sitting height, span, length of certain bones, skull measurements, etc. In police work, this has been largely replaced by fingerprinting although outlines are still used in the FBI "Wanted" sheets.

The means available to the forensic pathologist for identification are:

1. Complexion, racial color, eyes.

2. Likeness of features.

3. Occupation marks.

4. Clothes, articles in pockets, jewelry.

5. Deformities, birth marks, etc.

6. Injuries, scars, tattoos.

7. Finger printing.
8. Stature, weight.
9. Sex.
10. Age.
11. Teeth, dentures.
12. Hair.

Complexion

The body should be examined in daylight. Vital shades like pale, florid, sallow, etc., disappear soon after death; freckles, pimples, etc., last a little longer.

Bodies in water lose hair and skin. The color of the eyes changes from blue to grey to brown.

Likeness of Features

Death alters expression very rapidly so that little reliance can be placed upon this mode of identification. Decomposed bodies in particular are distorted by gas and should be looked at again after the autopsy when gas has escaped and fluids have drained so that the original shapes are better recognizable.

If bones only are available the facial characteristics of a skull may be reconstructed with the help of a sculptor.

Occupation Marks

Stains: Paint, dye, grease, flour, etc., may be found on the skin and clothing.

Debris under fingernails, in ears, or in pockets may provide clues.

Callosities and deformities may be characteristic of certain professions. The shape and condition of the hands will usually distinguish the laborer from the professional man or unemployed. Peeling potatoes causes superficial cuts on the fingertips; tailors may show callosities on the thumb from holding scissors, and needlepricks on the fingertips. Playing the violin or cello causes characteristic callosities. Metal-workers may show siderotic skin pigmentation. Nicotine stains on the fingers and the back of the incisor teeth mark the cigarette smoker; thick and burnt skin on the thumb and perhaps increased wear on certain teeth may identify a pipe-smoker.

These marks are helpful but not conclusive. Their presence is indicative of a certain job or habit; their absence does not exclude it.

Clothes, etc.

These are usually of great value: the maker's tags, laundry marks or dyer's marks provide useful information. "Invisible" ink is commonly used to mark clothes; they should, therefore, be examined under U. V. light.

Watch makers and jewelers often use private marks in repairs.

Cigarette packages bear code symbols indicating the date and place of manufacture.

Social security cards, drivers' licenses, etc., are, of course, good circumstantial evidence to establish a body's identity.

Deformities, Birth Marks, etc.

Congenital dislocations, cleft palates, harelips, moles, or port-wine stains are of great value and should be carefully noted.

Injuries, Scars, Tattoos

Old fractures, accidental or operative scars, marks from boils, etc., should be noted, described and measured.

If x-rays of the living person are available, the presence of arthritic and degenerative changes of the large joints and the spine are important features to note and compare.

Tattoos may occur anywhere on the body. Names, dates, symbols of occupation or trade (sailors, soldiers) furnish useful information. They also give an idea in what sort of circles the deceased moved around (obscene ornaments, etc.). The marks may become obscured in decomposed bodies, but they reappear if the superficial dermis is stripped.

In 1935, James Smith disappeared from Sidney, Australia. Two weeks later a shark was caught on the beach and sold to an aquarium. There it vomited a human arm which showed tattoo marks that were identified as Smith's.

Finger Printing

This is undoubtedly the safest and most accurate means of identification. In 782 A.D. the Chinese used fingerprints as substitutes for signatures. In 1853, Sir William Herschel, a civil servant in India, used this method to prevent Indian pensioners from collecting their pension more than once.

Its use in criminology was gradually adopted in England and later in France and Germany where the Bertillon system was in general use.

At the time of birth a fine pattern of ridges develops in the skin of the balls of the fingers, thumbs and parts of the palms and soles of the feet.

These ridges are arranged in

Whorls	25%
Loops	67%
Arches	6–7%
Composite forms	1–2%

and serve for primary classification.

Finer details, e.g., branching, coalescence, etc., permit sub-grouping.

Sixteen to twenty points of fine comparison are accepted as proof of identity. The chances of similar prints from different fingers are about 1 in 64 thousand million. Never yet in the world's crime records have two identical prints been seen, unless from the same fingers.

On decomposed or immersed bodies, difficulties may arise; often, however, glove-like pieces of skin can be removed and may give perfect prints.

Stature and Weight

About 1.2 inches in men and 1.5 inches in women should be subtracted from any stature measured in foot wear. Also, it should be taken into account that the corpse length is about 2 cm. more than the living stature.

If bones only are found, their measurements can be used for reconstruction of the stature by use of tables to be found in the standard textbooks on Forensic Pathology and Anthropology. Similarly, conclusions as to race, sex and age can be drawn with reasonable accuracy.

Sex

Even markedly decomposed or incinerated remains may contain tissue that is recognizable microscopically. The uterus resists decomposition longest, and sections from the pelvic region may show endometrial tissue.

Skin and mucous membranes may be used for nuclear sexing in mutilated remains where the genitalia are missing. And, of course, the well known sex differences of the human skeleton can be used to establish the sex of bodies.

Age

In recently dead people, this seldom presents difficulties.

Wrinkles, the distribution of hair (hair in the auditory meatus rarely begins to appear before 50 years of age). the state of the teeth, etc., may be used.

The ossification centers, the cranial sutures, degenerative joint changes are helpful to determine the age of skeletons.

Teeth and Dentures

In natural decomposition, teeth are practically industructible. They are, therefore, an excellent aid in the identification of remains and the estimation of age.

The cooperation of a dentist interested and experienced in the field of forensic dentistry is invaluable.

The following points should be noted: Number and situation of teeth present; number and situation of teeth lost including evidence of how long lost, (watch for teeth lost post-mortem); arrangement, irregularities, erosion, caries, fillings; bridge, crown work and dentures; the exact shape of edentulous jaws.

The identity of a murder victim occasionally rests entirely with the dental findings. The most celebrated cases are those of Prof. Webster being convicted for the murder of Dr. Parkman whose artificial teeth were found in a furnace (Boston, 1950) and Haigh's "acid-bath" murders in London in which the lost victim was identified by her dentist who recognized the acrylic resin dentures.

Hair

Color, texture, dyes, etc., should be noted. Racial characteristics are less reliable than commonly believed.

Conclusion

The identification of unknown human remains is always in direct proportion to the time, care and industry applied to the problem.

CHAPTER 6

Physical Evidence Utilization in the Administration of Criminal Justice

Brian Parker and Joseph Peterson

The Nature of Proof by Physical Means in Criminal Matters

Human activity necessitates changes in the real world in every instance. A thought involves a change in a neuron network. A movement involves a change in the molecular states of muscle fibers. A sound involves a change in the vocal passages. A spoken word involves these changes and a change in the molecular distribution of air. These changes in matter-energy configurations and relationships constitute physical links between an activity and its human agent. If these changes can be established, they provide a basis for inferring specific human intent to engage in the particular activity as well as direct physical connections. Through documenting those changes, the sequence of events can be proven which relate a given activity to a specific actor.

The conviction of the guilty and the exoneration of the innocent in the investigation of criminal activities has occurred time and again when attention was focused on material reality as extrinsic evidence. Success in this sense of criminal investigation is amply demonstrated in the annals of detection. Such cases as Dr. Webster's murder of Mr. Parkman, the St. Valentine Day multiple murders, and the English insulin murder have shown the value of scientific examination and interpretation of the physical traces left in the wake of human violence. From the beginnings of this century in the endeavors of such men as Gross, Reiss, and Niceforo, the contributions of scientific crime detection have been considered as useful, and often essential, to many areas of criminal investigation. More recently, the task force report on the police stated that "success in complicated investigation may depend in large part upon the scientific evaluation of pertinent data" and that Supreme Court decisions suggest "the

50

necessity of a more adequate police crime scene searching and pains-taking laboratory review." [14]

The demonstration that "each criminal violation must be shown to be in fact a breaking of the law, and must be linked to a specific individual" is the functional service of "crime" laboratories.[4] Performance in fulfilling this functional responsibility on a local basis is conceded to be minimal in most law enforcement operations.[14] The need for increasing such scientific services has been expressed in a number of technological and administrative terms such as proximity of services, timeliness of services, education and training of law enforcement personnel, education and training of experts, certification of experts, research and development in techniques, standardization of methods, environmental reference stan-dards, and local support.[14, 16, 17] This stress on prerequisites for increased performance assumes the performance to be vital throughout the ad-ministration of criminal justice. The record of individual successes, partic-ularly in murder cases, is an insufficient support for this assumption. Relevance is not guaranteed by mere expansion and increased involve-ment.

For the "crime" laboratory, "there remains a legitimate question as to the extent of its use." [1]

Behind the operational needs there is, as stated by Dr. Blumstein, "the fundamental need to discover the impact on crime of the many actions taken to control it. Very little is known to even a rough approx-imation about how much any prevention, apprehension, and rehabilita-tion program will reduce crime. And without such knowledge, how can we intelligently choose among them?" [16] The fundamental need pertains not only to know what exists, but also to know what could exist and what should exist in the relationship of the "crime" laboratory to the administration of criminal justice. "There comes a time when an expand-ing scientific profession needs to stop and examine its foundations and modes of operation." [18]

The "Crime" Laboratory as a Subsystem in the Criminal Justice System

In a physical sense, the effect of a criminal upon the site of his activity, and, conversely, the effect of the site upon the criminal consti-tute the "pertinent" sources of information to the investigative process. This nonverbal information, however, must be retrieved before any value in the way of an interpretation can be assigned. When the interpretation is communicated to the investigative process, the value conveyed is sub-ject to a reinterpretation by each decision maker involved. These re-interpretations are affected by the extent to which the retrieved informa-tion is part of the interpretative message and by information from other sources. The response engendered is the investigative assessment of the criminal incident. In turn, the criminal justice system generally is subject to this interplay of information, interpretation, and reaction. Problems in measuring "crime" laboratory impact occur all along the communication channels in the administration of criminal justice. This study was directed at the problem of retrieval which can be viewed in two aspects: documentary and technical.

The informational output of a "crime" laboratory, both relevant and irrelevant, depends upon the input—the documentary retrieval. This aspect is the collecting * of physical objects from the site of the crime which might determine the event sequence for a given violation and connect the criminal to that event sequence. Figure 1 is a schematic diagram of physical retrievals from crime sites and suspects and subsequent processes.[19] The diagram shows only networks for physical objects and suspects with but two of the informational channels in that network. Operational delays in movement along the networks are included. This simple model emphasizes the critical nature of documentary retrieval as a laboratory input. Stated in Willmer's conceptual terms [20, 21] the physical interaction of the site environment and the criminal during the course of a violation produces a number of constitutent signals. "The total signal is made up of a number of different messages that have different frequencies and similar interdependencies."[18] Since the choice of those physical objects bearing relevant signals from a crime site or a criminal is a unique selection, it is desirable to minimize the error of not collecting a significant object. Additionally, since the distribution at a site of physical objects bearing relevant signals is unknown, several objects collected may yield the same signal. This redundancy in collection must be tolerated. The collection, or documentary retrieval, is further complicated by physiological shortcomings of investigators, such as vision, and psychological ones including perception."[18]

Technical retrieval of nonverbal information from a physical object is, within a laboratory operation, a selection of strategies. The choice of a strategy, or a combination of strategies, rests upon the query posed by the individual case. Within a given strategy, the search plan is a set function. For example, the finding of an unexpected stain at a crime site will raise the query as to what is it and how did it get there. In the absence of additional information as to the suspected violation, a general retrieval strategy would be necessary. This is the most difficult type of analysis to perform since the content of nonverbal information could be present in a variety of forms. During an abstraction, the recovery of one

---

* "Collecting" is used in the sense of physical removal and locational coordinates relative to the site.

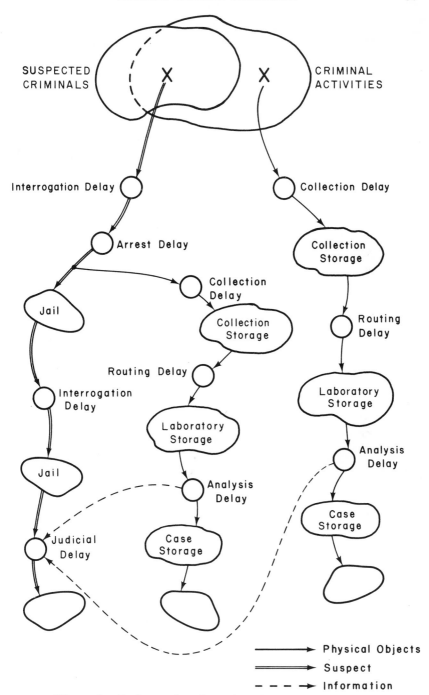

Figure 1. Pathways for Physical Evidence Retrievals.

form may change or obliterate another form. The decisions on strategies to use in technical as well as documentary retrievals are extremely critical because of this potential loss in informational content. In such circumstances, the general retrieval strategy must so order the analyses that the maximum amount of nonverbal information is recovered. Where additional information is available, e.g., a suspected homicide, and identification of the stain as blood and the determination of the direction of travel by the blood drops that produced the stain are types of possible abstracted information. Two retrieval strategies, one chemical and one physical, would be used. A simple removal of the stain would preclude the physical analysis; a photograph alone of the stain would preclude the chemical analysis. Another example of a technical retrieval strategy is cyclic in nature wherein subsequent steps in the series are determined by the preceding abstractions. One such series is where a liquid is first determined to be blood; then, of human origin; then, of a particular group; then, of a particular type; and then, possibly, to fall within various classifications of additional seriological factors. This aspect of technical retrieval of nonverbal information from physical objects has occupied much of the laboratory involvement in the administration of criminal justice. The allocation of resources to explore and develop this scientific examination and interpretation of nonverbal information is of basic importance. However, this necessary component of the "crime" laboratory function remains irrelevant unless physical objects are brought in for analyses.

Results

The number of cases where no physical objects could be retrieved were few in most offense classes. In the 63 suspected burglaries where this happened, five cases involved cleaned-up sites, four cases involved sites inaccessible to an observer, and 21 cases involved situations where it was thought the entry was by key or through an unlocked door coupled with removal of a single item prominently displayed, i.e., a portable color television. For one robbery there was an inaccessible site. This data is presented in Table I with totals and adjusted totals for cleaned sites, inaccessible sites, and minimal disturbance.

TABLE I
PROPORTION OF CASES WITH NO RETRIEVABLE
PHYSICAL OBJECTS

SUSPECTED OFFENSE	NUMBER OF CASES	WITHOUT OBJECTS	ADJUSTED°	PERCENTAGES No. OBJ.	ADJ.°
Burglary					
Residential	355	47	18	13	5
Non-Residential	114	7	7	6	6
Auto	78	9	8	12	10
Total	547	63	33	12	6
Auto Theft	85	5	5	6	6
Theft	45	12	12	27	27
Robbery	26	5	4	19	15
Rape	6	0	0	0	0
Assault/Battery	6	1	1	17	17
Murder	5	0	0	0	0
All Others	29	7	7	24	24
Total	749	93	62	12	8

° Totals adjusted for cleaned sites, inaccessible sites, and minimal disturbance.

Table II indicates the number of physical object categories filled for all cases in a suspected offense class with median values considering all cases and cases where physical objects were retrievable.

TABLE II
PHYSICAL OBJECT CATEGORIES PER CASE

SUSPECTED OFFENSE	NUMBER OF CASES	NUMBER OF PHYSICAL OBJECT CATE- GORIES FILLED	MEDIAN FOR ALL CASES	MEDIAN FOR CASES WITH RETRIEVABLE OBJECTS
Burglary				
Residential	355	1002	3	3
Non-Residential	114	479	4	4
Auto	78	168	2	2
Total	547	1649	3	3
Auto Theft	85	282	3	3
Theft	45	87	2	3
Robbery	26	47	1	2
Rape	6	31	4	4
Assault/Battery	6	15	3	3
Murder	5	22	6	6
All Others	29	85	2	4
Total	749	2218	3	3

The distribution about the median values for the physical object categories within given suspected offense classes can be seen in Table III.

TABLE III
DISTRIBUTIONS IN PHYSICAL OBJECT CATEGORIES

SUSPECTED OFFENSE	NUMBER OF PHYSICAL OBJECT CATEGORIES FILLED PER CASE											
	0	1	2	3	4	5	6	7	8	9	10	11
Burglary												
Residential	47	54	68	75	48	31	12	9	2	2	6	1
Non-Residential	7	6	14	22	21	10	12	11	5	4	2	–
Auto	9	23	16	17	7	4	1	–	1	–	–	–
Auto Theft	5	10	19	12	18	9	7	3	–	2	–	–
Theft	12	7	8	11	4	3	–	–	–	–	–	–
Robbery	5	8	4	5	4	–	–	–	–	–	–	–
Rape	–	–	1	1	2	–	–	–	–	2	–	–
Assault/Battery	1	1	–	2	2	–	–	–	–	–	–	–
Murder	–	2	–	–	–	–	1	2	–	–	–	–
All Others	7	4	4	3	4	1	4	–	–	1	1	–
Total	93	115	134	148	110	58	37	25	8	11	9	1

Table IV presents the total number of offenses in each physical object category for each suspected offense class.

TABLE IV

PHYSICAL OBJECT CATEGORIES PER SUSPECTED OFFENSE

PHYSICAL OBJECT CATEGORY *

SUSPECTED OFFENSE	1	2	3	4	5	6	7	8	9	10	11	12	13	14	15	16	17	18	19	20	21	22	Misc.	Total
Burglary Residential	111	125	107	50	65	72	51	63	62	27	23	43	47	15	15	15	16	26	9	17	7	10	26	1002
Non-Residential	73	49	20	41	25	33	10	34	14	20	20	10	15	24	17	18	4	12	11	5	6	10	8	479
Auto	37	28	7	22	6	3	11	2	4	5	7	3	3	6	3	3	4	2	3	1	0	0	8	168
Total	221	202	134	113	96	108	72	99	80	52	50	56	65	45	35	36	24	40	23	23	13	20	42	1649
Auto Theft	31	36	25	12	19	8	16	3	10	23	25	18	1	7	7	8	7	3	4	2	4	2	11	282
Theft	18	15	6	2	4	3	3	0	3	6	4	1	1	3	4	2	4	0	3	1	1	0	3	87
Robbery	2	6	3	0	0	2	4	1	2	8	4	1	3	4	0	1	0	0	0	2	3	0	1	47
Rape	0	2	3	1	3	2	5	0	2	3	1	1	0	1	1	0	0	0	1	3	1	1	1	31
Assault/Battery	1	2	1	1	0	1	1	0	0	0	0	0	1	2	0	0	0	1	0	0	0	0	1	15
Murder	2	2	2	1	1	1	1	1	1	1	0	2	0	2	1	0	1	0	1	0	3	0	1	22
All Other	7	6	3	11	7	4	4	2	1	3	4	1	1	1	1	1	10	3	3	2	5	3	2	85
Total	282	271	177	141	130	129	106	106	98	96	88	81	71	65	48	48	47	46	35	33	33	25	62	2218

* An explanation of Physical Object Category on following pages.

1. *Toolmarks*—This category includes all physical evidence where it was evident that one object, serving as a tool, acted on another object creating impressions, friction marks, or striations. A screwdriver, pipe, pry bar, fender of an automobile, or barrel of a gun could all produce toolmarks.

2. *Fingerprints and Palmprints*—All prints of this nature, latent or visible, are included. Bare foot prints, glove or other fabric prints would be included in this category also.

3. *Organic, botanical, zoological* material and unknown *stains*—Cases where matter of organic origin or stains of nonorganic nature were discovered. Excreta, all residues from trees and shrubs, and food items were typical examples.

4. *Glass or plastic fragments*—The presence of broken or chipped glass or plastic in an area suggesting it was the result of the responsible's actions or it might have been transferred to person(s) involved in the offense.

5. *Paint*—Liquid or dried paint in positions where transference would be possible to persons in that area. Freshly painted locations, cracked and peeling paint on window sills, and automobile collisions are leading examples.

TABLE IV (continued)

6. *Tracks and Impressions*—Includes skid and scuff markings, shoe prints, depressions in soft vegetation or soil, and all other forms of tracking. Conventional tool marks would not be included in this category.

7. *Clothing*—Instances where items of clothing are left, carried, removed or discarded by persons. Individual fiber characteristics are included in a separate category.

8. *Wood fragments*—Cases where forces have created fragmenting or splintering in areas where transference was likely. Prying, kicking, and chopping attempts at entry points were the most frequent examples.

9. *Dust*—All cases where "dust" (all types of surface contamination) was noticeably disturbed by someone.

10. *Cigarettes, matches, related ashes*—Discovery of any of these combustible items which were in such position that their relationship to responsibles was likely.

11. *Paper*, in various forms—There are two basic areas of identification for paper. First, where the paper itself might be traced to its original position or orientation, and second, where external information including latent prints and other contaminating substances might be present on the paper.

12. *Soil*—The presence of soil or soil-like material in locations where identification or individualization seemed possible.

13. *Fibers*, natural or synthetic—Fibers were often found near sharp corners or edges, or on objects where electrostatic or mechanical forces caused a transfer.

14. *Tools and weapons*—Cases where tools and weapons were found at crime scenes or in automobiles and there was a strong likelihood that they were involved in this or another criminal offense.

15. *Grease and oil*—Any lubricant or fatty substance, often possessing environmental contamination, that was in a position to suggest involvement in the crime.

16. *Documents*—Of such quality that their origin may be traced to a person or instrument. Suicides and robbery notes would be of this type. Also cases where instruments were stolen (check protectors) that could be traced back to a product of that particular instrument, in possession of rightful owner.

17. *Containers*—All bottles, boxes, cans and other containers which might hold residues or material of helpful nature.

18. *Construction and packing material*—All those substances commonly found in construction or packing areas, which don't belong to any of the other classifications.

19. *Metal fragments*—Industrial machining areas, scenes or objects of collisions, and other scrappings that would probably result in transfers to persons or objects in the vicinity.

20. *Hair*—Any animal or human hair discovered in an environment which could link a person with that particular area.

21. *Blood*—All suspected blood, liquid or dried, animal or human, present in a form to suggest a relation to the offense or persons involved.

22. *Inorganic and mineralogical substances*—All substances, and otherwise not belonging in another category, that could be classified under one of these headings, and bearing a relationship to the offense or offender.

Misc. *Other* category—Miscellaneous.

CHAPTER 7

Collection and Preservation of Scientific Evidence

The modern day medical examiner has often been called "The Medical Detective" because of the increasing application of scientific methods to the investigation of deaths coming under his jurisdiction.

In many of our cases the determination of the cause and manner of death has been materially aided by the proper evaluation of scientific evidence found and collected by the medical examiner during his examination of the room or place where the body was found. Hairs, blood stains, threads or pieces of cloth, mud and dust, medicine bottles or boxes are but a few of the items to look for that may be of importance in solving the mystery of a given death.

The laboratory technician is seldom able to personally supervise the collection, preservation, labelling, packing and transportation of physical evidence which he may later examine in the laboratory. He must usually rely entirely on the field investigator to properly recover and preserve those pieces of physical evidence pertinent to a given case.

A close understanding must exist between the laboratory technician and the investigator of their mutual problems and, unless this understanding exists, the full value of the presentation and proof of scientific evidence in court can never be realized. Laboratory findings should be considered by the investigator as a supplement to an investigation which has been thorough insofar as the subject matter is concerned.

The investigator must have some knowledge of the underlying principles of laboratory techniques and must know what the laboratory technician can, and equally important, what he cannot tell from evidence submitted for examination. The investigator must also know the laboratory's recommended procedures for methods of recovery, marking, preservation and forwarding of trace evidence.

In this bulletin are some of the recommended procedures for getting physical evidence to the laboratory in a condition suitable for performing scientific tests and in a manner that will meet legal requirements concerning such evidence.

Some genral rules will be given first and then different types of evidence will be discussed.

1. It seems unnecessary to say that physical evidence should reach the laboratory in as nearly as possible the same condition as it was when it was found at the crime scene but all too often material is submitted which has been so altered, tampered with or mutilated by investigators that any reliable testing procedures are utterly useless or impossible to perform.

2. Secondly, the investigator must be able to show a continuous chain of possession of evidence from the time it is discovered until the time it is introduced as evidence at the trial. It is desirable that evidence pass through as few hands as possible and that it be sent to the laboratory as soon as possible after its discovery. Written receipts showing the chain of possession are recommended. These should show the date, time and names of the transmitter and the receiver and the character or type of evidence involved.

3. Evidence material should be packed for shipment so as not to move about in the container during transit.

4. Each article should be wrapped and labelled separately. If several articles are submitted to the same laboratory then each should be wrapped and labelled individually and then all may be enclosed in one large bundle which is also labelled and wrapped.

5. Liquids should be placed in well stoppered containers properly labelled and then packed to safeguard against breakage during transit.

6. Wet stains upon cloth, paper or other objects should be *air* dried before packing to avoid putrefaction during transportation. Do not use a fan or artificial heat to dry such stains.

7. Powders, dust, hairs, specks of paint and other small particles of evidence require special care. They may be collected in small clean pill boxes, then sealed and labelled, or placed in one of the small clear plastic envelopes which have been developed in recent years. The label may be placed inside such envelopes which are then sealed with a stapler.

Bullets, firearms and fingerprints require special laboratory procedures and equipment which are not available in our laboratory. Such material should be turned over to the police or sent to the FBI Laboratory in Washington.

Weapons of Attack

These may be examined for blood, fibers, hairs, stains, embedded foreign material or fingerprints. Do not clean or wipe them in any manner. Care must be taken not to add to or destroy any fingerprints which might be present. Allow the object to air-dry if wet. Do not wrap such articles in cloth or paper, or wedge paper against them in the container.

The item of evidence may be laced securely to a flat piece of corrugated cardboard with heavy twine. For bottles and other irregular shaped objects containers have been devised using wooden dowels placed in holes in the top and bottom of the container in such manner as to hold the object stationary during transit.

Clothing

The clothing of the victim or suspect is often the source of valuable information. Do not shake or in any way attempt to clean articles of clothing sent in for examination. Very often the dust in the cuffs and seams of clothing, fibers and hairs invisible to the eye, and other fragile evidence may be destroyed by such cleaning.

Send the entire article of clothing. Do not cut out pieces bearing the area in question and submit them. Attach a label to each article submitted and wrap securely and separately. The clothing should not be folded across area which bear marks, stains or powder burns. A piece of clean white paper may be placed over such areas.

Firearms Identification

Firearms used in your cases are generally best left to the police to send to the appropriate laboratory for comparison tests. The medical examiner should examine the gun, however, and try to determine if the weapon in question was actually the death weapon. Cases have occurred where one caliber of bullet is removed from the decedent and yet the gun by his side was of a different caliber.

Bullets imbedded in wood or other substances should not be dug out but rather a portion of the material containing the bullet should be cut out or removed and sent to the laboratory. Removal of an evidence bullet from the body of a deceased person should be done by the physician performing the autopsy.

Blood Stains

Fresh blood is best gathered in a clean dry glass container. If obtainable, place a small amount of sodium oxalate or sodium citrate in the container. If a suitable container is not available the blood may be absorbed on clean white filter paper, blotting paper or as a last resort, a piece of clean white cloth. Air dry the article and place in a clean plastic or cellophane envelope, label and seal.

Send the entire garment of clothing or blood stained article where possible. Where it is impossible to submit the article bearing the stain, for example on floors or walls, the blood may be flaked off with a clean knife and collected in a dry pill box or plastic envelope. Use a different clean knife or other instrument for stains from different places.

Seminal Stains

Such stains will be found on clothing, sheets, blankets and other textile materials. Submit the entire article or garment, first being sure it is completely dry. Label and wrap each article separately and place in a suitable box or container for transportation to the laboratory.

Fingernail Scrapings

In homicides and other attacks against persons, including sex offenses, residue under fingernails of both victim and suspect may provide the investigator with valuable evidence. Minute particles of skin, blood, hair and cosmetics may be found which may possess indentification value.

Such scrapings should be taken with a clean knife and the residue from each finger placed in a separate clean dry container, sealed, labelled and forwarded to the laboratory.

Hair

The identification value of hair is more limited than certain other types of evidence but it may provide corroborative information. Hair may be found in the grasp of an assault victim, under fingernails, on clothing, bedding, and at various places on an automobile if such has been involved.

Place the hair on a sheet of clean paper, fold, seal and label and then place in another envelope or container to send to the laboratory.

If hair is found on a weapon of attack, send the weapon to the laboratory.

Where hair evidence is submitted, a generous sample of head, axillary and pubic hair from the victim or suspect should be submitted packed in separate containers, properly sealed and labelled. This hair should be pulled out, not cut off.

Fibers, Threads, Textiles, Twines, Cord, Rope

Small fragments of such items may be found at a variety of crime scenes and may furnish valuable information to the investigating officer. These items are packed in clean containers, sealed and labelled.

Drugs and Poisons

In suspected poisoning cases the laboratory will examine evidence such as foods, drugs, blood, and other material. In every suspected poisoning case make an immediate search for possible sources of the poisoning agent and container. If a suspected container is found, seal and label it and pack in a suitable container to avoid breakage during transit.

If the material is not in a suitable container for shipment then it should be placed in one provided by the investigator.

In suspected arson cases physical, mechanical or chemical methods may be employed for the timing and setting of fires. These include candles, kerosene and other inflammable liquids, matches, cigarettes, twines, fuses, clockwork mechanisms, sodium metal etc. Suspected material from such a scene should be placed in tightly stoppered containers, sealed and labelled.

CHAPTER 8

The Location of Hidden Objects

Barry J. Blain

It has been said that there are policemen in Great Britain who are unaware of the existence of the Home Office Police Research and Development Branch. This is probably the fault of the Branch publicity machine. However, even among those enlightened souls who know of us, there are many who know in very little detail about our day-to-day functioning. This article tries to draw attention to a very small area of the Branch's work in the hope of lifting at least part of the apparent veil surrounding it.

Mr. Peter Watts in the March edition of *The Police Journal*, described how the Branch is concerned with the scientific investigation of all aspects of police work, with the overall aim of increasing police efficiency. The major part of the studies concerns operational research into such topics as intelligence flow, beat patrol, traffic policing, computers for the police, and so on, One group, however, which is concerned more directly with day to day police activities is the Equipment Group. The Equipment Group deals with hardware, and maintains a very comprehensive file on police equipment, performs "Which"-type tests and field trials, carries out and supervises research and development, lends out equipment, and assists in police operations.

One topic we are studying in detail is the location of hidden objects. This is a problem closely related, technically, to the military problem of mine detection, but the range of target objects is much wider. It is probably a truism to say that a policeman can be looking for anything anywhere at any time. He might be looking for stolen gold bullion, a dead body, a smear of blood, bank-notes, a murder weapon, fingerprints, a missing person, and so on. The places searched might be a building, an open field, a car, a river-bed, a cesspool, or an overcoat pocket. The police also have to contend with political and sociological pressures. For instance, the concept of the liberty of the individual might prevent the police monitoring every person entering and leaving a dance hall or gambling club, in a search for weapons or drugs. There is the question of manpower effectiveness: how many officers should be detailed to carry out a search for a missing handbag, a blood-stained breadknife, a kidnapped child? The one aspect in which the police problem is less worrying than the military problem is that of safety: if a search is unsuccessful it is unlikely that anything is going to blow up in the detective's face, at least in the literal sense.

Kinds of Search

It seems that a detective is called upon to conduct two quite distinct kinds of search. The first kind is the search for clues and evidence at the scene of a crime, when he is looking for anything which might be important, and there is no way of telling beforehand what will turn up. Any object or disturbance or change in the original environment might be useful, and relevant finds could include a weapon, a single hair, a drop of drugged coffee, a chair out of place, a blood stain, a footprint or a cracked tile. In such a search the detective makes use of his five senses, coupled with the fantastic pattern recognition abilities of the experienced human brain. Scientific equipment is not necessarily of value, although some help can be obtained from simple technical aids such as a magnifying glass, a camera and lighting equipment.

In the second category of searching the object of interest is well defined. The police may suspect the existence of a vital piece of evidence, either through deduction or from a statement by a prisoner or witness. Occasionally a suspect will admit that he has thrown the weapon over a bridge or into a river, or it may be necessary to find a spent cartridge case, a cache of explosives or a supply of drugs. Alternatively, the police may be looking for specific stolen property such as bank-notes, gold bullion or a haul of silver. Finally there is often a need to search for a dead body. Although the case of "The Bodies on the Moor" is the notorious example which springs to mind, there are many more common and prosaic instances. Usually someone such as a child is missing, and the police have to mount a full-scale search, being reasonably certain that what they are looking for is a corpse. In this second category of searching there is a reasonable probability that equipment can be developed to reduce the workload on the police. We have concentrated our research almost entirely on this second category.

Equipment

A great deal of work is being done in assembling a large armory of detectors, and in developing specialized equipment for police purposes. Most progress has been made in the field of metal detection, but we are pressing ahead with techniques such as ultra-sonics, infra-red and thermal imaging and high definition sonar for other kinds of object. The technical problems which occur in this work are many and various, and thousands of words could be written on the subject. *The Police Journal* is probably not, however, the most suitable publication for detailed articles on electro-magnetic induction theory, the design of data-processing circuits, and the like.

A major problem which arises with every piece of new equipment is that of operational behavior. However good the instrument may be technically, it is useless for a real search unless it is ergonomically sound. Some faults just do not become apparent in any number of laboratory and field trials, but only emerge after the instrument has been operated in the police environment under the strained and urgent conditions of a real search. The kind of fault which might show up is that a handle is in the wrong place, a meter is too large or too small, the instrument cannot be held at the correct angle or at the optimum height from the ground, the batteries cannot be replaced in the rain, or the instrument is simply not robust enough for the job. This is why operational trials of equipment are, from our point of view, an absolutely essential step in the development and assessment of search instruments. It is also important to carry out operational tests in order to clarify the operational needs, and determine the type of environments which occur.

A New Service

An even more important reason for carrying out these operational trials is to develop the idea of a specialist technical service able to assist the police in searches, or indeed in other activities. The range of sensitive and sophisticated equipment which is available at the Branch with the corresponding expertise is not available for police use from any other source in the country, and possibly in the world. Some forces might have a metal detector on hand, and occasionally a local group of the Royal Engineers will be prepared to co-operate in a search. It must be remembered, however, that the Army is skilled primarily in detecting mines, not police objects. Also, the use of detection equipment is not quite as simple as it might first appear, as the choice of the best instrument depends on the object to be located and the environment, and a great deal of experience is necessary to get the best out of many kinds of detector. We hope, therefore, that when we use our instruments on a police search not only are we collecting data for ourselves, but we are providing a useful service to forces. It might be worth mentioning here that the Branch team is prepared to assist at any search, anywhere in the country, at very short notice if necessary, and that no red tape is involved: just a 'phone call to Horseferry House.

Searches

The first major police search undertaken by the Branch (see *Police Research Bulletin*, No. 8, October, 1968) involved finding bulldozers, mechanical diggers, and other civil engineering machines which had disappeared from various sites throughout the country, and were suspected to be buried in two sand quarries. At first sight, it appears ridiculous that a bulldozer cannot be found just by looking. However, when it is realized that they could be buried at a depth of 30 *ft.* or more in a 50 *acre* sand quarry, and that 2½m. *cu. yds.* of sand might have to be shifted, it becomes clear that a vast amount of spade work would be required.

The equipment taken to the scene by the Home Office team included mutual inductance metal detectors (for all types of metal at relatively short range), magnetometers (for iron and steel, at rather longer ranges), wooden canes, string, and a high quality spade. The idea was to clear the ground of surface "clutter," such as barbed wire and scrap metal, with the easy-to-use general purpose metal detectors, and then to cover the cleared ground with the more sensitive magnetometers. It turned out that the two quarries of interest had many steep banks, ridges and hollows, and extensive underwater areas and we found it impossible to carry out well-defined grid searches as carefully as we would have liked. Nevertheless with perseverance, and about 10 minutes assistance from a temporarily helpful bulldozer driver, most of the suspect areas were surveyed. At several points the magnetometers gave readings which could have been due to a large mass of steel such as a mechanical shovel at a considerable depth. Manual digging revealed 50-gallon oil drums at a depth of 8 *ft.* at two points, and an old plough or harrow, again at about 8 *ft.* below the surface, at another point. The major items of interest to the police were two unused steel lorry sides detected about 1 *ft.* inside a steep sand-bank by one of the mutual inductance devices.

In the summer of last year we assisted in the search for a key and a weapon ("a blunt instrument") required as evidence in the case of the murder of a woman. The search area was a half-acre garden, including much scrub land round a rather decrepit cottage. It was not possible to use a magnetometer as the area was too full of ferromagnetic clutter, and so the detectors used were of the induction type. The scrub land was covered with huge amounts of rusting chicken wire, and from the evidence of what we unearthed, the whole garden appeared to have been laid over an old breaker's yard. At one point, for instance, a Jaguar Mark VII engine was found, buried 3 ft. down. Nothing relevant to the case turned up, which was not surprising, as the weapon was found later (a wooden axe handle, and therefore undetectable by our instruments) at the roadside some distance away, and the key was found several miles along the road from the house.

In February, 1960, eight-year-old Iris Dorkins was found murdered on a common in the Southampton area, with 39 stab wounds. A 10-year-old suspect was found not guilty of the crime, and the case was not cleared up. Last autumn a man aged 22, held in custody at Southampton on another matter, admitted to the murder, and claimed that he had buried the murder weapon, a sheath knife, in soft mud in waste-land behind a garden in Bitterne. In 1960, a public footpath ran through this area, but by 1968 it had become very overgrown, and probably very changed in appearance. Nevertheless the man very emphatically identified, to within a yard or so, the place at which he claimed to have pushed the knife into the ground, just below the surface.

A day or two before we were called in the local police removed all bushes and undergrowth in an area 30 ft. by 30 ft., surrounding the stated point of burial. The ground was, however very marshy and wet, and on a slope, and it was again difficult to keep accurately to a grid pattern. One problem was that if a reading needed more than about 10 seconds at any one point, the operator was liable to find himself up to his knees in mud, and sinking fast. Even so, a very thorough search was made of the area, using sensitive magnetometers, and we removed much magnetic clutter, for example tin cans, rusty nails and the remains of an iron bedstead. A 10 ft. square was then marked out round the point of major interest, which was dug out to a depth of 1 ft., and several further instrument surveys were made. Although the detection depths of the pieces of scrap metal confirmed that a knife would have been detected at a depth of more than 2 ft., nothing of interest was discovered. It is possible that the very marshy nature of the ground caused the knife to sink to a depth of several feet, or that the top few inches of the soil had been washed away over the years, exposing the knife which had been taken by a passer-by.

Any Takers?

To the inevitable question "Have you ever found what you were looking for?" the answer must be in most cases "No." In fairness to ourselves, however, it must be pointed out that, first, no one else has found the item either, and second, we have usually been called in as a "last resort," after the police, the army and possibly the dogs have all made a thorough search. In nearly every one of the six or eight police searches we have carried out, we left the area reasonably confident that the object we had been looking for just was not there. This is presumably useful information for the officers in charge of the case.

I would like to conclude by restating that we are very keen to take part in any operational search which may turn up. There is no question of red tape or expense. All that is necessary is a call to Ron Walker, Norman Duncan, or myself, or to anyone in the Equipment Group of the Police Research and Development Branch. The telephone number is 01-834-6655.

Crime Detection and Scientific Techniques

Evidence of specific crime must be examined in the context of the offense. Although no two offenses are exactly alike, the investigator must gather certain evidence to prove his case.

A number of specific offenses and forms of evidence are discussed in this section in order to develop a frame of reference for the investigator. The section deals with homicide, forgery, fraudulent documents, ballistics, rape, blood tests and other offenses and investigatory techniques. One area not ordinarily associated with criminalistics, white collar crime, is also examined.

Certain information surrounding the assassination of President Kennedy and the subsequent investigation serves to illustrate techniques in the handling of such evidence. The investigation was detailed and the material presented in an understandable fashion.

Fingerprints and the development of their role in crime detection has served as a cornerstone in identification. The development of this science has led to the solving of many crimes as well as clearing many innocent persons.

The use of the breath as a measure of alcohol in the system has led to the development of the breathalyzer. Various forms of this device are now being used by the police in handling cases of drunken driving.

The importance of physical evidence cannot be overlooked. This point is emphasized by experienced investigators in their instructions to new officers.

CHAPTER 9

The Investigation of Deaths Due to Drowning

W. M. Jennings, M.D.

Drowning is a form of asphyxia which results from submersion or partial submersion, in a fluid. It is a form of smothering but is distinctive due to its characteristic circumstances and signs. The investigation of cases of drowning is important due to the fact that a large number of deaths, approximately 7,000 per year, and an estimated 7,000 near deaths, result from aquatic mishaps.

The majority of the victims die of obstruction of the air passages following inhalation of fluid. A certain small proportion die of asphyxia due to laryngeal spasm caused by sudden entry of cold fluid into the larynx. Others die of sudden cardiac arrest due to vagal stimulation following sudden entry of fluid into the air passages. The changes in the bodies of the victims of drowning are not distinctive, and hence it is important to be careful about the interpretation of the findings.

A person falling into water usually rises to the surface due to the natural buoyancy of the body. If he is unable to swim he usually makes irregular movements of his limbs, often in violent manner, in attempts to save himself. Violent attempts to breath air are made on reaching the surface and if the head is not quite above the surface he inhales and swallows certain quantities of water. The uncoordinated movements are not effective in maintaining position on the surface and the victim sinks, rising again with renewed physical activity. The number of times a person goes under depends upon his physical condition and endurance. The old saying that a drowning person goes down three times is nothing but an "old wives' tale." Sooner or later exhaustion sets in and the person finally sinks. Convulsive movements then occur with automatic respiratory efforts drawing more water into the bronchioles. Death occurs between two and five minutes after complete submersion, respiration ceasing first with heart beating for a certain time, following. (4)

External Signs of Acute Drowning

Providing putrefaction has not set in, the difficulties in recognition of a death from drowning are not as great as some believe. In most cases it is possible to determine whether the individual was alive or dead at the time of submersion. The special difficulty lies in distinguishing between accident, suicide, and homicide.(5)

Most bodies are pallid and cold, since cooling occurs twice as fast in water than in air. The rate of cooling is about 5°F per hour and the body usually attains the temperature of its surroundings within five to six hours following submersion.

Hypostasis is confined to the head, neck, and front of the chest as these parts are at a lower level than the rest in a drowned body and is reddish-pink in color, similar to some extent to that seen in carbon monoxide poisoning.

Goose-flesh, once thought to be an important sign is of no diagnostic value. Although frequently present, it can also occur in circumstances other than drowning.

The presence of foam in the nose and mouth is an important sign and if found on a body recovered from water is strongly suggestive of drowning. (4) It can occur in deaths due to other causes such as: strangulation, acute pulmonary edema, epileptic seizure, or electrical shock. However, other signs are present which make it possible to differentiate these cases. The foam is white or pinkish in color and composed of fine bubbles in a tenacious and persistent matrix. The foam may be wiped away but will reappear on pressure to the chest. (5)

The eyes may be congested. Petechial hemorrhages in the conjunctivae are rare.

Material such as sand, gravel, weeds may be found in the hands or beneath the finger nails. When objects are found tightly grasped in the hands it is a strong evidence of death from drowning. They also indicate that the person was alive when he entered the water. (4, 5).

Careful external examination is necessary if injuries which have occurred before submersion are to be recognized. These must be differentiated from injuries produced after death, e.g. lacerations and fractures caused by propellers.

Internal Signs

These signs are best seen before putrefaction takes place. Most attention should be turned toward the respiratory system. As with the external examination, foam is often found in the respiratory passages. The amount may vary from restriction to secondary bronchi and beyond to completely filling all the air passages. There may also be water in these passages, however, this is variable and not necessarily diagnostic. Other material found in air passages may be silt, small aquatic organisms and diatoms. Comparison of diatoms in water in which the body was submerged with those in water from air passages is valuable.

In cases of drowning, the lungs are bulky and ballooned. They are heavy, pale in color and pit on pressure. There are characteristic differences in lungs in cases of fresh and salt water drowning. In fresh water drowning, the lungs are emphysematous (called "emphysema agquosum"), crepitant and retain their shapes when removed from the body. When sectioned the individual portions also retain their shapes. The tissue contains some foam and very little fluid. On the other hand, the lungs in salt water drowning are heavy, jelly-like in consistency and markedly water-logged. They do not retain their shape when removed from the body and when sectioned considerable amount of fluid pours out.

The mechanism of the pulmonary picture is thought to be due to irritation of the respiratory mucosa by water which stimulates the secretion of mucus. Respiratory movements, often violent, whip this substance into a foam. The powerful inspiratory movements draw air deep into air passages but the expiratory efforts are inadequate to expel air, water, and foam. Thus a process occurs which progressively distends the lungs until death occurs from asphyxia. (5, 9, 10)

Due to inhalation of water and resultant obstruction to the pulmonary circulation, the right heart and large veins are distended with dark red blood. In fresh water drowning, because the inhaled fresh water has a lower concentration of chlorides than blood an osmotic pressure difference exists. Consequently the inhaled fresh water is drawn into the blood stream leading to increased blood volume and haemo-dilution. In salt water drowning, precisely the opposite happens. The salt water inhaled has higher salt content than blood and so haemoconcentration and water logging of the lungs result.

On the basis of these phenomena it is believed that measurement of choride content of the right and left heart can be of diagnostic value in suspected drownings. (4) These determinations are, however, of doubtful value because of mixing of blood between chambers in hearts, with patent septa and because of alteration due to changes of putrefaction. Several investigations of known drowning victims have failed to demonstrate choride differences in the majority of cases. (8)

Foreign material in the lungs and stomach fluid may be peculiar to the water in which the body was submerged. The drowning person usually swallows a great deal of water which should be examined grossly for mud, plants, and microscopically for plankton, algae, and diatoms. (4, 5)

Various organs and bone marrow of drowning victims has been found to contain diatoms. The water containing diatoms as well as algae and plant fibers penetrate the lung capillaries, reach the left heart and are carried throughout the circulation. In some cases where putrefaction or mutilation make examination of the lungs impossible, diatoms have been found in the marrow of the sternum and long bones of extremities to establish the diagnosis of drowning. The collection of marrow can be achieved without risk of contamination from outside by diatoms present on skin or clothing. Examination of one body buried at sea failed to reveal one single diatom. (2, 3)

There are many cases of drowning due to abnormal causes. Excellent swimmers have been found victims of drowning. One possible mechanism may be hyperventilation prior to swimming in order to extend time and distance. It is possible for these swimmers to lose consciousness due to oxygen lack before the impulse to breath. This blackout may cause the swimmer to drown, especially if under water. (7)

Some reflex mechanisms are thought to cause unusual deaths by drowning. An apnea and laryngeal spasm due to stimulation of receptors in the lung may cause such death. Also, lung receptors have been found to produce pulmonary hypertension and decreased systemic blood pressure without bradycardia. (9, 10)

Cardiac inhibition resulting from vagal stimulation has been suggested as a cause of death. The vagus may be stimulated by the sudden inrush of water into the naso-pharynx or larynx. A sudden blow to the abdomen may also produce the excitation. (5)

The final diagnosis is usually easy before putrefaction has begun. In cases complicated by decomposition the diagnosis is more difficult. It becomes a matter of inference based on circumstances of death and exclusion of other possible causes.

In all cases of drowning, it is important to perform the autopsy at the earliest opportunity so that putrefaction does not obscure the signs of drowning. It is significant to establish whether the person was alive before he entered water or not. The signs helpful in the diagnosis of drowning are objects firmly grasped in the hands, presence of foam and water in the air passages, presence of water in stomach, appearances of lungs and presence of diatoms in the internal organs and bone marrow.

REFERENCES

1. Editorial—*Oedema of the Lungs in Drowning.* J. Forensic Med. 8:97–8, 1961.

2. THOMAS, F., VAN HECKE, W., TIMPERMAN, J., *The Detection of Diatoms in the Bone Marrow as Evidence of Death by Drowning.* J. Forensic Med. 8:142–144, 1961.

3. TIMPERMAN, J., *The Detection of Diatoms in the Marrow of the Sternum.* J. Forensic Med. 9:134–136, 1962.

4. SMITH, S. and FIDDES, F. S., *Forensic Medicine,* J. and A. Churchill Ltd., London, pp. 263–273, 1955.

5. POLSON, C. J., 1962. *The Essentials of Forensic Medicine,* Pergamon Press, Oxford, pp. 331–359.

6. FULLER, ROGER H., 1963. *Drowning and the Postimmersion Syndrome: a Clinico Pathologic Study,* Military Med. 128:22–36.

7. DUMETRU, A. P. and HAMILTON, F. G., 1963. *A Mechanism of Drowning.* Anesthesia and Analgesia, 42:170–176.

8. GRIFFIN, GEORGE E., 1966. *Near-drowning: Its Pathophysiology and Treatment in Man.* Military Med. 131:12–21.

9. COLEBATCH, H. J. H. and HALMAGYI, D. F. S., 1961. *Lung Mechanics and Resuscitation after Fluid Aspiration.* J. App. Physiol. 16:684–696.

10. PASK, E. A., 1964. *The Physiopathology and Treatment of Drowning.* Brit. J. Anesth. 36:557–564.

CHAPTER 10

Statistical Features of Rape

Arthur Frederick Schiff, M.D.

The word "rape" is derived from rap meaning "to seize" or "to snatch." In turn, rap is born from the Latin *rapere, raptum* which means "to seize." Rape has been defined as "the unlawful carnal knowledge of a woman by force and against her will" (1), and as "the unlawful carnal knowledge of a woman by a man forcibly and against her will. That is, without her consent and against her utmost resistance." (2).

The author prefers a more comprehensive definition: *Rape is the carnal knowledge, to a lesser or greater degree, of a female, not the wife of the assailant, without her consent and by compulsion either through fear, force, or fraud, singly or in combination.*

There is general agreement that three elements belong to the crime of forcible rape: carnal knowledge, force, and the commission of the act without the consent of the female.

Carnal knowledge—or, to employ a common synonym, penetration —can be of any degree ranging from the slightest penetration by the male organ into the vulva, without the usual signs of virginity being erased, to complete sexual intercourse with emission of seminal fluid. DeRiver (3) states "the crime of rape is established on proof of penetration of the vulva only, without any invasion of the deeper parts as a necessary element."

The second component is the use of whatever force is necessary to overcome the victim's will to resist. In discussing English law, Professor Glaister (4) emphasizes the point that the victim must maintain her resistance to the last, giving up only when overcome by "unconsciousness, complete exhaustion, brute force, or fear of death." The Florida courts take a more lenient view. In forcible rape, the actual raw force can be transmitted to the mind. No hands may be laid upon the woman, yet she can be so intimidated by "an array of physical force" (5, 6) that she dare not resist, and, in fact, offers no resistance at all.

The third element of the triad is nonconsent. Even though force is used, if sexual intercourse is not against the will of the female, then no crime has been committed. On the other hand, if consent is given because of fear of personal injury the consent is considered void and the charge of rape stands (7).

In the United States, there is a definite increase in the known incidence of rape. The Federal Bureau of Investigation reported 22,460 cases of forcible rape in 1965. A year later the total climbed to 25,332 and the number reported for 1967 is 27,096. Table I depicts the rise in Dade County from 1964 to 1967. Whether the increase is due to a larger population, a deterioration of moral standards, a growing disregard for law and order, or a more strict enforcement is a probing question for the more knowledgeable psychiatrists and sociologists to consider.

TABLE 1

	1964	1965	1966	1967
White	85	82	88	99
Colored	108	96	112	130
Total	193	178	200	229

Reviews of indexed literature of the past decade (Cumulated Index Medicus 1957–1967) reveal an amazing paucity of statistics concerned with this crime. Books dealing with medical jurisprudence are comparably sparse not only on statistics, but on the subject itself; e.g., space allocated to the topic runs from 3 pages out of 239 (8) to 13 pages out of 1349 (9). Usually rape must share space in these few pages with "Other Sexual Assaults."

The purpose of this article is to present statistics derived from a series of 100 consecutive cases involving subjects of alleged rape which were seen and examined by the author in Dade County, Florida.

Place and Population

Dade County, the biggest of the 67 counties in Florida covers 2,352 square miles; however, this includes 650 square miles of the Everglades National Park, a flood control district along with bay and some ocean bottom, so that actually the vast area is reduced to 654 square miles of land for urban use and land "non-urban readily developable." There are 27 municipalities in the county, each but one with its own police force. There is also the Dade County Public Safety Department with jurisdiction over the whole county but mainly responsible for the unincorporated areas. As of July 1, 1967, the resident population was 1,181,840 with the addition of 300,000 to 400,000 more persons at the peak tourist month of March.

Results and Discussion

This series which excludes other sexual offenses such as child molestation, sodomy, and statutory rape, bridges a 14-month period from October 26, 1966, to December 27, 1967. Of the 100 females reporting sexual assault, 64 were black. Considering the fact that most of these crimes were either committed in or originated from predominantly Negro areas, it is not surprising that 64% had been perpetrated upon Negro women who are more available in these districts than are white women.

Age. The youngest victim was 6 years of age and the oldest 57. Cosgrave (10) declares "the oldest woman I have examined was a woman of 73 raped by her son of 44. The youngest, a child of 4½, live spermatozoa being isolated from what remained of the vaginal canal." Although the average age was 23.2 years, the group from 10 to 19 years was, by far, the largest at 47%. The next largest group was 20 to 29 years of age at 32%. The ages appearing most frequently were 13 and 14 at 8% and 9% respectively. Only 2% were below 10 and 3% above 50. Several conclusions may be drawn from these facts: Firstly, a young woman must be more desirable to a male than a wrinkled, gray haired oldster. Secondly, not only will a 13- or 14-year-old have less fight in her, making her more manageable, but she will be more easily immobilized by fear and threats. Thirdly, a youngster is more accessible and less difficult to accost than a more experienced adult. Also, in a càrryover of parental discipline, she may accede more readily to the demands of an older person.

Marital Status. Fifty-two victims were single while 48 had at one time or another been married. Of the latter, however, only 20 were married at the time of the attack. Hence, the unmarried, separated, or divorced woman—the one without a mate—seemed five times more susceptible to rape than her married counterpart, who either remained home with her mate or went out accompanied by him. Forty-one women, including 7 unmarried women, had given birth to one or more children (up to 8). Only 7, the youngest 6, the oldest 19, were virgins. This appears to reflect a current attitude of pride in nonvirginity with virginity considered as a stigma of juvenility.

Assailants. In 58 cases, there were lone assailants; in the remaining 42 cases, from 2 to 10 men were involved in the crimes, the most popular combination being a duo. Thus, approximately 181 men were involved (in instances of multiple assaults, accurate figures were difficult to obtain). Of these, 31 were white and the rest Negro. Of the single assailants, 19 were white and 37 Negro. In the multiple assault cases, 36% were performed by black males while 5% were perpetrated by white males. One case was an example of integration even in crime, two white men teaming up with a Negro to rape a 29-year-old Negress. In 15 instances, white women were allegedly raped by Negroes; in 2 cases a white man or men attacked colored women.

In 33% of the cases the assailant or assailants were known to the victims prior to the sexual confrontations. Here, the assaulter was either an overly ambitious boyfriend, a neighbor or neighbors, an acquaintance of the family, or even a member of the family. In one case, the assailant was a father-in-law; in two, brothers-in-law; and in one, a cousin.

In 7 instances, robbery accompanied rape. In 3 of these cases, robbery appeared to have been the prime motive, and rape was secondary, the thief merely taking advantage of the situation which presented itself.

Sixteen cases had their genesis in bars. The majority of the remaining cases began with a woman unwisely accepting a ride from a stranger, being abroad alone in a rough neighborhood at a late hour of the night, or visiting a man's abode for a little petting which soon got out of hand.

Location of Crime. Thirty-seven percent of the assaults occurred either in automobiles or on the ground in the immediate vicinity. Undoubtedly, because of its mobility or even as an enclosed semiprivate space, the automobile is favored by rapists. The second most popular site was the victim's dwelling or near vicinity (22%). Eleven percent took place in the living quarters of the assailants. The rest (30%) transpired in abandoned houses (6%) (of which Dade County has many due to the current building of expressways and condemnation of whole neighborhoods) or in open areas such as a schoolyard, a rock pit, a vacant lot, or an isolated wooded spot.

Injury to Victim. It may be conjectured that if a woman, facing sexual assault, resists to her utmost, she will sustain numerous injuries both locally (about and within the genitalia) and generalized (elsewhere on the body). However, as Smith (11) points out "it would be a great mistake to expect well-marked evidence of resistance in all cases." Graves and Francisco (12) call attention to the fact that "rape committed on married women and on women who have previously engaged in intercourse would be less likely to cause damage unless considerable violence was used." Nevertheless, if a woman is held to the ground, kicking, screaming, struggling, and making every effort to keep her thighs together, an examiner may reasonably expect to find some marks of violence. Injuries will vary from case to case, depending upon the amount of resistance offered by the victim, the force employed by the assailant, and even the mental attitude of the assailant. For example, the male may be a psychotic deriving sexual gratification from using more force than is necessary to accomplish his purpose. In discussing a New York City study of 250 sex offenders, Coleman (13) states that antisocial personalities with strongly aggressive tendencies were commonly observed in the group. Frequently, serious injuries were inflicted upon the victims.

Usually, when an adult female is overpowered by two or more males there is very little generalized injury, but much trauma may be found in the vaginal tract. In young children who do not understand what is happening and have little power of resistance, the same may be true.

One type of injury may occur while another is absent. Thus, in this series, a 6-year-old girl's genital tract was so badly traumatized she required immediate reparative surgery, yet the remainder of her body was almost free of damage. In the case of a 49-year-old woman, both eyes were swollen closed, her face was distorted by swelling, and she sustained fractures of both the maxilla and mandible. She was barely conscious, but there was only a slight injury to her genitalia. In a third case, a healthy 28-year-old airline stewardess had no injuries whatsoever. Although the official reports describe each recent abrasion, bruise, laceration, and scratch no matter how slight, they will not be considered as injuries here. Only gross injuries will be commented upon.

Sixty-two victims were classified as having no injuries at all, while 38 exhibited signs of trauma. Of these, 21% had generalized injuries mostly confined to the neck and head area. Ten percent showed some degree of trauma only to the genitalia, such as a recently ruptured hymen or tears of the vestibule or vaginal canal. Seven percent had a combination of local and generalized injuries. All generalized damage appeared to have been incidental to subduing the victim. All local injuries were incidental to sexual intercourse. A hymen was ruptured by a penis or tears were made because of a disproportion between a narrow or atrophic vagina and a large penis. Tears were also caused by over enthusiastic penile thrusting as well as by multiple assailants.

The ages of those injured ran from 6 to 57 years with an average of 24.8. It should be pointed out there is some question as to whether all 38 victims had been, in fact, sexually assaulted.

Credibility of Charges Made by Victims. Determining whether or not a female has been sexually attacked is, sometimes, an extremely difficult or even impossible task. Many an attorney in a courtroom requesting a "yes" or "no" answer from an examiner fails to realize he is not dealing with an exact science. The examiner must rely on whatever history he can elicit from the victim, law officers, and any witnesses, on physical signs which sometimes can be misleading, a sixth sense derived from long experience in interviewing patients, a good knowledge of psychology, and judiciously used intuition. Since no competent, unbiased witness is standing by during the commission of the crime, at best the conscientious examiner must also consider motive and must weigh the words and attitude of the victim carefully in arriving at a conclusion. At worst, he can only offer to the authorities whatever findings there be without comment.

The presence either of trauma, spermatozoa, or seminal fluid in the vaginal tract does not indicate sexual attack, nor, on the other hand, exclude it. Experience is the asset which allows the examiner to interpret the facts intelligently and decipher the puzzle that has been set before him. In some states, the life of a man may depend upon the examiner's competence and skill.

Although evidence—injury and/or proof of recent sexual intercourse —was detected in 83% of the cases, the author believes only 61% could be called and were, in fact, rape. Seven percent definitely were not rape and 15% were questionable. It is important to note here that although there was general agreement between experienced police investigators and this examiner as to the interpretation of the facts in the majority of cases, the author termed a few cases "questionable" within the framework of the three elements of rape while the investigators filed the cases as "unfounded." Paradoxically, in 8 cases, no evidence whatsoever was found, yet this examiner believed all of them to have been subjected to bona fide sexual assaults. This is not surprising since a woman, fearful of disease or pregnancy, may have douched before reporting the crime, thereby destroying all evidence. In addition, if the attacker wore condoms, and a few were thought to have used them, both chemical and microscopic tests would be expected to be negative.

Six percent showed no proof at all, but were classified as "questionable." Five percent had no proof and were definitely thought not to be rape. Why, one may ask, would a woman deliberately and falsely report she had been raped? Motives were many and were soon uncovered. One teen-ager, seeking revenge on a boy who had spurned her for another girl, enticed him into sexual intercourse in a schoolyard, then cried "Rape." When the severity of the charge and the penalty for the crime, along with the penalty for filing false information with the police, were explained to her, she quickly came forth with the truth. She had wanted "to teach him a lesson." Another teen-ager, returning home at a late hour to face waiting parents who had earlier ordered her to be home by midnight, used the same cry to turn punishment into concern. One woman, it was believed, was not paid for her services and so lodged a complaint with the police. Yet another, picked up by police for public drunkenness, declared falsely she had been sexually assaulted. Blackmail is sometimes a motive. Casper (14) discusses the case of a woman whose 11-year-old daughter was allegedly raped by a respected shopkeeper. Not only did the child display the signs of rape, but, in addition, had gonorrhea. Eventually, it was brought out in court that the child's mother had attempted to extort money from the accused and, having failed in this endeavor, turned the child over to her lover to produce physical evidence. The lover had gonorrhea; the shopkeeper did not.

Apprehension and Punishment. Because the majority of these crimes is committed in clandestine stealth, the assailant hurriedly perpetrating the act in a few minutes, then fading into anonymity, the job of apprehension is a difficult one. Nevertheless, the police agencies of Dade County have done creditable work in connection with apprehension.

After thorough investigation, 19% of the cases were marked "unfounded." In 45% assailants were not apprehended. Of the remaining 36%, 10 cases were resolved in the courts with the assailants being found guilty of rape or a lesser crime such as attempt to commit rape, or being allowed to plead guilty to a lesser charge. Then ten cases involved a dozen men. Three of the 12 were sentenced to life imprisonment. One case was dropped because the complaining witness disappeared. Six victims, for one reason or another, elected not to prosecute; two withdrew charges. One assailant is known to be entering court very shortly on a reduced charge, "assault with intent to commit rape."

The punishment, naturally, varies with the circumstances, the victim, the assailant, and even the judge. One assailant who pleaded guilty to a charge of intent to rape was given 20 years at hard labor in the state penitentiary while another who was found guilty of rape by a jury with a recommendation for mercy received 15 years in prison. Another assailant who raped a 6-year-old child was sentenced to life imprisonment. The author has never seen a jury bring in a verdict entailing the death penalty. Also, he has been impressed by the fact that the members of the jury before which he has testified all appeared serious, sincere, and dedicated to reaching a just verdict.

Summary

An analysis of 100 consecutive cases of alleged rape seen in the Dade County Medical Examiner's Office has been presented. These have been considered from the standpoint of age, marital status, assailants, location of crime, injury to victim, credibility of charges made by victims, and apprehension and punishment.

REFERENCES

1. TAYLOR, ALFRED SWAINE, *Principles and Practice of Medical Jurisprudence* (12 ed.). Keith Simpson (ed.). J. & A. Churchill, Ltd., London, England, 1955.

2. BLACK, HENRY CAMPBELL, M. A., *Black's Law Dictionary* (4th ed.). West Publishing Co., St. Paul, Minn., 1951.

3. DE RIVER, PAUL, *Crime and the Sexual Psychopath*, Charles C Thomas, Springfield, Illinois, 1958.

4. GLAISTER, JOHN, *Medical Jurisprudence and Toxicology* (11th ed.). Livingston, Edinburgh, Scotland, 1962.

5. Rice v. State, 35 Fla. 236, 17 So. 286, 1895.

6. Flowers v. State, 152 Fla. 649, 12 So.2d 772, 1943.

7. Green v. State, 135 Fla. 17, 184 So. 504, 1938.

8. MORITZ, ALAN R. and STETLER, C. JOSEPH, *Handbook of Legal Medicine*, C. V. Mosby Co., St. Louis, Mo., 1964.

9. GONZALES, THOMAS A., VANCE, MORGAN, HALPERN, MILTON, and UMBERGER, CHARLES J., *Legal Medicine, Pathology and Toxicology* (2d ed.). Appleton-Century-Croft Inc., New York, 1954.

10. COSGRAVE, MAY ST. JOHN, *Medical Examination in Alleged Sexual Offenses*, J. Forensic Sci. 3, 94–99, 1963.

11. SMITH, SIR SIDNEY and FIDDES, FRED SMITH, *Forensic Medicine* (10th ed.). J. & A. Churchill, Ltd., London, England, 1955.

12. GRAVES, LESTER R. and FRANCISCO, J. T., *A Clinical and Laboratory Evaluation of Rape*, J. Tennessee State Med. Assoc. 55, 389–394, 1962.

13. COLEMAN, JAMES C., *Abnormal Psychology and Modern Life*, Scott Foresman and Co., Chicago, Illinois, 1958.

14. CASPER, JOHANN LUDWIG, *A Handbook of the Practice of Forensic Medicine*, Vol. 3. The New Sydenham Society, London, England, 1864.

CHAPTER 11

Breath Testers

Evaluation of inexpensive, disposable devices for breath testing of blood alcohol concentration shows that the devices often produce high numbers of erroneous results.

The evaluation, conducted by the State Toxicology Laboratory of North Dakota State University (NDSU) and the Insurance Institute for Highway Safety, concluded that most of the devices "produced erroneous readings in practically all of the ranges of actual blood alcohol concentration where tests were administered."

Under field conditions "the results may be expected to be even worse, since this study was conducted under ideal conditions, without many of the problems expected in the field," the report notes.

A total of eight types of disposable screening devices from four manufacturers were evaluated. The devices tested were the Alcolyser H, Alcolyser (Iowa type), Alcolyser 100, Becton-Dickinson Device 1, Becton-Dickinson Device 2, Kitigawa Drunk-O-Tester, Sober-Meter SM-1 and Sober-Meter SM-6.

(The disposable devices tested are not to be confused with the more expensive, quantitative testing instruments—such as the Breathalyzer and Photo-Electric Intoximeter—which use photo-electric and other sophisticated chemical and physical methods, and whose results correlate well with actual blood alcohol concentrations.)

Manufacturers estimate sales of the disposable devices to be half a million units or more per year and say sales are increasing rapidly. Recent highway safety program emphasis on removing the abusive drinker from the driving population has lent impetus to the use of the inexpensive, disposable devices.

The devices, which range in price from less than one dollar to about two dollars each, are commonly used for pre-arrest screening tests, indicating whether the blood alcohol concentration of a suspect is above or below the legal limit. The devices "have been offered, in some instances, as tests that produce results that can be used as evidence," the report states.

Thirty-one states follow the Department of Transportation highway safety standard 308 which recommends that blood alcohol concentrations not higher than 0.10 percent by weight be used to legally define the terms "intoxicated" or "under the influence of alcohol." The remaining 19 states have limits higher than 0.10 percent or have no legal limit.

Each of the disposable screening devices tested consists of a small glass tube, containing an alcohol-sensitive chemical, and a breath-volume measuring device such as a balloon, plastic bag or air pump.

"In this evaluation all of the disposable screening devices were used as simple qualitative tests of the type that indicate whether the blood alcohol concentration of a test subject is greater than or less than 0.10 percent," the report points out. "Results indicating a blood alcohol concentration greater than or equal to 0.10 percent were recorded as positive and results indicating a blood alcohol concentration less than 0.10 percent were recorded as negative."

The report cautions that, "Before a law enforcement agency decides to use a device of this type—and if so, which particular device—it is imperative that the agency and the officers who will administer the test be aware of the results that may be expected, and in particular the two types of erroneous results: false positive readings and false negative readings."

It points out that readings obtained from the disposable devices may indicate that a person is legally intoxicated when his actual blood alcohol concentration is below the legal limit (a "false positive" reading). "If the device is being used for pre-arrest screening, errors of this type could result in arrests at actual blood alcohol concentrations below the recommended maximum legal limit.

"Clearly, both public and judicial acceptance of screening tests would be jeopardized if the screening tests employed were to result in false arrests of large numbers of motor vehicle operators who subsequently would be exonerated on the basis of accurate post-arrest quantitative tests," the report says.

On the other hand, readings from the same devices may indicate that blood alcohol concentrations are lower than the legal limit when, in fact, they are not (a "false negative" reading), thus possibly permitting "suspects who should be arrested (to be) set free. Since some violators would erroneously pass the test . . . this would dangerously limit the effectiveness of countermeasures utilizing such devices for screening tests," the report says.

"The need for a breath screening test for alcohol has been widely recognized for some time. However, devices producing excessive error, if widely used, will impede progress toward the development of effective countermeasures against the problem of the abusive use of alcohol as a source of road losses," the study concludes.

CHAPTER 12

The Kennedy Assassination:
Hairs and Fibers

Testimony on hairs and fibers was given by Paul M. Stombaugh of the FBI. Stombaugh has been a specialist in hairs and fibers since 1960, when he began a 1-year period of specialized training in this field. He has made thousands of hair and fiber examinations, and has testified in Federal and State courts in approximately 28 States. Stombaugh examined and gave testimony on the following objects: (1) The green and brown blanket found in the Paine's garage, Commission Exhibit No. 140; (2) the homemade paper bag found on the sixth floor of the Texas School Book Depository following the assassination, Commission Exhibit No. 142; (3) the shirt worn by Oswald on November 22, 1963, Commission Exhibit No. 150; and (4) the C2766 rifle, Commission Exhibit No. 139.

General Principles

Hairs. As shown in Commission Exhibit No. 666, a hair consists of a central shaft of air cells, known as the medulla; a cortex containing pigment granules (which give the hair its color) and cortical fusi (air spaces); and a cuticle and an outer layer of scales. Unlike fingerprints, hairs are not unique. However, human hairs can be distinguished from animal hairs by various characteristics, including color, texture, length, medullary structure and shape, shape of pigment, root size, and scale size. In addition, hairs of the Caucasian, Negroid, and Mongoloid human races can be distinguished from each other by color, texture, size and degree of fluctuation of diameter, thickness of cuticle, shape and distribution of pigment, and shape of cross-section. Moreover, even though individual hairs are not unique, the expert usually can distinguish the hairs of different individuals. Thus, Stombaugh, who had made

88

DIAGRAM OF A HAIR

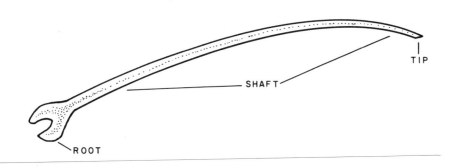

TIP

SHAFT

ROOT

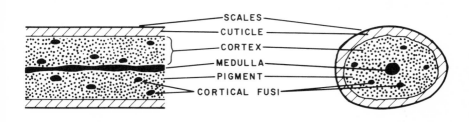

SCALES
CUTICLE
CORTEX
MEDULLA
PIGMENT
CORTICAL FUSI

LONGITUDINAL SECTION   CROSS SECTION

COMMISSION EXHIBIT No. 666

approximately 1,000 comparison examinations of Caucasian hairs and 500 comparison examinations of Negroid hairs, had never found a case in which he was unable to differentiate the hairs of two different Caucasian individuals, and had found only several cases in which he could not distinguish, with absolute certainty, between the hairs of two different Negroid individuals.

Fibers. Like hairs, the various types of natural and artificial fibers can be distinguished from each other under the microscope. Like hairs too, individual fibers are not unique, but the expert usually can distinguish fibers from different fabrics. A major identifying characteristic of most fibers is color, and under the microscope many different shades of each color can be differentiated—for example, 50–100 shades of green or blue, and 25–30 shades of black. The microscopic appearance of three types of fibers—cotton, wool, and viscose—is illustrated in Commission Exhibit No. 665. Two of these, cotton and viscose, were the subject of testi-

TEXTILE FIBERS

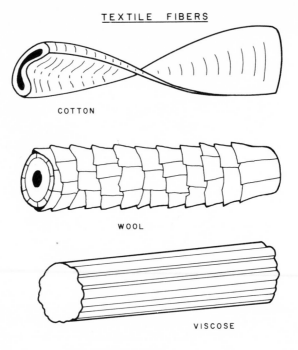

COTTON

WOOL

VISCOSE

COMMISSION EXHIBIT No. 665

mony by Stombaugh. Cotton is a natural fiber. Under the microscope, it resembles a twisted soda straw, and the degree of twist is an additional identifying characteristic of cotton. Cotton may be mercerized or (more commonly) unmercerized. Viscose is an artificial fiber. A delustering agent is usually added to viscose to cut down its luster, and under the microscope this agent appears as millions of tiny spots on the outside of the fiber. The major identifying characteristics of viscose, apart from color, are diameter—hundreds of variations being possible—and size and distribution of delustering agent if any.

The Blanket. Stombaugh received the blanket, Commission Exhibit No. 140, in the FBI Laboratory at 7:30 A.M., on November 23, 1963. Examination showed that it was composed of brown and green fibers, of which approximately 1–2 percent were woolen, 20–35 percent were cotton, and the remainder were delustered viscose. The viscose fibers in the blanket were of 10–15 different diameters, and also varied slightly in shade and in the size and distribution of the delustering agent. (The apparent cause of those variations was that the viscose in the blanket consisted of scrap viscose.) The cotton also varied in shade, about seven to eight different shades of green cotton being present, but was uniform in twist.

When received by Stombaugh, the blanket was folded into approximately the shape of a narrow right triangle. A safety pin was inserted in one end of the blanket, and also at this end, loosely wrapped around the blanket, was a string. On the basis of creases in the blanket in this area it appeared that the string had been tied around the blanket rather tightly at one time while something was inside the blanket. Other creases and folds were also present, as illustrated in Commission Exhibit No. 663. Among these was a crease or hump approximately 10 inches long. This crease must have been caused by a hard protruding object approximately 10 inches long which had been tightly wrapped in the blanket, causing the yarn to stretch so that the hump was present even when the object had been extracted. The hump was approximately the same length and shape as the telescopic sight on the C2766 rifle, and its position with respect to the ends of the blanket was such (based on the manner in which the blanket was folded when Stombaugh received it) that had the rifle been in the blanket the telescopic sight could have made the hump.

The string wrapped around the blanket was made of ordinary white cotton. It had been tied into a granny knot (a very common knot tied right over right, right over right) and the dangling ends had been further tied into a bow knot (the knot used on shoelaces).

After receiving the blanket, Stombaugh scraped it to remove the foreign textile fibers and hairs that were present. He found numerous foreign textile fibers of various types and colors, and a number of limb, pubic, and head hairs, all of which had originated from persons of the Caucasian race, and had fallen out naturally, as was shown by the shape of their roots. Several of the limb and pubic hairs matched samples of Oswald's limb and pubic hairs obtained by the Dallas police in all observable characteristics, including certain relatively unusual characteristics. For example, in both Oswald's pubic hair and some of the blanket pubic hairs, the color was a medium brown, which remained constant to the tip, where it changed to a very light brown and then became transparent, due to lack of color pigments; the diameters were identical, and rather narrow for pubic hairs; the hairs were very smooth, lacking the knobbiness characteristic of pubic hairs, and the upper two-thirds were extremely smooth for pubic hairs; the tips of the hairs were sharp, which is unusual for pubic hairs; the cuticle was very thin for pubic hairs; the scales displayed only a very small protrusion; the pigmentation was very fine, equally dispersed, and occasionally chained together, and displayed only very slight gapping; cortical fusi were for the most part absent; the medulla was either fairly continuous or completely absent; and the root area was rather clear of pigment, and contained only a fair amount of cortical fusi, which was unusual. Similarly, in both Oswald's limb hairs and some of the limb hairs from the blanket the color was light brown through its entire length; the diameter was very fine and did not noticeably fluctuate; the tips were very sharp, which is unusual; the scales were of medium size, with very slight protrusion; there was a very slight gapping of the pigmentation near the cuticle; there was an unusual amount of cortical fusi, equally distributed through the hair shaft; and the medulla was discontinuous, granular, very bulbous, and very uneven.

Other limb, pubic, and head hairs on the blanket did not come from Oswald.

The Paper Bag. Stombaugh received the paper bag, Commission Exhibit No. 142, at 7:30 A.M. on November 23, 1963. No foreign material was found on the outside of the bag except traces of fingerprint powder and several white cotton fibers, which were of no significance, since white cotton is the most common textile, and at any rate the fibers may have come from Stombaugh's white cotton gloves. Inside the bag were a tiny wood fragment which was too minute for comparison purposes, and may have come from the woodpulp from which the paper was made; a particle of a waxy substance, like candle wax; and a single brown delustered viscose fiber and several light-green cotton fibers.

The fibers found inside the bag were compared with brown viscose and green cotton fibers taken from the blanket. The brown viscose fiber found in the bag matched some of the brown viscose fibers from the blanket in all observable characteristics, i.e., shade, diameter, and size and distribution of delustering agent. The green cotton fibers found in the bag were, like those from the blanket, of varying shades, but of a uniform twist. Each green cotton fiber from the bag matched some of the green cotton fibers from the blanket in all observable characteristics, i.e., shade and degree of twist. Like the blanket cotton fibers, the cotton fibers found in the bag were unmercerized.

The Shirt. Stombaugh received the shirt, Commission Exhibit No. 150, at 7:30 A.M. on November 23, 1963. Examination showed that it was composed of gray-black, dark blue, and orange-yellow cotton fibers. The orange-yellow and gray-black cotton fibers were of a uniform shade, and the dark-blue fibers were of three different shades. All the fibers were mercerized and of substantially uniform degree of twist.

The C2766 Rifle. The rifle, Commission Exhibit No. 139, was received in the FBI Laboratory on the morning of November 23, 1963, and examined for foreign material at that time. Stombaugh noticed immediately that the rifle had been dusted for fingerprints, "and at the time I noted to myself that I doubted very much if there would be any fibers adhering to the outside of this gun—I possibly might find some in a crevice some place—because when the latent fingerprint man dusted this gun, apparently in Dallas, they use a little brush to dust with they would have dusted any fibers off the gun at the same time." In fact, most of the fibers Stombaugh found were either adhering to greasy, oily deposits or were jammed down into crevices, and were so dirty, old, and fragmented that he could not even determine what type of fibers they were. However, Stombaugh found that a tiny tuft of fibers had caught on a jagged edge on the rifle's metal butt plate where it met the end of the wooden stock, and had adhered to this edge, so that when the rifle had been dusted for fingerprints the brush had folded the tuft into a crevice between the butt plate and the stock, where it remained. Stombaugh described these fibers as "fresh," by which he meant that "they were clean, they had good color to them, there was no grease on them and they were not fragmented." However, it was not possible to determine how long the fibers had been on the rifle, in the absence of information as to how frequently the rifle had been used. Examination showed that the tuft was composed of six or seven orange-yellow, gray-black, and dark-blue cotton fibers. These fibers were compared with fibers from the shirt, Commission Exhibit No. 150, which was also composed of orange-yellow, gray-black, and dark-blue cotton fibers. The orange-yellow and gray-black tuft fibers matched the comparable shirt fibers in all observable characteristics, i.e., shade and twist. The three dark-blue fibers matched two of the three shades of the dark-blue shirt fibers, and also matched the dark-blue shirt fibers in degree of twist. Based on these facts, Stombaugh concluded that the tuft of fibers found on the rifle "could easily" have come from the shirt, and that "there is no doubt in my mind that these fibers could have come from this shirt. There is no way, however, to eliminate the possibility of the fibers having come from another identical shirt."

CHAPTER 13

Checlass: A Classification System for Fraudulent Checks

E. H. W. Schroeder

Any agency which investigates crimes involving fraudulent checks requires a system for classifying and filing the large number of checks it receives. In the fraudulent check file in this laboratory, checks were originally classified and filed according to name, age, modus operandi, handprinting, typewriting, check protector and rubber stamp impressions, and company names. When a check was being examined it would be classified and checks with matching classifications drawn from the file. Only then would the handwriting be compared.

This system was very useful but had one serious drawback. If the passer of a check changed his name or if his check did not fall into any of the above classifications, such a check could not be linked with any of the checks in the file, although the file might contain checks written by him. To overcome this deficiency a system using handwriting as its primary classification was developed in this laboratory after similar systems for handwriting and check classifications were studied in relation to the requirements of our fraudulent check file (1, 2, 3, 4, 5, 6). This system was first employed in 1966 and although it was successful, its effectiveness depended upon the use of trained document examiners. Also, only 250 writings on checks could be classified by one examiner in a year because of the time-consuming measurements that were required. The increase in work called for a speedier system which could be operated by personnel not qualified as document examiners. This meant that the characteristics used should be easily recognizable and the modes in which they occur easy to define. In addition these characteristics had to satisfy the following criteria:

1. High frequency of occurrence,
2. Distinct variations from one person's writing to another's,
3. Tendency to remain constant within a single writing.

Exhaustive tests of approximately sixty handwriting characteristics on more than three thousand checks led to the selection of the following characteristics:

A. Sex
B. Wording on the amount line
C. Filler strokes
D. Relative height of letters (ratio)
E. Variations in the cents symbols following the printed $
F. Width of writing
G. Payer signature
H. Type of payee
I. Date
K. First letter of amount in words
L. Peculiarities
M. Capital M and N
N. Capital T
O. Capital F
P. Numeral 3
Q. Numeral 4
R. Capital S
S. Capital A
T. Capital C
U. Capital D

Descriptions of Classifications

A. Sex: The sex of the check passer is inferred from the named used or, in case of doubt, from the police report.

Class 1—Male
Class 2—Female

B. The wording on the amount line:

Class 1—Standard—Only the dollar amount is specified in words, e.g.:

Fifty-six ————————
twelve ————————

Class 2—Others, e.g.:
Fifty-six Dollars ————
Forty-one & three cents
No more than forty ——
Forty and ————————
———— 40 ————

(Handprinting and typewriting are included in these classifications.)

C. Filler strokes on the amount line:

Class 1—Standard—Either there is no filler stroke present or there is a plain, relatively straight stroke on the right of the written dollar amount, e.g.:

Forty

Forty ————————

Class 2—There is a plain, relatively straight stroke on the left of the written dollar amount.

Class 3—Other

(Handprinting and typewriting are included in the classifications of the filler strokes.)

D. Relative height of letters (ratio): The heights of upper zone letters like b, d, f, k, l, and capital letters are compared with those of middle zone letters like a, c, e, i, m, o, w.

Class 1—Standard—The former are approximately 2½ times as high as the latter, e.g.:

Class 2—They are more than 2½ times as high as the latter, e.g.:

Class 3—They are less than 2½ times as high as the latter, e.g.:

E. Variations in the cents symbols following the printed $:
Class 1—Standard—Neither xx nor strokes present, e.g.:

Class 2—xx present, e.g.:

Class 3—Other, e.g.:

F. Width of writing:
Class 1—Standard—The average length of the downstrokes of the letters m, n, and u is approximately equal to the distance between successive downstrokes, e.g.:

Class 2—The downstrokes are further apart, e.g.:

Class 3—The downstrokes are nearer, e.g.:

G. Payer signature:
Class 1—The payer signature has only one given name or an abbreviation
     of such name, with no initials, e.g.:
     John Doe, Ed. Doe, Geo. Doe, Robt. Doe
Class 2—Other, e.g.:
     Doe, J. Doe, John F. Doe, John Frank Doe
(Mr., Mrs., Sr., Jr., etc. are ignored.)

H. Type of payee:
Class 1—The payee is an individual.
Class 2—The payee is a store, company, etc.

I. Date:
Class 1—The month is written or typed, in full or abbreviated,
        (a) with a capital followed by small letters,
        (b) to the left of the day,
        (c) the day is expressed only in figures,
   and (d) the figures are not followed by a suffix, e.g.:
     December 1, 1970; Dec. 1, 70.

Class 2—Other, e.g.:

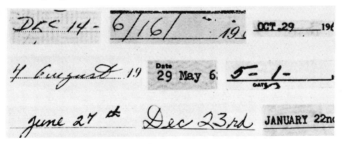

K. First letter of amount in words:
Class 1—Standard—The written dollar amount starts with a capital letter.
Class 2—The written dollar amount starts with a small letter.
(Handprintings and typewritings are included.)

L. Peculiarities:
Class 1—Standard—None of the characteristics described in classes 2 and
     3 are present.

Class 2—Additions, handwritten, handprinted, typed or rubber stamped are inserted to increase the check's plausibility, e.g.:

(Addresses, telephone numbers and remarks such as "Plus exchange" are ignored.)

Class 3—The check has indications of foreign authorship or bears typewriting, check protector, or rubber stamp impressions, but does not fall into class 2; or the writing on the check is distinctly tall, short, large, or small, e.g.:

M. Capital M and N:

Class 1—The letter does not fall into class 2 or class 3.

Class 2—The stroke preceding the first downstroke of a capital M or N
consists of a loop, wedge, or retrace, e.g.:

Class 3—The letter is handprinted, e.g.:

N. Capital T:

Class 1—The letter consists of one stroke, e.g.:

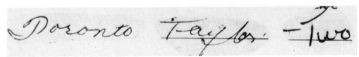

Class 2—The letter consists of more than one stroke, e.g.:

O. Capital F:

Class 1—The letter consists of one stroke, e.g.:

Class 2—The letter consists of two strokes, e.g.:

Class 3—The letter consists of more than two strokes, e.g.:

P. Numeral 3:
Class 1—It does not fall into class 2.
Class 2—The first element consists of a loop, wedge, or retrace, e.g.:

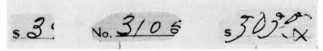

Q. Numeral 4:

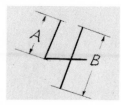

Class 1—Length A is greater than, or approximately equal to, one half
of length B, $[A \geqq \frac{1}{2} B]$, e.g.:

Class 2—$A < \frac{1}{2} B$, e.g.:

Class 3—Closed form, e.g.:

R. Capital S:
Class 1—The initial stroke is low, e.g.:

Class 2—The initial stroke is high, e.g.:

S. Capital A:
Class 1—The letter is oval or circular and there is no long introductory
    stroke, e.g.:

Class 2—The letter is oval or circular and has a long introductory stroke,
    e.g.:

Class 3—Other, e.g.:

T. Capital C:
Class 1—There is no long initial stroke as illustrated in class 2.
Class 2—There is a long initial stroke, e.g.:

U. Capital D:
Class 1—The letter is written in cursive writing and the final curve
    proceeds to the left of the staff, e.g.:

Class 2—The letter is written in cursive writing and the final curve
    remains on the right of the staff, e.g.:

Class 3—Other, e.g.:

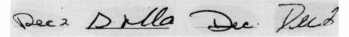

Rules for Classification

1. Characteristics which do not fall clearly into a class are ignored.
2. If a characteristic falls equally into two classes it is classified in both. If it falls preponderantly in one class it is classified in that class.
3. Check protector impressions are ignored, except in characteristic L. Peculiarities, Class 3.
4. Ticks are disregarded.

So that a classifier may make the classifications more readily a table of characteristics is appended (Table I).

Results

Six hundred checks were separately classified in this laboratory by two persons. Approximately 95% agreement was found. The average time taken by one person to classify twenty checks was one day.

It is seen that this method is reliable and requires no special training in handwriting examination. It makes use of handwriting characteristics and habitual ways of filling out checks which distinguish one person from another. It is speedy and enables the operator of a check file to deal with large numbers of checks. Hence the system lends itself to computerization. A computer program has been set up and tested at this laboratory and it is expected that use of a computer will be routine before long.

Summary

A system for classifying the writing and other characteristics of fraudulent checks is described. Checks are classified according to the sex of the writer, his handwriting characteristics and the habitual format of his checks. The system uses twenty characteristics which may appear in one of two or more well-defined modes. Ten of these characteristics usually appear on all checks in one of these modes. All the characteristics can be recognized by persons not qualified as document examiners and checks may be classified at the rate of four per hour. A computer program has been set up for the system and tested at the Centre of

TABLE I
CHARACTERISTICS EMPLOYED IN CLASSIFICATION
FOR COMPUTER PROGRAMMING

Sex
11 Male
12 Female

Amount Line-wording
13 Standard
14 Other

Filler Strokes
15 Standard
16 Stroke on the left
17 Peculiar strokes

Relative Height
18 Standard

19 Distinctly high

20 Distinctly low

Cents variations
21 Standard
22 xx present
23 Strokes present

Width
24 Standard

25 Wide writing

26 Narrow writing

Payer signature
27 John Doe, Al Doe
28 Other

Type of payee
29 Individual
30 Store or company

Date
31 March 5, 70; Mar 5, 70
32 MAR 5, 70; 5–3–70;
   Mar 5th

First letter
33 Capital letter
34 Small letter

Peculiarities
35 Standard
36 Additions
37 Foreign authorship,
   typewriting, check
   protector; tall, short,
   large, small writing

Capital M & N
38 Plain stroke

39 Reverse move-
   ment

40 Handprinted

Capital T
41 One stroke

42 Other (incl.
   handprinted)

Capital F
43 One stroke

44 Two strokes
   (incl. hdpr.)

45 Other (incl.
   handprinted)

Numeral 3
46 Plain stroke

47 Reverse move-
   ment

Numeral 4
48 Standard

49 Long endstroke

50 Closed form

Capital S
51 Standard

52 Starting high
   (incl. hdpr.)

Capital A
53 Standard

54 Long initial stroke

55 Other (incl.
   handprinted)

Capital C
56 Standard
   (incl. hdpr.)

57 Long initial stroke

Capital D
58 Curve to left

59 Curve on right

60 Other (incl.
   handprinted)

Forensic Sciences. It enables an operator to retrieve checks on file which correspond to the questioned check in a sufficient number of characteristics.

REFERENCES

1. BATES, B. P., *Identification System of Questioned Documents*. Police 8, No. 2, 1963.

2. BRADFORD, R., *The Bradford System*. Ralph Bradford, Supt. Records, Long Beach, P.D., California.

3. LEE, C.D. and ABBEY, R. A., *Classification and Identification of Handwriting*, D. Appleton & Co., N.Y.

4. LIVINGSTON, O. B., *A Handwriting and Pen-Printing Classification System for Identifying Law Violators*. J. Crim. L., 49, No. 5.

5. MALLY, R., *Identification and Handwriting*. Bundeskriminalamt Laboratory, Wiesbaden, Germany.

6. MOORE, J., *Handwriting Classification*. Description of the system employed by the Criminal Investigation Department of the Nottingham City Police, Nottingham, England.

CHAPTER 14

Disguised Handwriting: A Statistical Survey of How Handwriting Is Most Frequently Disguised

Edwin F. Alford, Jr.

In conducting handwriting comparisons, the document examiner must consider many aspects of the writing. The significance of individual writing characteristics is one of these. Here, correctness of evaluation is often dependent on the ability of the examiner to properly recognize various elements of disguise which are often introduced into a writing. Not only should the basic rules governing disguised writing be understood but also the examiner should be familiar with the diverse factors involved in producing such writing.

A person intent on producing an effectively disguised writing must both eliminate his natural and unconscious writing characteristics and simultaneously substitute alien features. Ideally, this is done in a manner to preclude suspicion based on the pictorial quality of the writing. Such a task is formidable and usually results in failure. Writing habit is so ingrained in most writers that it is impossible for them to entirely discard automatically formed elements. Many features of the writing are beyond the awareness of the writer and therefore cannot be modified. Other characteristics are not altered, simply because the writer lacks the skill necessary to make the change.

Even if a writer were moderately successful in eliminating his own writing habits, the substitution of alternate characteristics presents a most difficult obstacle. To be successful, a writer must change both conspicuous and inconspicuous elements. The alternate forms for letters and numbers must be consistently utilized and, at the same time, the writing must exhibit some semblance of naturalness.

The average writer attempting a perfect disguise is not equal to the challenge. The task is too complex. Most writers are ignorant of the factors involved and therefore their manner of disguise is relatively simple. The methods employed and those features most often subject to change are generally familiar to the document examiner. Nevertheless, the examiner must be on the alert. And, he must be competently qualified to recognize disguising features so that obvious characteristic differences are not wrongly attributed to disguise and concordant features are not overlooked just because they are camouflaged.

This paper endeavors to explore, in a systematic way, the most common methods persons employ in trying to alter their writing and also to determine the frequency of occurrence of the particular features that were changed. No attempt has been made to determine how many different elements of disguise each writer utilized.

Methods

Format of Specimens Used for Survey.   In implementing the study only "request" writings were used rather than including writings examined in actual cases. This offered better control and resulted in more equitable appraisal of those features considered. Also, the format of request specimens insured inclusion of disguise elements that might occur randomly in actual cases. While realizing that persons actually attempting to disguise for nefarious purposes might be motivated to greater effort and possibly the disguise would be more "thought-out" and practiced than in the case of those merely honoring a request to attempt disguise, it was believed the request specimens would still be fairly representative of the basic features of methodology.

Implementation of the study dictated the desirability of using a simple form for the request specimens. While providing maximum benefit, the simplicity of a form would not overburden the respondent with lengthy writing tasks. The form devised consisted of two identical pages. Two "check-size" blocks were drawn across the top of each page. Immediately below spaces approximating the size of postal cards were drawn. Each writer was asked to write his own name in one of the "check" spaces and three different names in the other. Similarly, an address was to be written in one of the "postal card" spaces and a short text in the second. The writers were asked to first furnish specimens of natural writing on one page. A disguised version of that writing was then requested on the second page. No information was furnished regarding possible methods of disguise.

By a study of the writing requested such elements of disguise as slope, size, capital and lower case letter forms, etc. could be considered. In addition, it was also possible to consider spacing, spelling and arrangement habits as related to checks, addresses and texts.

Criteria Used in the Study. Many handwriting features do not readily lend themselves to statistical evaluation. Because of the normal variations inherent in all handwriting, meaningful measurements can become impracticable. Heights, angles, ovals, etc. fluctuate, the slope of a writing is not necessarily consistent, and even the general forms of letters are subject to varying degrees of normal change. The value assigned a given individual handwriting feature varies due to the subjective nature of the evaluation process. This limits the feasibility of a precisely accurate statistical approach to the evaluation of handwriting. For this study, no attempt was made at critical measurements. The results reported are not represented to be exact. They are offered as valid observations based on interpretations of those features changed. The statistics cited were derived from the 135 samples collected. The conclusions and principles stated were drawn from both the samples and numerous actual cases examined involving disguised writings.

There is an infinite number of ways for a person to attempt to disguise handwriting. Studies in this project were restricted to those features of disguise considered major (or most likely to occur), based on previous examining experiences.

The success of the attempt to disguise was not considered in treating the collected data. If an obvious attempt was made to disguise through the alteration of a specific characteristic it was included in the statistics, even if the writer lacked the capability to utilize that mode of concealment throughout the writing. In some instances, isolated changes in writing habit were classified as disguise because by their nature they clearly indicated the intent of the writer to implement them as such.

In accordance with the above factors, the findings reported are based on interpretations of disguise elements consistent with the experience and examining acumen of the author.

Results

Study of the 135 sets of writings collected confirmed the general views of document examiners regarding the prevalence of certain methods employed by writers to effect a disguised handwriting.

Slope. It is generally accepted that the most popular methodologic feature of disguise is a marked alteration of the slope or slant of writing. Of the 135 samples examined, 50 writers, or 37 percent, attempted to change slant when producing the disguised writing. Sixty percent of those changing the slope of the writing converted their normal forward slope to a vertical writing, while 16 writers (32 percent) substituted a pronounced back slope in place of their usual forward slope (Fig. 1).

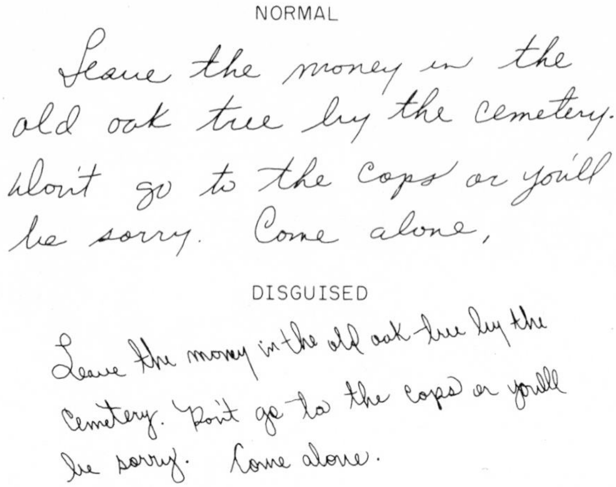

NORMAL

DISGUISED

Figure 1. Change of slope utilized to disguise. Other modifications are slight. Use of back slope changes pictorial appearance.

Examination of the undisguised writing revealed approximately 9 percent of all writers wrote normally with a vertical or backhand slant. Three of those writers changed from a back to a forward slope and one normally employing a vertical writing shifted to a back slope.

As previous examining experience had indicated, the introduction of a pronounced departure from the normal slope was, for the most part, neither consistent nor successful. Rarely was the writer able to maintain an unnatural slope uniformly.

Awkward (Unaccustomed) Hand. Only 8 persons (6 percent) of the 135 tested resorted to the use of the awkward hand as a means to conceal their writing identity. This may seem to be a low number. In view of the fact that writing produced with the unaccustomed hand often does not closely resemble that written with the normal, it would appear many writers would adopt this mode of disguise. The fact that relatively few rely on the use of the awkward hand may be attributed to an inability to produce writing which would be considered artistically acceptable for the purpose for which it was intended. Also, many persons do not consider themselves capable of writing with the unaccustomed hand.

Handprinting. Not unexpectedly, handprinting or block lettering was not employed as an alternate form of writing signatures on checks. (In actual practice, forged checks examined in the U. S. Post Office Department Crime Laboratory occasionally do contain handprinted endorsements.)

Six of those persons furnishing specimens did resort to handprinting to camouflage the address or text portions of the writing. Additionally, several of those persons obviously made an effort to even disguise the printing, a finding that may be surprising to some examiners.

Size. The size of a writing may normally vary according to the circumstances surrounding the writing act. Since the normal and disguised writings collected for this analysis were written under like circumstances in each instance, any radical alteration of size was interpreted to be an element of the disguise attempt. The percentage of those changing the size of the writing was nearly the same as the percentage of those changing the slope. Approximately 35 percent of the writers (48 persons) wrote larger or smaller than normal. Thirty-one persons wrote larger while 17 individuals diminished the size of the writing. It was noted that the larger writing tended to be somewhat more ornate or fanciful whereas the writing became less embellished when written smaller.

Arrangement. Arrangement features include paragraphing, placement of writing relative to the "base line," line spacing, margins, address alignment and endorsement placement.

An examination of the arrangement habits on the samples collected confirmed the commonly held belief that such traits are rarely considered by the person attempting to disguise. In fact, it was observed that arrangement characteristics are quite consistent. Many distinctive arrangements were noted among the 135 specimens taken, but only three persons changed their writing regarding this feature; and none of those changes involved the manner of writing the "checks." Two of the changes involved the arrangement of the message portion of the form and only one person changed the arrangement of the address portion (Fig. 2).

Angularity. It is generally recognized that the reason for altering slope in disguising handwriting is because it drastically changes the overall appearance of the writing. Since a change in the angularity of a writing also may have a profound effect on the pictorial aspect it was decided to ascertain if this quality of a handwriting was commonly altered as a mode of disguise. Various factors may influence the angularity or roundness of writings, and it was difficult to judge whether a variation of such was a planned part of the disguise or merely resulted due to other modified elements. Tabulations regarding angularity were restricted to those instances where it was believed the change was deliberately introduced as a means to disguise. These showed 32 percent of the writers changed the appearance of the angularity of their writing.

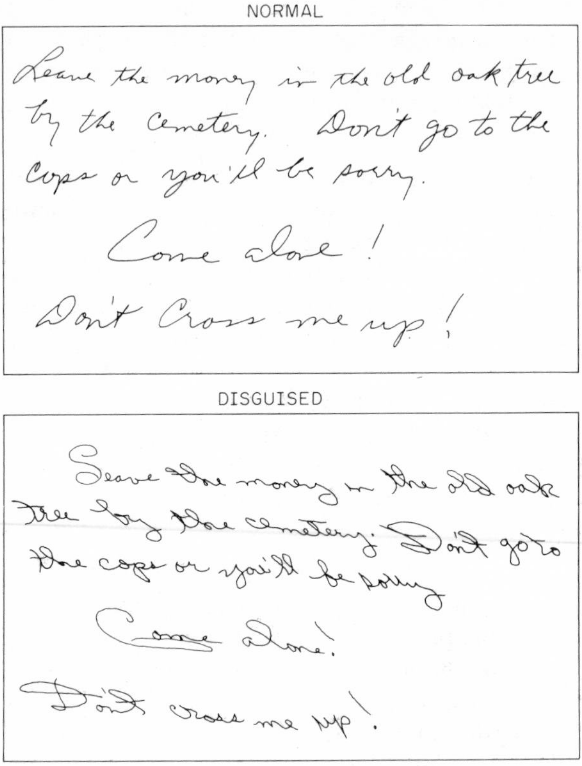

NORMAL

DISGUISED

Figure 2. Arrangement habit unaffected by attempt to disguise. Slope altered, attempt made to change approach strokes, substitute forms used for capital letters and upper and lower extensions modified.

Seventy percent of those persons wrote a more rounded hand while 30 percent made the writing appear more angular (Fig. 3).

Spacing. Like arrangement habits, spacing characteristics are almost never tampered with by those seeking to mask their true writing identity. Of the 135 individual writings studied, none was materially altered regarding spacing habits. It was observed that spacing changed proportionally, i.e., wide spacing became wider in certain instances, but most disguised writing was spaced amazingly similar to the natural writing. Even persons possessing highly unusual and identifying characteristics retained those idiosyncrasies in the disguised text writing.

Spelling. It was not anticipated that persons would misspell endorsements on the "check" blocks on the handwriting forms since such sig-

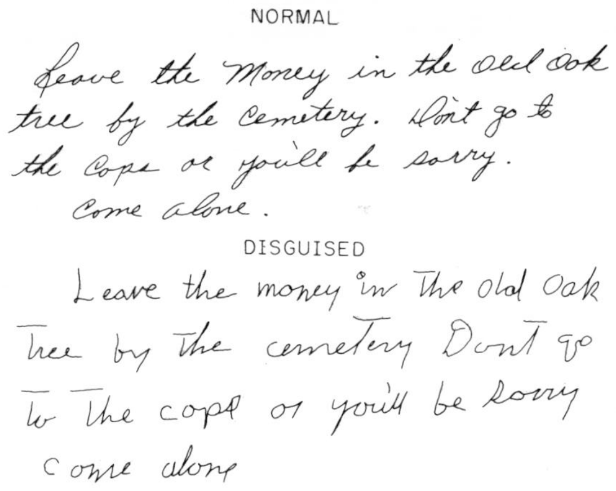

NORMAL

Leave the money in the old oak tree by the cemetery. Don't go to the cops or you'll be sorry. Come alone.

DISGUISED

Leave the money in The old Oak Tree by The cemetery Don't go To The cops or you'll be sorry Come along

Figure 3. Example of use of increased angularity to disguise. Writer also changed upper and lower extensions and altered placement of *T* cross.

natures would normally be viewed with suspicion if not spelled in conformity with the "correct" spelling. Experience through examination of anonymous letters in the laboratory did indicate, however, the possibility of deliberate incorrect spelling and grammatical errors in text writing as a means to preclude identity. The test writings did not support this supposition. None of the writers deliberately changed spellings.

Approach Strokes.   The absence or presence of approach strokes can influence the visual complexion of writing quite significantly. The survey conducted disclosed approximately 37 percent of the disguised writings contained some attempt to modify the approach strokes, although in almost all cases the writer was not able to persist in the alteration. The fact that some determined endeavor had been made to change the approach strokes was deemed sufficient to include that writing in the statistics.

It was noted that alteration of the approach was, in almost all cases, confined to the letters *t, i, b* and *h*. Other letters were largely ignored. Further, most writers appeared to direct their efforts toward changing only one letter. For example, a person omitting the normal approach stroke of the letter *t* would continue to place approach strokes on the letters *i, b* and *h* in the disguised writing.

Alteration of introductory strokes is not likely to be an effective means of disguise (especially for extended writings) in view of the fact most writers seem to concentrate their efforts toward only a single letter and are not able to maintain the change regarding that character.

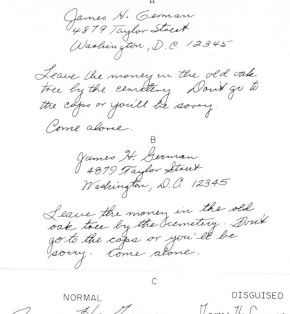

Figure 4. A. Normal writing by one person. B. Disguised writing by same person. Approach strokes altered in text writing but not in address. Note also that writer changed number forms in disguised writing. C. Terminal strokes modified. Writer also used different writing instrument to produce disguised address.

Of the persons attempting to modify the approach strokes, 54 percent deleted approach strokes and 46 percent added such strokes (Fig. 4).

Terminal Strokes. The findings regarding terminal strokes generally paralleled those of approach strokes except the letters selected for alteration were not the same. In the case of terminal strokes the change was almost inevitably restricted to the small letter *s*. Other letters were very seldom altered. Twenty-eight percent of the writers changed the finishing strokes to some extent. Fifty-three percent of those persons added, extended or embellished the terminal stroke and 47 percent omitted or diminished that feature (Fig. 4).

Upper and Lower Extensions. Because of their visual prominence, upper and lower extension letters are particularly susceptible to careful attention by the writer intent on deception. The survey of this feature disclosed that approximately one-half of the writers endeavored to reject their normal method of forming the upper and lower loops and to substitute alternate forms. Apparently lower extensions are more conspicuous to the average writer since twice as many instances of lower loop alterations were recorded than of those formed above the base line of writing. Most often, writers normally using loops resorted to plain or retraced extensions while fewer of those normally employing retraced or plain extensions changed to looped formations. In many instances, the size or shape of loops were altered. Also, not unexpectedly, changes were more frequent and more consistent regarding the first or last letter of a word. Upper and lower extensions were frequently not altered when they occurred within a word (Fig. 2).

Some writers naturally form looped extensions in certain letters and not in others. Where mutual variation was present in both the normal and disguised writing that sample generally was not counted as reflecting altered extensions as a mode of disguise. In several such samples, however, it was noted that the writer contrived to have the disguised writing contain both forms in diametrically opposed fashion. For instance, a writer using a looped form y and a retraced p may try to disguise by using a retraced y extension and a looped p. Four of the writings studied reflected an attempt of this nature.

Additionally, it was ascertained that most individuals did not encompass both upper and lower extension changes as a manner of disguise. Most writers were obviously content to change either one or the other. Relatively few tried both.

Capital Letters. Another area of disguise adopted by a great many writers involved the design of capital letter formations. Approximately 80 percent (115 writers) attempted to alter the forms of these letters to at least some degree. Somewhat surprising was the fact that in many instances the writers did not adhere to a changed letter form successfully, but rather frequently lapsed back to their normal style of that letter. Only half of the specimens disclosed efforts to substantially modify more than several of the capital letter designs whereas the other half reflected attempts to reshape only one or two selected letters (Fig. 5).

Lower Case Letters. It is generally accepted that lower case letters forms usually offer the best examining basis for determining identity regarding disguised writing. Statistics gained from this study confirm this. With the exception of a certain few letters, lower case styles remained basically unaffected even when written by those employing drastic measures of disguise concerning other features.

Several of the lower case letters do offer alternate forms which lend

NORMAL   DISGUISED

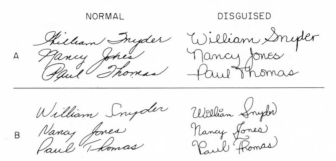

Figure 5. "A" written by one writer, "B" by another. Capital letters altered in each instance. Additionally, disguised writing "A" is more rounded than normal writing—writer "B" uses circle *i* dot as element of disguise.

themselves well to substitution, and these are sometimes adopted by the person striving to conceal his true writing habits. Those most commonly changed are the *r, e, s, k* and *t*. The conventional *r* may be replaced by the arcade style (sometimes referred to as a "speed *r*"), or, in some instances the block form of the letter is adopted. The "Greek *e*" may be substituted for the usual formation of that letter. The block form of the *s* is often utilized instead of the typical lower case version. Similarly the block form *k* may be used in place of the generally used copybook *k* or the more unusual Locker copybook style. The *t* is most often altered when it is the last letter of a word. The writer improvises various means of forming the cross bar.

A comparison between the normal and disguised writings assembled showed the frequency of change of those lower case letters listed above to be as follows:

1. The *r* was changed on 22 of the specimens.

2. Fourteen samples contained alternate forms of the letter *e*.

3. In 13 writings the *s* was significantly changed.

4. Substitute forms of the *k* were depicted on 7 of the hand-writing specimens.

5. Alternate methods of forming the *t* were noted on 27 samples.

Most of the writers restricted their efforts at concealment to one or two of the letters mentioned although some attempted to change several. In spite of the fact that the writers were not required to furnish lengthy specimens, consistent adherence to a substitute form of a letter was impossible for the majority (Fig. 6).

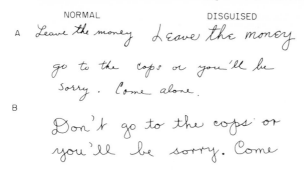

Figure 6. Example of use of alternate form of *e*. B. Example of change of *r* and *s*. Both writings by same writer.

"I" Dot or Period.   Although it was not initially contemplated that the *i* dot or period be included in the study, the prevalence of change made regarding this feature as an element of disguise dictated otherwise. Nearly 15 percent of the writers changed the *i* dot and/or period. Sixteen persons used a circle formation for the *i* dot or period when disguising. Those persons normally used the conventional form of that feature. Four of the individuals who normally employed the circle form of the *i* dot or period reverted to the conventional style when effecting a disguise (Fig. 5).

Numbers.   The identification value of any writing is significantly enhanced if numbers are included in the material studied. In addition to extending the range of character forms available for examination, figures are in themselves sufficiently individual to warrant opinions regarding authorship. The variety of figures encountered in routine document examinations establishes the uniqueness of numerals. In spite of this awareness by document examiners, it is believed by some that numerals are often overlooked by the writer groping for a deceptive expedient. It is theorized that the average person assumes numbers are written alike by everyone and, additionally, most persons are not familiar enough with numbers to invent an alternate form.

Statistics derived from this study indicate that there is a general awareness of the individuality of number forms and many writers possess the facility to effectively modify the figures they normally use. Many adopted the style of numbers associated with printed matter in place of the conventional written forms, some added serifs to normally plain figures, and others incorporated the "foreign" designs such as the familiar "German" 7.

Seventy percent of the disguised writing studied contained at least some changed number forms (Fig. 4).

Summary

Disguised writings are frequently encountered by the examiner of questioned documents. Recognition of the various elements associated with disguise is most important. Wrongly attributing differences to disguise, or overlooking possible identifying features because they are masked, could lead to serious error.

A survey was initiated to statistically analyze methods and elements of disguise. Request writing samples were collected from 135 persons. These were studied to determine the most common methods of disguise used by those intent on writing deception and also to determine the frequency of change of the disguise elements employed.

Elements studied included use of the awkward hand; change of slope, size, letter forms and numbers; alteration of upper and lower extensions; deceptive spelling and arrangement habits; altered approach and terminal strokes; change of angularity of writing, etc. Observations regarding the various aspects of disguise are reported.

It was noted that the elements most often changed are those which most drastically affect the pictorial appearance of the writing. Other features altered are those which lend themselves well to modification or substitution.

The study showed most attempts to disguise are neither consistent nor successful.

CHAPTER 15

Tool Marks: An Aid in the Solution of Auto Larcenies

Susan M. Komar

The number of auto larcenies in the United States is reaching tremendous proportions and the rate is steadily increasing. One reason for the criminal's success in this field is that he knows that there is little chance that he will be caught, and even if caught, his sentence will be mild compared to the punishment for other, more risky crimes. The lack of sufficient evidence in auto larceny cases is one of the major difficulties that the law enforcement agent faces. Stealing cars in order to strip them and sell the transmission, battery, and other major component parts is also on the increase. Here, too, the investigator faces the problem of insufficient evidence.

Tool mark identification has proven itself an invaluable aid in the field of criminal investigation and should not be overlooked in cases of auto larceny, especially involving auto strippings. It is obvious that the offender must use tools of some sort to loosen and remove the nuts, bolts, and other items which secure the battery, transmission, engine, and other parts of the car which he finds profitable to remove. In doing this, he must often use a considerable force on the tool—a force sufficient to cause that took to leave its "fingerprint" in the form of a tool mark on the parts removed. These marks can then be compared to test marks made with tools found on suspects, thus increasing the possibility of linking them to the crime.

Since there are so many of them on a car, lug nuts provide a very good source for tool marks from auto strippings. The force required to remove these lug nuts from the wheel is usually sufficient to cause clearly identifiable tool marks. These marks are characteristic of the particular

119

tool which caused them, and they can be reproduced in 'the laboratory provided the proper tool is submitted.[1]

One difficulty in the comparison of tool marks on lug nuts is to find a suitable medium on which to make the test marks. This material must be strong enough to withstand the twisting force which must be applied to obtain a suitable test mark, and yet, it must be soft enough not to cause any alterations in the suspect tool. This test material must also have a hexagonal shape of the same dimensions as the nut.

A method previously attempted in this laboratory required the casting of a hex-head bolt in lead. This gave the proper shape to the test material, but when a strong, twisting force was applied, the lead simply gave under the stress and twisted with the force, making it impossible to obtain a suitable test mark.

Recently, a new method of making test marks for lug nut comparisons was tried and found to be quite satisfactory. The test material used was a three-quarter inch hexagonal rod of aluminum. (See Fig. 1.) This immediately solves the problems of shape, dimensions, and resistance to stress. Since the aluminum is a softer metal than that of the lug wrench, the danger of altering or damaging the tool is also eliminated.

The procedure for making the test marks is as follows: a length of aluminum rod is wrapped in a cloth (to prevent stray marks) and tightly gripped in a vise with about an inch or two of the rod protruding from the side in order that the socket end of the wrench can be fitted over it. The necessary force and twist is applied causing the wrench to make a clear, identifiable tool mark suitable for comparison.[2] Since the procedure is easy to repeat, many test marks can be made, varying the force and angle of application.

The small piece of aluminum containing the test mark can then be examined along with the lug nut under a comparison microscope. (See Fig. 2a.) At times the test or questioned mark will contain much more detail than the one to which it is being compared, thus making the comparison difficult. Greene and Burd [3] have suggested applying a layer of magnesium smoke to both the test and questioned marks. This can be done by igniting a short length of magnesium ribbon and holding the material containing the mark just above it in the trail of smoke, moving either the ribbon or the material to obtain an even coating. (See Fig. 2b.)

---

[1] John E. Davis, *An Introduction to Tool Marks, Firearms, and the Striagraph* (Charles C Thomas Publisher, 1958).

[2] D. Q. Burd and P. L. Kirk, *Tool Marks—Factors Involved in their Comparison and Use as Evidence*, 32 Journal of Criminal Law and Criminology, 679 (1941–42).

[3] R. S. Greene and D. Q. Burd, *Special Techniques Useful in Tool Mark Comparisons*, 41 Journal of Criminal Law, and Criminology, 523 (1950).

Figure 1. Lug nut (left) and test material (right) containing tool marks made by the same lug wrench. Brackets indicate the areas actually matched.

This procedure eliminates the smaller, more detailed striations, enhances the larger characteristics, and provides a uniform color making the comparison less difficult.

Employment of the method described for making test marks for lug nut comparisons in case work has recently led to the positive identification of a lug wrench as having made the tool marks on several lug nuts recovered from the scene of an auto stripping. Figure 1 shows the lug nut containing the questioned mark used for comparison. Pictured with the lug nut is a short length of aluminum rod on which a test mark (indicated by arrows) was made with the suspect wrench. It can be seen here that the size and shape of the test material is the same as that of the lug nut. Figure 2a is a photomicrograph of the match between the test (left) and questioned mark (right) taken at a magnification of 10x. Figure 2b shows the same match as Figure 2a after magnesium smoke application. Note that the smaller, more confusing details are eliminated while the more significant striations are enhanced. Note also that the magnesium smoke method seems to make the match more evident.

Figure 2. Photomicrograph (mag. 10x) of the match between the test mark (left) on the aluminum rod and the questioned mark (right) on the lug nut.

The identification of tool marks on lug nuts can be used to link several auto larcenies with the same tool and, hence, the same person or persons. This can be done by establishing an open file and classifying the lug nuts according to some appropriate category such as the geographical area in which they are found or according to the make of car from which they were taken.

The procedure for making suitable test tool marks for comparison to questioned marks found on lug nuts from stolen and stripped autos is simple, easily repeatable and relatively successful. It increases the possibility of collecting sufficient evidence from the crime scene and, in this way, could become an invaluable aid in curbing the rising auto larceny rate.

CHAPTER 16

Fingerprinting:
A Story of Science
vs. Crime

The history of modern law enforcement has proven that science and crime are natural opponents: science flourishes with discovery while crime thrives in concealment. The conflicting relationship between the two was emphasized dramatically on August 30, 1968, when experts of the 47-year-old Identification Division in Washington, D.C., identified, from latent fingerprints found on a ransom note, a kidnapper who held a 4½-year-old boy he had taken at gunpoint from a California mother only 2 days before.

Notwithstanding the importance of this identification in the efforts of FBI Agents to return the ransomed child unharmed to the safety and comfort of his parents, the overriding significance of this latent fingerprint identification lay in the certainty with which scientific method has enabled law enforcement to identify an individual from the billions of persons who inhabit this earth. By its ability to expose the criminal and his acts, science has indisputably asserted itself as the precursor of modern law enforcement.

At daybreak on August 29, 1968, an FBI Agent at Friendship Airport, Baltimore, Md., was handed an envelope which had arrived by a commercial airliner departing from Los Angeles, Calif., late the previous evening. Alerted that the package contained a ransom note found the day before in the investigation of a kidnaping case by the Los Angeles FBI Office, the Agent lost no time in rushing it directly to FBI Headquarters in Washington, D.C.

Typewritten in capital letters of a common style on a piece of unwatermarked white bond paper torn from a larger piece, the note stated:

HAVE 250,000.00 DOLLARS IN USED 20 DOLLAR BILLS. PUT BILLS
IN A CLOTH BAG LIKE A LAUNDRY BAG. DO NOT HAVE WRAPPERS ON

BILLS PUT THEM IN THE BAG LOOSE FOLLOW DIRECTIONS CLOSELY OR
YOU WILL NEVER SEE THE BOY AGAIN HIS SAFETY DEPENDS ON MY
SAFETY

BE AT CORNER OF LA CIENEGA & BEVERLY BLVD. AT 7:30 PM TONIGHT
I WILL CONTACT YOU BY THE PHONE AT BEVERLY PARK ON BEVERLY
BLVD.

Examination by experts in the FBI Identification Division later that same morning produced two latent fingerprints on the note. However, comparison of these with the fingerprints of known or suspected kidnapers, extortionists, and strong-arm criminals effected no identification.

Surveillance and Apprehension

The Los Angeles FBI Office in the meantime, with the cooperation of the victim's parents, was involved in hectic surveillance attempting to cover numerous ransom payoff locations which the wary kidnaper changed repeatedly during the evening of August 28th, and the following day, through telephone messages to the victim's father and by cryptic notes left at prearranged locations. In the course of this round-the-clock surveillance, Agents observed shortly before midnight on August 29, 1968, in the vicinity of one of the designated payoff locations an unknown male furtively copy a pay telephone booth phone number and thereafter depart in a car. Immediately checking the license plate number observed on the car, the Agents discovered it was registered to a recently paroled convict who had been convicted in Federal Court four years earlier for transporting a stolen motor vehicle across State lines.

Descriptive data concerning this suspect were telephonically furnished to the FBI Identification Division in the early morning hours of August 30th, where an arrest record for him, based on fingerprints, was found. These fingerprints were then compared with the two latent prints on the ransom note and found to be identical.

The investigators were relentlessly closing in around the kidnaper with a swiftness that he could not have possibly imagined. Within a few hours following his identification, the kidnaper, with the victim child, was spotted by FBI Agents as he attempted to intercept an intermediary who carried the ransom money in a laundry bag to a prearranged drop. Apparently sensing that something was amiss, the desperate kidnaper fled the area in a car, with the victim, before the payoff could be made. Although realizing his desperation and potential to carry out his threat to harm the child should his own safety be at stake, investigating Agents had no choice but to pursue him in a high-speed chase. While his car careened through a business section of Los Angeles at dawn on August 30th, the kidnaper emptied his revolver firing at pursuing Agents, wounding one of them in the arm. Finally, the pursuing FBI cars gained positions in which they could force the kidnaper to stop. The defiant kidnaper, clutching his young victim as a shield, continued to "fire" his gun at the first Agent who approached the car. Fortunately, the empty revolver resounded only with the "click" of its firing pin striking empty cartridges. Most fortunately, the kidnaped child was not seriously harmed and suffered only the trauma of his abduction and a few minor abrasions from being tossed about in the speeding automobile.

Before Scientific Methods

In the identification and arrest of the kidnaper, science again demonstrated that it is an extraordinary ally in the exposure of crime and criminals. The kidnaper's record in the FBI Identification Division cataloged his arrests for nearly a dozen serious crimes in seven States spanning a period of 21 years. Knowledge of these facts caused FBI Agents to take the necessary forthright action in effecting his apprehension and releasing his helpless captive.

Had this kidnaper been arrested a century ago when scientific methods first began to illuminate law enforcement procedures in identifying criminals, his previous background of lawlessness would most likely have gone unnoticed. Since using an alias was the practice of felons even before the advent of fingerprinting, it would have been improbable for police to associate an arrested person with any crime—particularly in a distant area—other than the one for which he had come to their attention. Police in those days relied only on their memories, sketchy descriptions, and a few photographs of some widely sought fugitives in establishing the identity of arrested persons. These methods were not always reliable. By the simple expedient of furnishing a new name with each arrest, criminals were quite successful in concealing their past nefarious activities. The absence of an infallible identification system obliged law enforcement agencies to deal with crime on a catch-as-catch-can basis. No procedures were available to law enforcement officials for accurately assessing crime, nor was there any basis of knowledge for devising programs and techniques to control crime.

Latent Fingerprints

Serious research into fingerprinting did not begin until the mid-19th century. Moreover, it was not until 1892 that identification of a latent fingerprint impression found on a wooden door figured in the solution of crime—a double murder in Argentina. Students of fingerprinting recognized early in their research that skin secretions of body fluids often leave clear fingerprint impressions on many objects that are touched. Later it was discovered that these latent impressions can be photographed and lifted by adhesive material without marring their identifying characteristics.

Latent fingerprints are of paramount importance in the solution of crime since they frequently, as in the case of the kidnaper, furnish an indelible and indisputable record of a criminal's presence at a crime scene. To the few who had long studied the subtle ridge patterns on human fingers, there was never any doubt of the momentous significance of their labors.

The singularity of fingerprint impressions had been recognized even in ancient societies as a special mark. However, the possibility of devising a workable system of identification from these curiously distinctive patterns on the tips of fingers did not materialize until the last half of the 19th century.

Henry Classification System

In 1901, England and Wales officially introduced fingerprinting for criminal identification. The English system was based on a classification formula designed by Sir Edward Richard Henry, then Inspector General of Police in Bengal, India, who had been stirred by the work of other fingerprinting pioneers. Using his gift of analysis and organization, Henry soon devised a workable identification process for the immutable and distinctive characteristics of fingerprints. It is the basic Henry Classification System, with modifications and extensions, which is used by the FBI and identification bureaus throughout the United States today.

Following introduction of fingerprinting in police departments in England, fingerprint identification departments were increasingly established throughout United States law enforcement agencies. Despite the vastness of this country and its substantial population, it did not, in the early 20th century, provide a true test for the newly found science of fingerprint identification. Compelled by an historical enmity toward centralized political—particularly police—power, the American experience produced an intricate array of law enforcement agencies whose jurisdictions honored the profuse political and geographical areas that emerged in the country's expansion westward. The complexity of this law enforcement network inhibited the growth of fingerprint identification departments as well as cooperation among those few police departments that adopted this identification procedure.

Valuable Fingerprint Collection

In 1896, the International Association of Chiefs of Police had established the National Bureau of Criminal Identification in Chicago, Ill., for the compilation and exchange of criminal identification data; this Bureau was later moved to Washington, D.C., where it gradually acquired a valuable fingerprint collection. However, it was not until 1924 that the full potential of fingerprint identification was realized in United States law enforcement. In that year, the FBI Identification Division was founded with little more than 800,000 fingerprint records comprised of those from Leavenworth Penitentiary and the National Bureau of Criminal Identification. Today, fingerprint records in the FBI's Identification Division represent over 86 million persons. However, less than 20 million of these individuals have prints in the criminal files; the remainder are in the civil files.

With thousands of contributing law enforcement agencies which, by the end of 1970, had grown to nearly 15,000, the FBI Identification Division has brought to realization the most ambitious dreams of fingerprinting pioneers and has given testimony of the value of scientific methods and procedure in the detection of criminals. FBI technicians have never found two fingerprints exactly alike in all details unless they were produced by the same finger. Throughout FBI history, nearly 43 million fingerprints of criminals and more than one-half million fugitives have been identified through its fingerprint files. In 1970, nearly 75 percent of all arrest prints received were identified with fingerprints of persons having prior criminal records.

One of the most important services in the detection of crime is provided by the FBI Identification Division's Latent Fingerprint Section. Classified under a special system are the fingerprints of a selected group of notorious criminals. This special latent fingerprint section of the criminal files makes it possible for a single latent print uncovered at the scene of a crime to be searched for a duplicate among the single fingerprint impressions of these felons whose past criminal background suggests their continued involvement in serious crimes.

Statistics

In fiscal year 1970 the Latent Fingerprint Section received 30,339 requests for latent print examinations. In these cases 3,555 suspects were identified, and more than 292,000 pieces of evidence were examined. In the past 7 years the number of latent fingerprint cases submitted to the FBI Identification Division has more than doubled, while the number of suspects identified in examinations during this same period has more than tripled. This significant rise in latent fingerprint cases in recent years is indicative of improved law enforcement training in scientific examination of crime scene evidence.

Aside from the detection of crime and criminals, the FBI fingerprints records have also served humanitarian interests in the identification of victims of major tragedies. Since 1940, the FBI Disaster Squad of identification experts has furnished assistance in 90 major disasters. In the last 75 disasters in which this squad rendered aid, it was possible to identify through fingerprints or palm prints more than 76 percent of an estimated 1,876 victims.

Most striking, however, in this era of rising lawlessness have been the achievements of the FBI Identification Division in the solution of crime. Scarcely 1½ hours after two police officers were last seen alive, their bullet-punctured bodies were found in the early morning of May 5, 1964, behind a shopping center in Fredericksburg, Va. A total of nine gunshots had snuffed out the lives of these officers. One was found slumped behind the steering wheel of the police patrol car while the other officer's body lay on the pavement outside the passenger side of the car. Fingerprint examination of the patrol car uncovered more than 60 latent impressions which were submitted to the FBI Identification Division for examination.

Three days later in faraway Inkster, Mich., police attempted to stop a suspicious driver, who, surprisingly, reacted by speeding away. In the course of his flight with the police in pursuit, the suspect's car collided with another, killing an innocent driver. The suspect's car proved to be stolen and contained the revolvers and handcuffs of the slain Fredericksburg police officers. The suspect steadfastly insisted in subsequent interrogation that an accomplice shot the officers while he waited in a nearby car; however, his fingerprints, after being submitted to the FBI, were matched with one of the latent prints found on the murdered officers' patrol car. This evidence and the fact that the existence of his alleged accomplice could not be established were instrumental in his conviction for the murders.

Investigation of Plane Crash

One of the most unusual crime identifications experienced by FBI experts resulted from the crash of a commercial airliner in a pasture at Danville, Calif., in May 1964. The last radio message from this ill-fated flight was that of an agonized male voice, presumably the pilot, shouting, "We've been shot, we've been shot. Oh my God help!" A few moments later the plane disintegrated in a thunderous impact with the ground, which killed all three crewmembers and the 41 passengers aboard. The mutilated remains of the victims as well as fragments of the aircraft were strewn over a half-mile area. Among this grisly debris were found a revolver with six empty shell casings still in its chambers and the severed hands of one of the crash victims.

Fingerprints of the hands were identified with prints of a foreign passenger who was visiting the United States. Investigation determined that he had purchased the gun found at the crash scene the evening before the flight and told an acquaintance the day of its departure that he intended to shoot himself. The identification of these hands with a gun-toting passenger in a suicidal frame of mind led to other evidence at the crash scene which formed a persuasive argument that he was responsible for the apparent midair shooting of the pilot. Unfortunately, the exact events that led to this crash will be forever lost in the silence of its victims.

Criminals have frequently attempted to conceal or obliterate their fingerprints to avoid detection in the course of lawless pursuits. These efforts have been to no avail. An unusual case in point occurred in the summer of 1968 at a county seat and manufacturing center of a northwest State. At 2 p.m. on an August afternoon, two armed, masked men entered a bank of this city where they took at gunpoint more than $2,000 of the day's cash receipts. One of the bandits carried out his role with more than unusual confidence for such a dangerous crime. Taking the precaution of coating his hands in a plastic film before the robbery, be believed that he would leave no tell-tale fingerprints at the crime scene.

The robber and his accomplice escaped in a getaway car which they abandoned a few blocks from the bank and departed the area in a second vehicle which could not be traced to them. In the excitement and haste of switching cars, however, the cautious bandit unwittingly peeled the plastic film from his hands, the shreds of which he left lying on the front seat of the abandoned car. FBI Agents examining the getaway car discovered the plastic film the inside surface of which contained the imprint of the bandit's palm and fingerprints. FBI latent fingerprint experts identified these prints with a man who was then being sought as a fugitive from a prior crime. This fingerprint identification disclosed both bandits' involvement in a series of other bank robberies in the United States and led to their eventual capture in Canada.

Attempt to Change Pattern

Intentional mutilation of the fingers has also been attempted by criminals in order to disguise or obliterate their fingerprint patterns. While these attempts have a history among criminals dating back to the very origins of fingerprint records, no successful case of evading identification by intentional mutilation has ever come to the attention of the FBI.

One recent case involved the arrest of a swindler by a Nevada police department. His fingerprints showed the core areas of all 10 fingers bore scars which obliterated the central portions of the patterns. During a previous incarceration at a California penitentiary, and with the encouragement of a fellow inmate, he had cut an "X" in the center of the fingerprint pattern on each of his fingers and thereafter cauterized the wounds with a red-hot soldering iron. Painful though this procedure was, the swindler took comfort in the assurances of his prison "friend" that he would never again be identified with a crime through fingerprints.

The FBI Identification Division, however, was able, through the remaining patterns of his fingerprints, to identify them with his prior fingerprint records, which traced his involvement in crime over a 15-year period.

Research has shown that in superficially scarred skin tissue the original ridge detail which forms a fingerprint pattern reappears with time. In any event, mutilation and skin grafts, which have also been used in an attempt to conceal fingerprint identity, themselves may form a distinctive pattern which is identifiable.

On the afternoon of May 10, 1969, a young female graduate student and part-time social worker had a chance meeting on a Baltimore, Md., street with a woman laden with groceries who asked for help in carrying her packages to a nearby apartment house. Arriving at the apartment, the student was accosted by a male, noticeably inebriated, who would not permit her to leave. He raped the young woman in the apartment and held her against her will for several days. In telephone calls to her father, the captor demanded $10,000 for the girl's release. He later sent demand notes to the father. FBI Identification Division experts found on these notes latent fingerprints which positively identified the abductor and his female accomplice. Subsequently both were apprehended and charged with extortion. The man was sentenced to 60 years' imprisonment, and the woman was sentenced to 25 years.

Science and Law Enforcement

Science in general, and specifically in fingerprint identification, has given law enforcement a far greater capacity to detect those who commit crime. While the science of modern law enforcement has developed a remarkable proficiency, the increasing opportunities for crime in our open society and the mobility of our population have often permitted the criminal that necessary step ahead to escape detection and apprehension.

To learn the true identities of criminals hours or even days following a confrontation by arrest, interrogation, or their association with crime through evidence quite often is not enough to secure their whereabouts or establish guilt beyond a reasonable doubt. The easy flight of felons to remote sanctuaries following the first signs of suspicion linking them with a crime, together with the ever-present possibility of their destruction or concealment of vital evidence, makes it imperative that a law enforcement officer have necessary criminal identifying information available to him at the time and place when most needed. Often this is while the officer is routinely walking his beat or patrolling a highway. To bridge this gap between confrontation of the criminal and discovery of his background requires that a law enforcement officer, at all times, be within easy access to essential law enforcement information that will permit him to discharge his duty with the swift decisiveness that the occurrence of serious crime demands and the public has a right to expect.

Again, with science in the forefront, the gap is narrowing. Development contracts, underway over the past several years, are nearing fruition in the effort to computerize the FBI's massive fingerprint files. This system will have the ability to electronically read, classify, and retrieve a previously entered record. With high-speed, computerized exchange of information already established in the Nation's law enforcement communications network, the FBI's National Crime Information Center, the fingerprint files of the FBI Identification Division will provide a lightning-fast response to inquiries concerning crimes and criminals. No longer will a dangerous wanted criminal be able to continue his flight after having been arrested on a minor charge and released while his identity and criminal background are being determined. No longer will a clever suspect's protestations during interview serve him in concealing his criminal record or prevent his immediate association with fingerprint evidence found at a distant crime scene. In time and with additional research in this area, it is anticipated that latent fingerprints uncovered at a crime scene could be, with appropriate computer classification, transmitted instantly to the FBI Identification Division for matching or elimination purposes. In the future it is quite conceivable that a criminal's identity may be instantly determined by simply placing his hand on an electronic scanner unit at police headquarters—or perhaps one mounted in a patrol car!

Promise For the Future

The story of modern law enforcement contains many feats of scientific methods in crime detection. The promise that science holds for the future of law enforcement, however, bids to far outrival its most notable accomplishments of the past. This century of modern law enforcement began with scientific methods of identifying criminals, and this basic police science, now secured in fingerprinting, is experiencing a startling renewal with the advent of computer technology. The pursuit of concealment goes on, but the margin for the criminal is narrowing. In this, all law enforcement and the public can rejoice.

CHAPTER 17

The Kennedy Assassination: Wound Ballistics Experiments

Purpose of the Tests

During the course of the Commission's inquiry, questions arose as to whether the wounds inflicted on President Kennedy and Governor Connally could have been caused by the Mannlicher-Carcano rifle found on the sixth floor of the Texas School Book Depository Building and Western Cartridge Co. bullets and fragments of the type found on the Governor's stretcher and in the Presidential limousine. In analyzing the trajectory of the bullets after they struck their victims, further questions were posed on the bullet's velocity and penetration power after exiting from the person who was initially struck. To answer these and related questions, the Commission requested that a series of tests be conducted on substances resembling the wounded portions of the bodies of President Kennedy and Governor Connally under conditions which simulated the events of the asassination.

The Testers and Their Qualifications

In response to the Commission's request, an extensive series of tests were conducted by the Wound Ballistics Branch of the U.S. Army Chemical Research and Development Laboratories at Edgewood Arsenal, Md. Scientists working at that branch are engaged in full-time efforts to investigate the wound ballistics of missiles in order to test their effects on substances which simulate live human bodies. The tests for the Commission were performed by Dr. Alfred G. Olivier under the general supervision of Dr. Arthur J. Dziemian with consultation from Dr. Frederick W. Light, Jr. Dr. Olivier received his doctorate in veterinary medicine from the University of Pennsylvania in 1953. Since 1957 he has been engaged in research on wound ballistics at Edgewood Arsenal and is now chief of the Wound Ballistics Branch. His supervisor, Dr. Dziemian, who is chief of the Biophysics Division at Edgewood Arsenal, holds a Ph. D. degree from Princeton in 1939, was a national research fellow in physiology at the University of Pennsylvania and was a fellow in anatomy at Johns Hopkins University Medical School. Since 1947, Dr. Dziemian has been continuously engaged in wound ballistics work at Edgewood Arsenal. In 1930, Dr. Light was awarded an M.D. degree from Johns Hopkins Medical School and in 1948 received his Ph. D. from the same institution. After serving a residency in pathology, he worked as a pathologist until 1940 when he returned to Johns Hopkins University to study mathematics. Since 1951, Dr. Light has been engaged in the study of the pathology of wounding at Edgewood Arsenal. All three of these distinguished scientists testified before the Commission.

General Testing Conditions

The Commission made available to the Edgewood Arsenal scientists all the relevant facts relating to the wounds which were inflicted on President Kennedy and Governor Connally including the autopsy report on the President, and the reports and X-rays from Parkland Hospital. In addition, Drs. Olivier and Light had an opportunity to discuss in detail the Governor's wounds with the Governor's surgeons, Drs. Robert R. Shaw and Charles F. Gregory. The Zapruder films of the assassination were viewed with Governor and Mrs. Connally to give the Edgewood scientists their version. The Commission also provided the Edgewood scientists with all known data on the source of the shots, the rifle and bullets used, and the distances involved. For purposes of the experiments, the Commission turned over to the Edgewood testers the Mannlicher-Carcano rifle found on the sixth floor of the Depository Building. From information provided by the Commission, the Edgewood scientists obtained Western bullets of the type used by the assassin.

Tests on Penetration Power and Bullet Stability

Comparisons were made of the penetrating power of Western bullets fired from the assassination rifle with other bullets. From the Mannlicher-Carcano rifle, the Western bullet was fired through two gelatin blocks totaling 72½ centimeters in length. As evidenced by Commission Exhibit No. 844, which is a photograph from a highspeed motion picture, the Western bullets passed through 1½ blocks in a straight line before their trajectory curved. After coming out of the second gelatin block, a number of the bullets buried themselves in a mound of earth.

Under similar circumstances, a bullet described as the NATO round M–80 was fired from a M–14 rifle. The penetrating power of the latter is depicted in Commission Exhibit No. 845 which shows that bullet possesses much less penetrating power with a quicker tumbling action. Those characteristics cause an early release of energy which brings the bullet to a stop at shorter distances. A further test was made with a 257 Winchester Roberts soft-nosed hunting bullet as depicted in Commission Exhibit No. 846. That bullet became deformed almost immediately upon entering the block of gelatin and released its energy very rapidly. From these tests, it was concluded that the Western bullet fired from the Mannlicher-Carcano had "terrific penetrating ability" and would retain substantial velocity after passing through objects such as the portions of the human body.

Tests Simulating President Kennedy's Neck Wound

After reviewing the autopsy report on President Kennedy, the Edgewood scientists simulated the portion of the President's neck through which the bullet passed. It was determined that the bullet traveled through 13½ to 14½ centimeters of tissue in the President's neck. That substance was simulated by constructing three blocks: one with a 20-percent gelatin composition, a second from one animal meat and a third from another animal meat. Those substances duplicated as closely as possible the portion of the President's neck through which the bullet passed. At the time the tests were conducted, it was estimated that the President was struck at a range of approximately 180 feet, and the onsite tests which were conducted later at Dallas established that the President was shot through the neck at a range of 174.9 feet to 190.8 feet. At a range of 180 feet, the Western bullets were fired from the assassination weapon, which has a muzzle velocity of approximately 2,160 feet per second, through those substances which were placed beside a break-type screen for measuring velocity. The average entrance velocity at 180 feet was 1,904 feet per second.

To reconstruct the assassination situation as closely as possible both sides of the substances were covered with material and clipped animal skin to duplicate human skin. The average exit velocity was 1,779 feet from the gelatin, 1,798 feet from the first animal meat and 1,772 feet from the second animal meat. Commission Exhibit No. 847 depicts one of the animal meats compressed to 13½ to 14½ centimeters to approximate the President's neck and Commission Exhibit No. 848 shows the analogous arrangement for the gelatin. The photograph marked Commission Exhibit No. 849 shows the bullet passing through the gelatin in a straight line evidencing very stable characteristics.

Commission Exhibit No. 850 depicts the pieces of clipped animal skin placed on the points of entry and exit showing that the holes of entrance are round while the holes of exit are "a little more elongated." From these tests, it was concluded that the bullet lost little of its velocity in penetrating the President's neck so that there would have been substantial impact on the interior of the Presidential limousine or anyone else struck by the exiting bullet. In addition, these tests indicated that the bullet had retained most of its stability in penetrating the President's neck so that the exit hole would be only slightly different from the appearance of the entry hole.

Tests Simulating Governor Connally's Chest Wounds

To most closely approximate the Governor's chest injuries, the Edgewood scientists shot an animal with the assassination weapon using the Western bullets at a distance of 210 feet. The onsite tests later determined that the Governor was wounded at a distance of 176.9 feet to 190.8 feet from the sixth-floor window at the southeast corner of the Depository Building. The average striking velocity of 11 shots at 210 feet was 1,929 feet per second and the average exit velocity was 1,664 feet per second.

One of the shots produced an injury on the animal's rib very similar to that inflicted on Governor Connally. For purposes of comparison with the Governor's wound, the Edgewood scientists studied the Parkland Hospital report and X-rays, and they also discussed these wounds with Dr. Shaw, the Governor's chest surgeon. The similar animal injury passed along the animal's eight left rib causing a fracture which removed a portion of the rib in a manner very similar to the wound sustained by the Governor. The X-ray of that wound on the animal is reproduced as Commission Exhibit No. 852. A comparison with the Governor's chest wound, shown in X-ray marked as Commission Exhibit No. 681, shows the remarkable similarity between those two wounds.

The bullet which produced the wound depicted in Commission Exhibits Nos. 851 and 852 was marked as Commission Exhibit No. 853 and possessed characteristics very similar to the bullet marked as Commission Exhibit No. 399 found on Governor Connally's stretcher and believed to have been the bullet which caused his chest wound. Those bullets, identified as Commission Exhibits Nos. 399 and 853, were flattened in similar fashion. In addition, the lead core was extruded from the rear in the same fashion on both bullets. One noticeable difference was that the bullet identified as Commission Exhibit No. 853, which penetrated the animal, was somewhat more flat than Commission Exhibit No. 399 which indicated that Commission Exhibit No. 853 was probably traveling at somewhat greater speed than the bullet which penetrated the Governor's chest. After the bullet passed through the animal, it left an imprint on the velocity screen immediately behind the animal which was almost the length of the bullet indicating that the bullet was traveling sideways or end over end. Taking into consideration the extra girth on the Governor, the reduction in the velocity of the bullet passing through his body was estimated at 400 feet. The conclusions from the animal shots are significant when taken in conjunction with the experiments performed simulating the injuries to the Governor's wrist.

Tests Simulating Governor Connally's Wrist Wounds

Following procedures identical to those employed in simulating the chest wound, the wound ballistics experts from Edgewood Arsenal reproduced, as closely as possible, the Governor's wrist wound. Again the scientists examined the reports and X-rays from Parkland Hospital and discussed the Governor's wrist wound with the attending orthopedic surgeon, Dr. Charles F. Gregory. Bone structures were then shot with Western bullets fired from the assassination weapon at a distance of 210 feet. The most similar bone-structure shot was analyzed in testimony before the Commission. An X-ray designated as Commission Exhibit No. 854 and a photograph of that X-ray which appears as Commission Exhibit No. 855 show a fracture at a location which is very similar to the Governor's wrist wound depicted in X-rays marked as Commission Exhibits Nos. 690 and 691.

The average striking velocity of the shots was 1,858 feet per second. The average exit velocity was 1,786 feet per second for the 7 out of 10 shots from bone structures which could be measured. These tests demonstrated that Governor Connally's wrist was not struck by a pristine bullet, which is a missile that strikes an object before hitting anything else. This conclusion was based on the following factors: (1) Greater damage was inflicted on the bone structure than that which was suffered by the Governor's wrist; and (2) the bone structure had a smaller entry wound and a larger exit wound which is characteristic of a pristine bullet as distinguished from the Governor's wrist which had a larger wound of entry indicating a bullet which was tumbling with substantial reduction in velocity. In addition, if the bullet found on the Governor's stretcher (Commission Exhibit No. 399) inflicted the wound on the Governor's wrist, then it could not have passed through the Governor's wrist had it been a pristine bullet, for the nose would have been considerably flattened, as was the bullet which struck the bone structure, identified as Commission Exhibit No. 856.

Conclusions From Simulating the Neck, Chest, and Wrist Wounds

Both Drs. Olivier and Dziemian expressed the opinion that one bullet caused all the wounds on Governor Connally. The wound to the Governor's wrist was explained by circumstances where the bullet passed through the Governor's chest, lost substantial velocity in doing so, tumbled through the wrist, and then slightly penetrated the Governor's left thigh. Thus, the results of the wound ballistics tests support the conclusions of Governor Connally's doctors that all his wounds were caused by one bullet.

In addition, the wound ballistics tests indicated that it was most probable that the same bullet passed through the President's neck and then proceeded to inflict all the wounds on the Governor. That conclusion was reached by Drs. Olivier and Dziemian based on the medical evidence on the wounds of the President and the Governor and the tests they performed. It was their opinion that the wound on the Governor's wrist would have been more extensive had the bullet which inflicted that injury merely passed through the Governor's chest exiting at a velocity of approximately 1,500 feet per second. Thus, the Governor's wrist wound indicated that the bullet passed through the President's neck, began to yaw in the air between the President and the Governor, and then lost substantially more velocity than 400 feet per second in passing through the Governor's chest. A bullet which was yawing on entering into the Governor's back would lose substantially more velocity in passing through his body than a pristine bullet. In addition, the greater flattening of the bullet that struck the animal's rib (Commission Exhibit No. 853) than the bullet which presumably struck the Governor's rib (Commission Exhibit No. 399) indicates that the animal bullet was traveling at a greater velocity. That suggests that the bullet which entered the Governor's chest had already lost velocity by passing through the President's neck. Moreover, the large wound on the Governor's back would be explained by a bullet which was yawing although that type of wound might also be accounted for by a tangential striking.

Dr. Frederick W. Light, Jr., the third of the wound ballistics experts, testified that the anatomical findings alone were insufficient for him to formulate a firm opinion on whether the same bullet did or did not pass through the President's neck first before inflicting all the wounds on Governor Connally. Based on the other circumstances, such as the relative positions in the automobile of the President and the Governor, Dr. Light concluded that it was probable that the same bullet traversed the President's neck and inflicted all the wounds on Governor Connally.

Tests Simulating President Kennedy's Head Wounds

Additional tests were performed on inert skulls filled with a 20 percent gelatin substance and then coated with additional gelatin to approximate the soft tissues overlying the skull. The skull was then draped with simulated hair as depicted in Commission Exhibit No. 860. Using the Mannlicher-Carcano rifle and the Western bullets, 10 shots were fired at the reconstructed skulls from a distance of 270 feet which was the estimated distance at the time those tests were conducted. It was later determined through the onsite tests that President Kennedy was struck in the back of the head at a distance of 265.3 feet from the assassination weapon.

The general results of these tests were illustrated by the findings on one skull which was struck at a point most nearly approximating the wound of entry on President Kennedy's head. The whole skull, depicted in Commission Exhibit No. 860, was struck 2.9 centimeters to the right and almost horizontal to the occipital protuberance or slightly above it, which was virtually the precise point of entry on the President's head as described by the autopsy surgeons. That bullet blew out the right side of the reconstructed skull in a manner very similar to the head wounds of the President. The consequences on that skull are depicted in Commission Exhibits Nos. 861 and 862, which illustrate the testimony of Dr. Alfred G. Olivier, who supervised the experiments. Based on his review of the autopsy report, Dr. Olivier concluded that the damage to the reconstructed skull was very similar to the wound inflicted on the President.

Two fragments from the bullet which struck the test skull closely resembled the two fragments found in the front seat of the Presidential limousine. The fragment designated as Commission Exhibit No. 567 is a mutilated piece of lead and copper very similar to a mutilated piece of copper recovered from the bullet which struck the skull depicted in Commission Exhibit No. 860. The other fragment, designated as Commission Exhibit No. 569 which was found in the front seat of the Presidential limousine, is the copper end of the bullet. Commission Exhibit No. 569 is very similar to a copper fragment at the end of the bullet which struck the test skull. The fragments from the test bullet are designated as Commission Exhibit No. 857 and are depicted in a photograph identified as Commission Exhibit No. 858. A group of small lead particles, recovered from the test bullet, are also very similar to the particles recovered under the left jump seat and in the President's head. The particles from the test bullet are a part of Commission Exhibit No. 857 and are depicted in photograph designated as Commission Exhibit No. 859. That skull was depicted as Commission Exhibit No. 862.

As a result of these tests, Dr. Olivier concluded that the Western bullet fired from the Mannlicher-Carcano rifle at a distance of 270 feet would make the same type of wound found on the President's head. Prior to the tests, Dr. Olivier had some doubt that such a stable bullet would cause a massive head wound like that inflicted on the President. He had thought it more likely that such a striking bullet would make small entrance and exit holes. The tests, however, showed that the bones of the skull were sufficient to deform the end of the bullet causing it to expend a great deal of energy and thereby blow out the side of the skull. These tests further confirmed the autopsy surgeon's opinions that the President's head wound was not caused by a dumdum bullet. Because of the test results, Dr. Olivier concluded that the fragments found on and under the front seat of the President's car most probably came from the bullet which struck the President's head. It was further concluded that the damage done to Governor Connally's wrist could not have resulted from a fragment from the bullet which struck President Kennedy's head.

CHAPTER 18

The Role of Criminalistics in White-Collar Crimes

Quon Y. Kwan,
Ponnusamy Rajeswaran,
Brian P. Parker,
and Menachem Amir

The role of criminalistics [1] has been overlooked in the critical area of white-collar crimes. These crimes receive the least publicity in the news and the least attention from criminologists, and yet the President's Commission on Law Enforcement and the Administration of Justice estimates that the economic liability of white-collar crime dwarfs crimes of violence and organized crime. Furthermore, white-collar crimes present perils more alarming than crimes of violence because they are invisible; they undermine the practical fabric of trust within a free society, they portend fair competition and honesty in free trade, and they injure the public welfare. This discussion will deal with the development of criminalistics in confronting the challenge of white-collar crime including the assimilation of the role of other scientists who function more or less as criminalists in these investigations.

A definition of white-collar crime is prerequisite to the discussion of the role of criminalistics in white-collar crime. White-collar crime is defined, in this study, as legal and normative deviation from the violator's occupational role. Controversy still exists as to the definition of this form of illegal behavior, since Sutherland who introduced this concept (1), maintained that it involved mainly violators in high social standing in business occupations. Cressy expanded the concept to include violations

---

[1] A definition of criminalistics drawn up and adopted by the California Association of Criminalists at its 21st Semiannual Seminar on May 26, 1963 at Ventura, California, which has been accepted by most practicing criminalists is that, "Criminalistics is that profession and scientific discipline directed to the recognition, identification, individualization, and evaluation of physical evidence by application of the natural sciences to law-science matters." This definition will be further amplified later on in this discussion.

of financial trust such as embezzlement (2). Clinard added offenses that violate the well-being of the national welfare and economy as exemplified by black-market operations (3).

Quinney extended the concept to cover any occupational deviation and violations of professional ethics which pervade the entire strata of socio-economic classes which are then not necessarily confined to the white-collar class (4). In brief, we define white-collar crime as it is specifically related to criminalistics, as any endeavor or practice involving the stifling of free enterprise or the promoting of unfair competition; a breach of trust against an individual or an institution; a violation of occupational conduct, or the jeopardizing of consumers and clientele.

White collar crime was found to be both legally and sociologically different from conventional crimes. Thus, the controversies over its criminological appropriateness center around the following issues, which will only be mentioned but not elaborated in this paper.

1. The nature of white-collar crimes. The arguments around this issue were settled by defining white-collar crime as both deviations, not necessarily illegal, and illegal behavior occurring during the violator's exercise of his occupational role, regardless of his social status.

2. The legal basis of white-collar crimes. Although the term, white-collar crime, is now a misnomer, it is used mainly as a synecdoche for a class of "mala prohibita," an already defunct or a doubtful classification of crimes. Other legal issues involved, which are beyond this paper, and which differentiate white-collar crimes from conventional offenses are the origin of white-collar offenses i.e. their "mala prohibita" nature; the determination of legal responsibility, or intent especially when corporations or other economic organizations are involved.

3. The issue of the social status of the offender, or can violators of white-collar laws be considered criminals in the conventional sense of such a term. This is due to the fact that Sutherland originally described upper-class violators who neither think of themselves nor are commonly thought of as criminals.

4. The issues involving enforcement, trial procedures and sanctions used to "punish" white-collar violators. These issues arise since some of the violators are only deviating from their occupational role which are not legal violations, and if they are defined as legal violators, they are customarily "punished" by civil and administrative action, rather than by the conventional criminal procedure.

The descriptive characteristics and modus operandi of white-collar crimes makes this type of crime unusual and different from the majority of crimes studied. Most white-collar criminals do not come from destitute backgrounds but are the progeny of good upbringing. In some white-collar crimes, offenders fail to see their victims; their victims are either diffuse or impersonal, e.g. the consumer public or the government. Further, the white-collar criminal believes that his offense involved no physical harm or infliction of injury. It is because of this particular belief of an intangible realm of unseen harm to the victims that society and even some criminologists categorize white-collar crimes as completely separate from the so-called hard-core conventional crimes such as murder, rape, or burglary. Contrary to this notion, white-collar crimes do thrive in a tangible atmosphere and have certain similarities to the so-called conventional crimes. There is, indeed, a set of white-collar crimes that do have an element in common with conventional crimes. This occurs when white-collar crimes are committed through the medium of material objects. The overlapping of the set of white-collar crimes and the set of conventional crimes is depicted in the common intersection of the Venn diagram as shown in Figure 1.

The model described above is based on the set theory of mathematical logic. It is perhaps the most lucid means of precisely portraying the role of criminalistics in the solution of white-collar crimes problems where the intersection or the link between criminalistics and white-collar crimes is the physical evidence that may be present. This is in accordance with the definition of criminalistics. The circumstances in which physical evidence arises in the commission of a white-collar crime will be considered in the discussion of contemporary investigations of these crimes as related to criminalistics.

The Etiology of Criminalistics and White-Collar Crime

The role of criminalistics in white-collar crime evolved from the manner in which crimes were classified. Historically, Anglo-American jurisprudence had defined the law in terms of prohibiting acts that were "mala in se" or inherently evil. For example, behavior that was "mala in se" was the infliction of harm or death on fellow citizens or the damage or theft of property. Since the common law dealt with only these types of crimes against persons and property, the investigation of these so-called conventional crimes has and to a great extent dominates the discipline of criminalistics. This concept of crime was revolutionized in 1939 by Sutherland's iconoclastic introduction of "mala prohibita" crime, which specifically referred to what was termed white-collar crime. In this sense, the social injustice and damage of the covert crimes came to be recog-

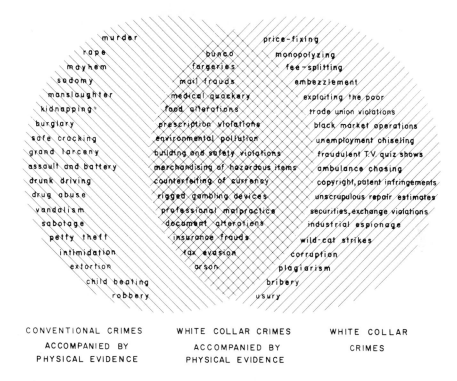

CONVENTIONAL CRIMES	WHITE COLLAR CRIMES	WHITE COLLAR
ACCOMPANIED BY	ACCOMPANIED BY	CRIMES
PHYSICAL EVIDENCE	PHYSICAL EVIDENCE	

Figure 1.

nized. The methods by which these crimes were controlled—suits for civil torts, civil liability, negligence or malpractice—were futile because of the recidivism and prevalence of these offenses. The exigency of white-collar crime induced law, as a means of social control, to apply the stigma and severity of criminal sanctions to these offenses. This resulted in a vast expansion of the law, whose provisions now include the motor-vehicle code, health, welfare and safety codes, building and fire codes and codes of business, and professional ethics. The concurrent trend resulted in the extending of the functions of the natural science criminologist (criminalist) to the detection of violations of these newly legislated codes aimed primarily at white-collar crimes. Where physical evidence emanates from the perpetration of these crimes, the significance of criminalistics lies in the scientific interpretation of the circumstances and recognition of such media in detecting violations that would otherwise evade justice. The fact finding process by the utilization of criminalistics then becomes the most essential part both in law enforcement and the administration of justice.

The contention that criminalistics does have a role in the solution of white-collar crime is substantiated by the employment of criminalists by specialized agencies outside of police departments or general law enforcement bureaus. Those trained in criminalistics and scientists who function as criminalists are found deployed in State and Federal Food and Drug Administrations; insurance companies and independent testing laboratories, for example, Underwriter's Laboratory, the U.S. Post Office, Customs Service Agency, Internal Revenue Service, State Gambling Commissions, Federal Trade Commission, City Fire Departments such as Los Angeles, and other bureaus. These agencies enforce codes regulating white-collar crime and differ from general law enforcement agencies in that they were created for the specific enforcement of *ad hoc* codes. One such *ad hoc* agency—the Michigan State Public Health Department maintains a laboratory which it officially designates as a Crime Detection Laboratory (5). Similarly, the New York State Racing Commission employs a forensic chemist whose function is to investigate unfair competition by the detection of doping of racing horses. These are some of the several examples of the role of criminalistics in white-collar crime.

Although criminalistics originated as an application of the natural sciences in law enforcement and the administration of criminal justice, criminalists are no longer so confined in their functions and the sole scientists so engaged. The assimilation of other scientists into the area of criminalistics is necessary in confronting the special problems posed in combating white-collar crime. Thus there are textile chemists, wood technologists, nutritional and food scientists, biologists, pharmacologists, metallurgists, medical experts, and many other applied scientists including statisticians engaged in enhancing the role of the natural sciences in law enforcement and the administration of justice either functioning as consultants to criminalists or in the capacity of criminalists offering expert testimony in a court of law in their particular area of expertise. An example of the utilization of applied scientists and technologists in the legal enforcement of white-collar criminal codes involves toxicologists and engineers. They are encountered in the various county air pollution control boards who detect and control the illegal discharge of toxic contaminants and pollutants by "white-collar criminals" of the commercial and industrial sectors. Implicit in their role in the detection and control of these violations and in the procedural hearings before a quasi-judicial commission or a court is precisely that of criminalists. The criminalist, for obvious reasons, cannot be expected to be an expert in every technical area where there is a tenable violation of the law or inquiry into the establishment of a fact. Thus, an entomologist may have to be consulted for the identification of a part of an insect that may have infected a stock of food resulting in the illness of consumers or an astronomer may be requested by a court to examine the shadows in a surveillance photograph to verify the time when a bribe was offered. Such novel situations resulting from enforcing codes against white-collar crime necessitates the broadening of the concept of criminalistics. For where a criminalist may be aware of the evidentiary value of an item of evidence, he may not be an expert in the evaluation of that particular item of evidence. In a similar manner, the scientist trained as a chemist, bacteriologist, or whatever the field may be, "must re-orient himself so that he can adapt his abilities to criminalistics" (6). Furthermore, he must be responsible not to a corporation or a governmental institution but to the entire system of the administration of justice. Hence, it must be emphasized here that criminalistics is not limited to the criminal justice system but extends into areas of civil litigations. Thus, criminalistics may be re-defined as a "multidisciplinary coordination of the natural sciences engaged in the administration of justice" (7). A result of this assimilation has been the propensity to use the term forensic sciences; however, the lack of convention permits the interchangeability of the terminology—criminalistics, police science, forensic chemistry, and forensic sciences. Further, it is extremely difficult to delineate hard and fast boundaries for criminalistics, or for that matter, any other disciplines included in the term forensic science because of the considerable overlap among them. For example, forensic sciences include the specialized areas of forensic medicine, toxicology, and document examination in which criminalistics may share a common base as in firearms identification; chemical analysis; ink, typescript, and paper identification, respectively. For this reason the term *criminalistics* is maintained for purposes of discussion and with special reference to *white-collar crimes* in this paper. A further justification for this may be that the term originated from the German, "System der Kriminalistik" of Dr. Hans Gross, one of the earliest pioneers of scientific investigation, familiar to all scholars and practitioners of criminalistics in different areas.

The termination of the above preliminary discussion with the assimilation of natural scientists in other fields as criminalists leads to the contemporary investigations of white-collar crimes in criminalistics with reference to five major areas: food and drugs, false advertising, tax evasion, insurance frauds, and questioned documents.

Food and Drug Violations

Food and drug violations are the most flagrant of white-collar crimes because they constitute a direct hazard to the population. Because present day food is processed on a mass production basis, greater opportunities are afforded for exploitation by degradation, contamination, and even poisoning of edibles. Inferior food substitution lends itself to the application of criminalistics in the context of food and drug analysis. The dangers of poisoned foods and unscrupulous drugs had been known from early times and through the leadership of Dr. Harvey W. Wiley, chief forensic chemist for the U.S. Department of Agriculture, the Food and Drugs Act and Meat Inspection Act of 1906 was finally passed. This marked the approach of the end of an era of *caveat emptor* for the naive public. The establishment of the federal Food and Drug Administration provided the resources for the detection of contamination, spoiled foods, unsafe levels of chemical additives and pesticides, food coloring, toxic cosmetics, drug impurities, and drug counterfeiting.

The more serious infractions of the white-collar criminal in the food and drugs area is the vending and distribution of biologically contaminated, putrefied, or spoiled food. At one time the tomato industry was ignominious for processing tomatoes under unsanitary conditions including the packaging of putrid rejected tomatoes in pastes, sauces, and catsup. Formidable outbreaks of food poisoning by fatal botulism and salmonella have been virtually eliminated because of inspections made mandatory by public health laws.

A further recurring problem is food poisoning by chemicals. The problem consists of detecting intolerable levels of additives such as pesticides, food coloring, artificial flavoring, leavening agents, and spoilage retardants. In addition, seafoods and different types of meat are treated with additives to tenderize, freshen, and flavor them. While a 100% inspection of all meat, fish and poultry is not practicable, the chemical poisoning often goes undetected until sickness or death results. For example, an innocent-looking compound such as sodium nitrite, very similar in appearance to ordinary common table salt was identified as the toxic agent in a spree of 152 poisoning cases, including one fatality. Sodium nitrite reduces the ability of erythrocytes to carry oxygen throughout the body thereby internally suffocating the victim. In this instance, seafood impregnated with sodium nitrite was traced back to a wholesaler and criminalists reconstructed the sequence of events leading to its presence in the seafood by an examination of the wholesaler's establishment. While it was common practice to clean fishes that were filleted with a simple saline or brine solution, crystals of sodium nitrite were found in the dust on the concrete floors, on the cutting tables, and under the hoops on the brine barrels at this establishment. This was suspected since it was a highly common though illegal practice to freshen spoiled fish with sodium nitrite since it removed its slime and stagnant odor. A record of a chemical warehouse selling sodium nitrite on a rush delivery with the firm's president personally authorizing and accompanying the 400 lb.

order of the compound negated any accidental contamination of the brine, leading to conviction of the seafood firm (8).

In another type of white-collar crime, food may be adulterated or mislabelled by the substitution of some of its components without necessarily adding harmful ingredients. In this form of cheating starch may be added to cocoa, vitamins may be omitted from enriched bread or the substitution of a water-sucrose mixture in orange juice and making up for the deficiency from the natural product by adding extra amounts of Vitamin C. The latter involved the crime of orange juice adulteration by the Cal-Tex Citrus Juice, Inc. of Houston, Texas in 1958. In addition to analysis of their product, surveillance of the company's plant revealed the shipment of unmarked quantities of sugar and syrup and a large discrepancy in the amount of fresh oranges entering the plant and the volume of finished orange juice produced. In refuting the firm's contention that the Food and Drug Administration data was derived from analysis of California and Florida oranges, it was shown there was no distinction between oranges grown between these two regions and those of Texas grown in two different seasons. Further, trace analysis showed a high degree of identity between the water content of the orange juice and the Houston municipal water supply with respect to the high fluoride levels present in both. The disposition of the case was the conviction of the firm's executives in May, 1960 (9).

To cite a more recent violation, eclectic criminalists acquired a method of species individualization of food products from biochemists in 1964. This technique was formulated by researchers A. C. Wilson, G. B. Kitto, and N. O. Kaplan of Brandeis University (10). Contracted by the Bureau of Commercial Fisheries in Gloucester, Massachusetts, their studies were directed towards employing enzymatic methods of identification to differentiate between closely related fish species. Cod and haddock, both common Atlantic salt water fish belong to the same taxonomic family, Gadidae. Haddock is more expensive and tasty than cod, but when marketed in the form of frozen fillets the two cannot be differentiated easily from each other by laymen. On the basis of the application of this new technique of individualization and additional tests on enzymes these workers were able to show that enough samples of frozen fish fillets and breaded fish sticks were mislabelled haddock, when they were actually the cheaper cod. On the results of this finding, offending commercial processors were warned of this intentional misbranding of their products. This mode of individualization has now been extended to a total of 26 fish species. Further, it has been adapted as an additional technique to differentiate other zoological species where adulteration of beef hamburgers and pork frankfurters can be detected.

Another major responsibility of food and drug analysts, toxicologists or criminalists in the investigation of white-collar crimes concerns the testing for control or purity of pharmaceutical preparations for consumer protection. For the same rationale that the consumer expects unadulterated and properly labelled food, a medical patient expects guaranteed quality in the drugs sold to him. However, some pharmaceutical companies either by accident, negligence, or even deliberate action, manipulate or contaminate the ingredients of their drug products. Such an accidental incident occurred in San Francisco recently where isonicotinic acid hydrazate tablets were administered to hospital adolescents to cure them of tuberculosis. The strange appearance of certain feminine traits in the boys was brought to the attention of field forensic drug chemists. Analysis indicated that the drug was contaminated with stilbestrol, a potent female hormone. The contamination was traced back to New York where it was discovered that the same items of equipment in the factory were used to manufacture different drugs. Faulty dust control and insterility accounted for not only intracontamination but also cross-contamination with botanicals, insecticides, and penicillin. (Penicillin, itself, although once hailed as a miraculous antibiotic has been found to be fatal to many people who are allergic to the drug.) Through analogous procedures, more than fifty companies were compelled to destroy contaminated, impure, and insterile stocks of drugs in August 1965 (11).

Another problem in the drug area that falls within the scope of criminalistics investigations of white-collar crimes is the detection of counterfeit pharmaceuticals. Encountered here is a combination of black market activity, grand larceny, misrepresentation, and also the vending of dangerous drugs. This kind of white-collar crime is viable because of the willful complicity of the interstate cafe owner and especially the street corner druggist in their distribution. The pharmacists are offered the "high quality" counterfeit pills at bargain prices, whereas it is well known that high quality pharmaceuticals cannot be merchandised at such low prices. In defying their ethical obligations to suspect the nature of these drugs, these pharmacists are accomplices in white-collar crime.

While the source of raw materials and sometimes the finished drug is a diversion from the legalized channels of production and distribution, e.g. pilferage and embezzlement, some white-collar criminals are able to crudely manufacture their own preparations with the aid of unethical chemists, and without the required stringent controls required for legitimate drugs. Patients may therefore be purchasing a counterfeit drug whose pharmacological effects little resemble the genuine drug prescribed with the tragic consequences that the physician may be misled in his management of the case. The commonest counterfeited drugs are imitations of amphetamines and barbiturates and bear a counterfeit trademark of a reputable pharmaceutical company in order to mislead the purchaser as to its origin. Tablets and capsules are distinctive for different pharmaceutical companies for their preparations. Further, they have distinctive stamped punch marks including registered trademarks. The identification of these characteristics is within the realm of criminalistics, when the source of the preparations can be traced, and the question as to their authenticity resolved.

The most notorious of drug violations is quackery. Unorthodox drug remedies and panaceas are promoted by charlatans who prey on those afflicted with terminal, incurable, or painful diseases such as cancer and arthritis. An estimated $250 million is taken from arthritis sufferers alone by these quacks (12). Senior citizens are the predominant targets of these white-collar criminals. Nevertheless, the suffering patient is always prone to try any remedy to save his life or alleviate his pain. The tragedy lies not in the wasted money but in believing these drugs are effective, where the victim lingers and does not receive adequate treatment until it is too late. Hundreds of such preparations have been evaluated and some purported to induce such impossible feats as longevity. The old-fashioned quack drugs were no more than concoctions of simple chemical compounds and medicinal herbs. The more ill-famed tonics were Hoxsey's formula and Mill rue (13). The latter drug falsely asserted to counteract almost all diseases including phocomelia in newborn babies whose mothers had been prescribed thalidomide, (which, further, was also banned by the Food and Drug Administration).

While the Food and Drug Administration documents what may be a prototype service of a local crime laboratory in the detection of white-collar criminality, recently, the Phoenix Police Laboratory uncovered that a variety of "mineral salt tablets" alleged to cure cancer was a quack. Analysis revealed that the tablets contained almost 99% lactose with only traces of minerals stated on the label on the bottle. This led to the prosecution and conviction of the promotor of the quack cancer curing tablets for practicing medicine without a license by the State of Arizona in April 1965 (14).

The gamut of radio therapy, neuro-linometers, microdynameters, electronic wands, Electron-O-Rays, and other devices of the "electromagnetic era" constitute another form of therapeutic quackery in which the criminalist engages in demonstrating the spurious nature of these devices and exposing another area of white-collar crime. These fake medical devices are purported to diagnose or heal by producing a weak magnetic field or emiting short-wave radio frequencies. A pseudo-religious center or pseudo-scientific institution is often used as a cover for practicing this kind of electronic therapeutic quackery. While such devices were known to have an earlier origin, in 1900 the Spectrochrome was promoted by D.P.F.

Ghadiali and claimed over thousands of devotees. A forensic examination revealed that it consisted of an ordinary light bulb whose rays were focused through pieces of colored glass. The colored rays were supposed to be attuned to the body's "radioactive forces" when rays of a particular wavelength, depending on different phases of the moon, were expected to cure specific ailments. A device called the "Radioscope" followed in 1924 which supposedly measured "emanations" associated with different diseases of the body and thrived until the 1960's. By turning several knobs on these worthless electrical machines, the instruments "can tune into any human body in the world." In 1963, a criminalist for the California State Public Health Department was instrumental in securing evidence that a Hollywood radio-therapy center known as Drown Laboratories was using such spurious devices. Operated by a chiropractor and her assistants, the contrivances were used to diagnose different ailments, especially cancer, even in the absence of the patient (15).

False Advertising

The second major area in white-collar crime in which criminalistics has played a key role is in the detection of false advertising in consumer production. Through a host of clever pseudo-scientific statements, half-truths, innuendos, hyperboles, and some scare tactics, wholesalers and retailers have been able to deceive many a customer into purchasing their products. When purchasers are induced into buying misidentified goods, their desires are effectively thwarted. The notion that the dissatisfied customer will punish the producer by not buying his product again is no remedial or punitive answer. Not only has the misrepresentation achieved its unjustified reward in the initial purchase, but many products are *not* based on repeated purchases for profitable production. In addition, by the time that product is replaced, the misdescription is forgotten. It is the function of criminalists and other investigators in the Federal Trade Commission to detect such criminal misrepresentation in trade and commerce.

Firm principles of deceptiveness cannot be established because of the lack of adequate standards. In appellate challenges by businessmen against the Federal Trade Commission, the standard of deceptiveness determined by the model consumer is lowered by whatever variables existing in this unwary person and also by giving the businessmen the benefit of the doubt. However, when a more comprehensive audience passes along an assertion to those less knowledgeable, the standards of deceptiveness are not the same. For example, a product description is understood by the retailers but not by the consumers.

So far, scientific evidence has provided the best criteria for judging deceptiveness. Serious infractions are considered to have occurred when an advertisement ascribes a quality, ingredient, or effectiveness to a product which, *ipso facto*, it does not possess (16). While an assertion may be ambiguous in meaning of which the less common is used to deceive the consumer, the same assertion may also convey useful information to a segment of consumers and a misleading impression to another. Illustrative examples of each type resolved by scientific evidence are cited below.

The case of Federal Trade Commission vs. Algoma Lumber Co., which became renowned because it was appealed to the U.S. Supreme Court, exemplifies the ascription of a quality to a product which it did not have. A forestry expert for the Federal Trade Commission identified a stock of cheap pine wood as yellow "pinus ponderosa" when it was described in the East as "white pine" and sold as such (17). Botanically, there are two groups of the genus of pine trees—yellow ponderosa and white ponderosa. The former grows in California and is accepted in the Western markets as "white pine." However, the defendant sold the same yellow pine in the East also as "white pine," which conflicted with the native Eastern white pine, to which it was basically inferior. The ruling of the Court was that the designation of quality was deceptive since it denoted a superior product in the contest region.

The age of spirits has also been the subject of misleading advertising. Forensic chemists of the Alcohol and Tobacco Tax Division of the Treasury Department, which is responsible for enforcing the Federal Alcohol Administration Act regulating liquor ingredients, bottling, and labelling, developed a partial solution with the application of nuclear chemistry utilizing a tritium dating technique. Large quantities of tritium had been discharged into the atmosphere following experimental detonation of hydrogen bombs beginning in 1952. Tritium combines with atmospheric ozone to form an isotope of heavy water and returns in this form through precipitation into the Earth's water cycle. An age or vintage verification of say, bourbon whiskey manufactured after 1952 could be made by characterization of its tritium content.

Another classic white-collar criminal violation involving false advertising concerns the clothing industry. Criminalists, like textile chemists are also able to differentiate between natural and synthetic fibers, and identify animal fibers. Dr. Henry Harap in his *Education of the Consumer* made a careful forensic scientific survey of the major forms of mislabelling in the clothing industry where inferior textiles and furs are substituted or blended with the real material and advertised as the latter. For example, "Irish linen" handkerchiefs are often found to contain only 50% linen. Similarly synthetic rayon is substituted for silk. The chief furs in the U.S. are limited to a small group of skins in which the terminology of the retail trade is hardly ever mentioned. "This is because furs are clipped, dyed, and pulled in such a way as to resemble those which are superior in wearing quality and warmth. The pelts of animals from warmer zones, such as woodchuck and oppossum are sold under the names of animals in the colder climates. Such furs are inferior in suppleness and durability of leather, denseness, and silkiness of under hair, fullness of protective hair, and because dyed, are brittle and less durable in general" (18). Expert testimony introduced in the "Truth in Fabrics" hearing in the 1920's prompted the Federal Trade Commission to reveal that 90% of the fur sold domestically was not marketed under its correct name (19). One cause for misleading consumers as to fiber content and durability of wearing apparel is the attempt by industry to sell at lower and more moderate prices and broadening the market base.

By way of variation, a more interesting example of false advertising may be cited in the motion picture industry. In 1933, the Federal Trade Commission was engaged in verifying the authenticity of the celebrated film "Ingagi." (Ingagi was alleged to be an African word for gorilla.) This film was produced by Congo Pictures, Ltd., of Los Angeles and was advertised as a true record of an African Safari expedition by a renowned scientist Sir Hubert Winstead and Captain Daniel Swayne, American hunter and collector of rare museum species (20). The scientific investigation of the film challenged the zoological existence of an animal new to science called a "tortadillo" and strange anthropomorphic beasts that were partly simian. A lexicographic survey revealed that the title of the film, "Ingagi" was fictitious as no such word existed in any of the African languages. Corroborative field investigations proved that both men were also fictitious; the "tortadillo" was fabricated by equipping a turtle with wings, scales, and a long tail; human beings suitably attired in skins represented gorillas; the pygmies and strange anthropomorphic beasts were enacted by costumed Negroes of various ages. Further, the background of the Griffith Park Zoo in Los Angeles was featured as the scenery for the jungle shots.

Another form of gross misrepresentation and false advertising in more subtle forms involves the ascription of a non-existent effectiveness to sundry and non-prescriptive remedies. They are differentiated here, from medical quackery as mentioned earlier, because of their semi-medicinal nature and their innocuous effects if consumed (as opposed to adverse drug effects). In this form of misrepresentation the seller informs the buyer that his product is in a position to treat an illness or malady without medical supervision. It is broadly insinuated, rather than blatantly asserted, that the product has extensive curative powers. Misleading advertisements of this type have been used in the "Geritol" commercials which purported to cure people who feel tired and worn out by supplying iron to their iron-deficient blood. Similarly, Caldwell, Inc. advertised and marketed a laxative to cure unmanageable children of constipation (21). While self-diagnosis could be hazardous and often misleading, submissions made before the Federal Trade Commission indicated that lethargy is not necessarily a condition of iron-deficiency, nor is constipation a disease but a symptom of an ailment (22). These few illustrative advertisements reveal that in many instances the consumer of such products is misled into believing that a cause is cured when in fact, only an anxiety has been relieved and the ailment still is present.

Tax Evasion

The government is itself a frequent victim of white-collar crime in which it is cheated by tax evaders. Tax evasion is a chicane practiced by all segments of society, but the greatest temptations occur in the white-collar sector. The most dangerous form of tax evasion is that resulting from the artful juggling of loopholes and exemptions—avoidance. Hermann Mannheim indicated, "The really dangerous tax offender does not evade; he avoids" (23). While a great deal of talent and imagination is directed to exploiting every tactic and device to avoid the tax burden, it is an equally intriguing and challenging problem in criminalistics to expose this facet of white-collar crime utilizing physical evidence.

Many people make sizable tax deductions by charitable donations in large sums more as an outlet for tax evasion rather than philanthropic reasons. This has been recently related to the boom in the purchase of extravagant paintings and objects d'art, which are then over-evaluated by "fee-happy" art appraisers. These are then donated to a local art gallery and written off as a tax deduction. This has led to the spawning practice of conniving art authentication. As a result, the Internal Revenue Service maintains a staff of forensic chemists to investigate these appraisals by examining the physical objects. Since the latter may be authentic and valuable certain non-destructive techniques of analysis are employed. Such a technique was adapted from one developed by the Brookhaven National Laboratories in 1962 utilizing X-ray fluorescence (24). Atoms in the mineral pigments are temporarily excited by bombardment with a fine needle beam of electrons (electron beam microprobe) or with neutrons and their fluorescent pattern sequentially photographed on X-ray film. The fluorescent patterns of mineral pigments of a painting are characteristic of their elemental composition. By comparison with bonafide paintings of the same artist the authenticity of the questioned painting may be established.

Art forgery, *per se*, whether or not committed for fraudulent sale and subsequent tax evasion, is also white-collar crime. X-ray shadowgraphs were used to expose the spurious Van Gogh works marketed by Otto

Walker because Van Gogh's highly individual art proved remarkably susceptible to this type of examination. In the noted trial of Van Meegeren for the Vermeer art forgeries, testimony was produced that the X-rays revealed images beneath a new coating of paint. Van Meegeren had apparently purchased old and relatively worthless paintings, carefully painted them over with a Vermeer imitation, and induced a craquelue assisted by numerous aged cracks from the old painting to produce a 17th century effect.

In a similar manner, ancient Roman Arezzo pottery was shown to be a forgery. Scientists at the Brookhaven National Laboratory examining Mediterranean relics for archeologists detected that the pottery differed in chemical composition from genuine Arezzo (25).

Another form of tax evasion is the avoidance of payment of tariff duties on imported articles. As related to objets d'art, the U.S. Customs Service Agency uncovered a forgery for a museum curator. Since by law, only imported articles of artistic antiquity produced before 1830 are exempt from duty, the Agency chemists were interested in the verification of the age of an antique tapestry imported from Europe. Although the curator vouched for its antiquity, analysis revealed that the tapestry's threads were stained with coal tar dyes, and the latter were not in use before 1857. As a result the museum was saved from the embarrassment of exhibiting a forged antiquity.

Similarly, criminalistics has served to detect improper classification of imports by shippers, who attempt to pay a lower rate of duty than that imposed by the Tariff Acts. Precise quantitative and qualitative methods of analysis of the contents of imports and some regulated exports have thwarted deliberate tax evasion and removed subjectivity from unintentional and often erroneous appraisals of customs duties. For example, X-ray instrumentation analysis was employed in establishing that material declared as "ordinary zirconium oxide" was in fact stabilized pure zirconium oxide, dutiable at 15% value. This type of examination has been extended to the determination of calcium fluoride in fluorspar, silica in glass sand, the composition of ferro-alloys, and in the identification of teflon (26).

A more significant role of criminalistics in the U.S. Customs Service Agency is not so much tax evasion but protection of the stability of the domestic economic market from foreign competition. Where a product is imported in such a manner as to avoid tariff duties because of its different physical form is an aspect of white-collar crime analogous to black market operations. By way of illustration, a product imported under the trade name of "Lioxin" in the 1960's was shown to be an impure form of vanillin which could be economically purified to conform to vanillin of the U.S. Pharmacopeia. Since the price of "Lioxin" was so low as to upset the domestic vanillin trade it was subjected to a tariff duty based on the retail value of the domestic vanillin product.

One of the most important areas of white-collar criminality and tax evasion concerns the Alcohol and Tobacco Tax Division of the U.S. Department of Treasury. During the Prohibition Era, its major task was in tracking down illegal distilleries. Since a heavy excise tax, which produces approximately 5% of all federal revenues is imposed on alcoholic beverages, the Division's laboratory has expanded its facilities (27). It is said that enough "moonshine whiskey" is distilled domestically especially along the "moonshine belt" across the Southeastern states to reduce the collection of taxes by 35% (28). Detection of this liquor is important because when it is transported across some state lines as contraband, it is sold at less than half the price of the regular liquor because of nonpayment of the excise tax.

In a precedent-establishing case, both in law enforcement and the administration of justice, criminalists identified the source of contraband liquor leading to the conviction of several liquor dealers for tax evasion. Illicit whiskey had been seized from a low-slung rented trailer transporting 2,400 gallons of the contraband from a still in Atlanta, Georgia to a distribution point in New York City. Samples of red clay soil clinging to the bottom and tires of the truck were scraped and compared with sample soil specimens from tire tracks in the vicinity of the illicit still in Atlanta utilizing neutron activation analysis. Trace studies of the elemental compostion of the two soils' contituents established a common source of origin. This physical evidence was of substantial value in associating the contraband seized in the Brooklyn raid with the Atlanta operators and was the first instance where the results of neutron activation analysis (29) was accepted in a U.S. District Court (U.S. vs. Anderson, et al.).

Insurance Frauds

Insurance frauds constitute another portion of white-collar crimes whose detection and investigation is dependent upon the science of criminalistics. This is why some major insurance companies contract with consulting criminalists. Practically all claims for insurance coverage require proof that the insured item or person sustained injury or destruction. This means that there must be some physical verification such as the decease of a policy-holder, vandalism, a traffic accident, workman's injury, or the loss of funds (possibly through embezzlement) from a federally insured bank. The white-collar crimes considered under this category are generally of the type committed by a party against a corporation. The cause can be an unsharable problem as discussed by Cressey or some greedy purpose. The crime is enacted by a man who, for example, decides he needs a new car, and vitiates his archaic 1956 Buick, or the benefactor-son who plants a bomb aboard an airplane which his $100,000 insured mother is on. The fraud need not be limited to the feigning of the act as an accident; there is also the unscrupulous doctor and the automobile mechanic who "pads" the bill to be paid by the insurance company with superficial, exorbitant, and unnecessary expenditures.

In this category of white-collar crimes, the criminalist's function is principally to determine if the given incident was intentional or accidental from examination of the physical evidence. For example, a criminalist investigating the burglary of an insured jewelry item may find no toolmarks or tampering on the safe from which it was missing; also, the window screen may be found to be cut from the inside of the house. The conchoidal fractures of the broken glass window may indicate the breakage originated from the inside, too. Since the only occupant of the house and the only person in possession of the safe's combination is the owner, the criminalist would infer an insurance fraud in which the owner had "framed" a burglary.

The best illustrating example of criminalistics investigation of insurance frauds is the study of arson. Fires have been known to be set by respectable persons and businessmen for the purpose of defrauding the insurance company. Arson for profit is always the first motive to be considered. The heinous social injustice that is not realized is the criminal responsibility for the death of citizens and firemen trapped in rescue or suppression attempts.

An insurance agent or broker may be a firesetter using arson as a device to awaken a community into purchasing fire insurance or to collect a greater monetary commission. Secondly, a corrupt claims adjuster may collaborate with policyholders or potential buyers to defraud the insurance company and thus create or augment the existing white-collar crime. The period of the depression, 1930–35, was marked by the notorious era of arson torch rings and firesetting by businessmen in conspiracies with insurance agents and public claims adjusters. The infamous Brooklyn arson ring included one such broker who gained the reputation of being able to guarantee a fire with every policy he wrote. Another ring included the "brains" of an unscrupulous attorney; in his position, he was able to use all legal loopholes and means available to defy apprehension and to counsel policyholders to commit arson. One other inducement for arson is the careless writing of fire insurance policies—over insurance—when policies are issued far in excess of the value of the insured property. This may be part of the plan of the white-collar criminal insurance agent or an outcome of the highly competitive nature of the insurance business. It is interesting to note here that insurance fraud is a white-collar crime committed *against* the corporation or institution whereas before only white-collar crimes committed *by* the corporation with the consumer public as the victim had been considered.

There are numerous instances whereby fire has been used to dispose of unwanted property at the expense of the insurance company: a house too old to live in is burned down, scrapping of machinery, liquidation of surplus or unsaleable quantities. There is also arson committed as a white-collar crime for making profit but not at the expense of the insurance company: the chance to get rid of a competitive business, the opportunity to seek a rebuilding contract, display of vanity for seeking employment or promotion, a situation where salvage profits over storage, the liquidation of real estate before it can be inherited, etc. Whatever the case might be, the crucial question that the criminalist is always confronted with is is whether a fire was accidental or incendiary. There has always been a tendency to regard fire as an unfortunate accident than a possible arson. The event of a fire is usually associated with "spontaneous combustion," electrical overloads, or lightning; even a cigarette planted in a bed appears to be an innocent cause of a fire. Thus, incendiarism is the most suitable and unsuspecting means of replacing unwanted furnishings and paraphernalia or collecting high premiums or for other personal gain. Another reason for using fire as a means of committing insurance frauds is that it destroys incriminating evidence making the investigation of arson the most difficult of all crimes. The major obstacle to arson investigation is on the part of some of the detectives and criminalists spuriously assuming all evidence is consumed in a fire.

Fires have also been known to be used for covering up other white-collar crimes such as embezzlement and pilferage. Embezzlers have attempted arson to disguise incomplete and unbalanced books. In some cases, books are tented with burning newspaper stuffed into them. Experimentation with combustible materials shows that books are the hardest to burn because of high inorganic salt content in high quality paper and small surface area, and thus can be recognized as physical evidence in arson. Managers, foremen, and inventory clerks are in favorable positions to conceal their pilferage by arson. By writing off the pilfered merchandise as fire loss, they are able to carry on this white-collar crime. An interesting example of such a case occurred in a southern textile mill which was destroyed by a fire of unknown origin. Although incendiarism could not be implicated, insurance agents were hesitant about honoring a claim for thousands of dollars worth of coats and suits. The owner's description of the destroyed clothing items detailed specific textures, models, and buttons and was submitted to a forensic chemist. The forensic chemist indicated that a particular type of button in the description was fireproof and arranged for tediously sifting through the ashes and debris to establish the number of coats consumed in the fire. The search for these pieces of physical evidence resulted in a finding that there were no such buttons. The arson investigation concluded in discovering that the plant's stock of clothing had been hauled off, a fire was set, and a false claim had been submitted (30).

The establishment of proof of arson in the administration of justice is very difficult indeed. Criminalistics evidence may be labelled as "insufficient" to prove guilt beyond a reasonable doubt in a criminal court since the rules of evidence are very exacting and whatever meager scientific evidence is meaningless if there is so much as one small link missing. Criminalistics, however, does not stop serving the interest of justice here but enters into the civil court. The insurance company simply refuses to honor the claim for loss from an insured person believed to be linked with a suspicious fire. In turn, the insured must commence a civil suit to recover his loss. Since only a preponderance of evidence is required to fight a suit, the testimony of the criminalist regarding the suspicious nature of the fire and possible link of the insured may be sufficient. Where the same criminalistics evidence would hardly have been accepted in a criminal court, it still serves administration of justice in cases of civil litigation. Such an action is a deterrent to arson because it eliminates or hinders the lucrative nature of the fraud, and this is the role criminalistics plays in checking as well as detecting white-collar crime.

Questioned Documents

There are numerous instances where white-collar crimes are frequently detected through the alteration, obliteration, or forgery of a binding legal document: a bookkeeper "doctors" a few numbers to embezzle some money, a counterfeiter prints up a set of credit cards, a postage franking stamp is altered, an administrator adds several heirs to a will, the date of expiration of a contract is postponed, the specifications of a building contract are changed to substitute inferior products. In brief, the document is a written agreement made with stipulations and conditions between two or more parties and is intended to provide a permanent record where memory is untrustworthy. Despite this intention, documents are not failsafe but are fallible to dishonest manipulation. The surreptitious alteration or forgery of a document is indubitably a criminal breach of trust and an instrument of the white-collar criminal. Some criminalists have ventured into this area of examination or specialize entirely in this area. However, for the most part they are handled by specialists designated as Examiners of Questioned Documents, and they function as such even though they may be attached to forensic science or criminalistics laboratories. Consequently the role of criminalistics in this area of specialization and white-collar crime is more often supplementary and of a routine nature, such as the identification of inks and papers by chemical analysis, determining the individuality of die stamps, and the restoration of erased or tampered writings and markings on different types of surfaces. A discussion of the role of the Examiner of Questioned Documents in white-collar crimes is hence a separate and extensive area of study.

Conclusion

There are many other white-collar crime areas to which criminalistics has been applied. We can add others including various aspects of consumer-safety and quality-control, such as testing of hazardous gas heaters and dangerous firecrackers, also the rigging of gambling machines and other devices, the detection of fish, game, and wildlife code violations and numerous civil cases involving forensic questions of liability and malpractice. These are areas in addition to the five already discussed. Unfortunately, criminalistics cannot solve all the problems of detection and investigation of white-collar crime because of an inherent lack of physical evidence. Nevertheless, it has been demonstrated that criminalistics does play a role outside of the normal police crime laboratory in the administration of justice and law enforcement of nonconventional crime.

REFERENCES

1. SUTHERLAND, E. H., *White Collar Criminal*, 5 American Sociological Review, 1–12, Feb., 1940.

2. CRESSEY, B. R., *The Criminal Violation of Financial Trust*, 15 American Sociological Review, 738–743, Dec., 1950.

3. CLINARD, M. B., *The Black Market: A Study in White Collar Crime*, 1952.

4. QUINNEY, R., *The Study of White Collar Crime: Toward a Reorientation in Theory and Research*, 55 Journal of Criminal Law, Criminology, & Police Science, 208–214, June, 1964.

5. Michigan (State) Department of Health, *Seventy-Seventh Annual Report of the Commissioner of Michigan Department of Health*, Lansing, Michigan: 1949), p. 6.

6. PARKER, B. P., *Government Review—Science and Crime*, 70 Technology Review, 10, 1968.

7. *Ibid.*

8. NEAL, HARRY E., *The Protector*, 1968, p. 33.

9. *Ibid.*, p. 53.

10. WILSON, A. C., *et al.*, *Enzymatic Identification of Fish Products*, 157 Science, 82–83, July, 1967.

11. Food & Drug Administration, *FDA Report on Enforcement & Compliance*, Washington, D.C.: Sept., 1965.

12. LANGER, G., *Growing Old in America: Fraud, Quackery Swindle the Aged and Compound Their Trouble*, 140 Science, 470, May, 1963.

13. Changing Times, *What the Health Hucksters Are Up To*, The Kipling Magazine, 221, Sept., 1964.

14. Food & Drug Administration, *FDA Report on Enforcement & Compliance*, Washington, D.C.: May, 1965, p. 20.

15. *Berkeley Daily Gazette*, Vol. LXXXVI, No. 241, Oct. 10, 1963.

16. FRITCH, B. E., *Illusion or Deception: The Use of "Props" and "Mock-Ups" in T.V. Advertising*, 72 Yale Law Journal, 148, Nov., 1962.

17. 291 U.S. 67, 1934, FTC vs. Algoma Lumber Co.

18. SCHLINK, F. J., *Your Money's Worth*, 1920, p. 109.

19. *Ibid.*

20. HARDING, T. SWAIN, *The Popular Practice of Fraud*, 1935, p. 59.

21. ALEXANDER, G. J., *Honesty and Competition*, 1967.

22. *Ibid.*

23. MANNHEIM, H., *Criminal Justice and Social Reconstruction*, 1967, p. 146.

24. SEABORG, GLENN T., *Science & Humanities: A New Level of Symbiosis*, 144 Science, 1200, 1964.

25. *Ibid.*

26. SELLERS, B. and ZEIGLER, C. A., *Applications of Radioisotope Excited X-Ray Techniques*, 1 Proceedings of the First National Symposium on Law Enforcement Science & Technology, 353, 1967.

27. SURFACE, WILLIAM, *Inside Internal Revenue*, 1967, p. 172.

28. *Ibid.*

29. Activation Analysis in Court, 7 Nuclear News, 31, June, 1964.

30. BATTLE, BRENDAN P., *Arson: A Handbook of Detection & Investigation*, 1954, p. 50.

The Computer: Its Role and Potential in Criminal Justice

During recent years, the use of the computer has been extended to almost every facet of American society, including the area of criminal justice. The computer offers a vast potential to the law enforcement community that is unparalleled. Through information storage and retrieval processes, the investigator has millions of facts at his fingertips, thus avoiding the need to dig through bulky and cumbersome police files.

Although the true potential of the computer in the administration of justice is still a thing of the future, giant strides have been made in adapting this technology to law enforcement and the detection of crime. Computer application is not limited to administrative matters, but can be readily used by the investigator in the gathering and evaluation of evidence.

Limited only by the imagination of the user, the computer can serve to index and cross index all types of information that will be of value to the investigator. It can catalog stolen items; cross index MO's (*modus operandi*) of criminals; keep current information on known criminals; firearms information; wanted persons; and the list goes on. All this is in addition to its value in the management of the criminal justice agency. The system can be adapted for use by industrial security personnel in developing information on industrial espionage, personnel risks, credit information, and the development of new techniques in the detection of shoplifting and employee dishonesty.

Because of its vast possibilities, the computer has become

one of the major advances of the century in the developing system of justice. Not to be overlooked is the value of the computer in crime prevention, by assigning patrol cars and personnel to high crime areas.

This section deals with the value of the computer to law enforcement and as a tool in the detection of crime. An attempt is made to acquaint the student with some of the rudimentary knowledge of the computer and how it operates. Such an approach is necessary since to many persons the workings of the computer seem shrouded in mystery. The various applications of the computer in criminal justice are discussed in order to offer the student a better understanding of this technology and its future applications.

The Federal Bureau of Investigation has taken the lead in adapting the computer to use in the criminal justice system with the establishment of the National Crime Information Center (NCIC). Linked to all of the states, the NCIC is serving as a repository of information on criminal activity throughout the nation, as well as gathering information on stolen property. Through the use of the NCIC network, police agencies throughout the country are able to assist each other in the apprehension of wanted persons and the recovery of stolen property.

Confidentiality of computer information cannot be minimized. In the development of such information systems, great care must be taken to preserve the rights and privacy of the individual. As computers grow more complex and the state of the art advances, computers will be linked together sharing information and compiling more accurate files. Still unresolved, this problem of confidentiality must be met head on because of its importance to every individual.

Generally, the computer is not seen as an investigative tool in crime detection. However, with the many advances in the technology there can be no doubt of its value. In recent years extensive research has been conducted on computerizing fingerprint files.

One final note is addressed to the securalists, who are criminalists involved in industrial security. Through the use of the computer, many criminals are committing thefts of corporate secrets as well as company assets. Such activity demands that the system be developed for the security of the computer in the corporate field as well as those operated by governmental agencies.

CHAPTER 19

A Simple Tool
for Complex Problems

Robert P. Shumate

The application of computer systems to law enforcement during recent years has caused police administrators at every level to face problems of the computer age. Even the small communities throughout the United States are finding themselves part of larger computer systems through terminals connected to central information repositories.

Police administrators in dealing with this problem have had to attempt to penetrate much of the hocus-pocus surrounding computer technology. While it is unlikely that police administrators will find themselves technically involved in computer systems, they do face the need for understanding the capabilities and limitations of what computers will do in order to deal effectively with them. This, in effect, places the police administrator in a position of having to absorb a considerable amount of technical knowledge concerning computer operations. This absorption of technical knowledge has been compounded by many myths which have grown up around computers.

The purpose of this session is to try and debunk some of the myths that surround computers and to describe, in principle, the way in which computer systems actually operate. Computer systems, as a matter of fact, are relatively simple devices in the way that they work, and stripped of the technical jargon they are easily understood by the layman.

We will start by describing exactly what a computer system is and what components make it up. Actually, a computer can be thought of as consisting of three major parts or elements which can be combined in any way desired to produce a system which will serve particular needs.

First I will describe what is referred to as the central processing unit which, in one way, is the heart of the computer. The CPU performs all of the logical and arithmetical functions of which a computer is capable.

165

Actually a computer can perform only relatively simple tasks, such as additions, subtractions, multiplication and division, as well as some logical functions. These logical functions involve the ability to compare to numbers or characters and determine whether or not they are equal, not equal, greater than or less than each other. However, the central processing unit, by being able to combine these very simple functions, is able to perform extremely complex tasks. In addition to the arithmetic and logical functions the central processing unit is the portion of the computer which analyzes instructions, which are called a program, and perform a step at a time various tasks.

The second major component is what we call storage. Storage consists of two types: storage, often called memory, which has limited capacity and is used for temporary storage of data and for the storage of instructions which tell the computer what tasks to perform; the second type of storage is referred to as peripheral storage and is made up of cards, tapes, disks and drums; it is used to store large amounts of data which will be used by the system in its problem-solving activities. Storage in the computer is very analogous to file cabinets in a manual system of filing and storing data. The various computer components that make up the storage allow data to be classified and organized in some fashion and retained for use as required.

Input-output devices make up the third broad area of components. These are devices which permit the users of computers to communicate with them and to obtain data which is retained in storage. I will discuss in more detail the type of input-output devices that computers use, but, in general, they represent the means by which data is entered to a system and by which information is obtained from the internal devices of the computer and brought back to the user. It is the way in which a person communicates with the activity occurring inside the computer. Today some of the major advances in computer technology are being made in the input-output area. There are new types of devices being developed that allow the users of the system to communicate more easily with the computer itself.

These three major components can be combined to produce a computer system in almost any way that is desired. Some computers have large amounts of memory; others put emphasis on input-output devices which can be used to serve many purposes. There are in existence today computing systems within the law enforcement area which use hundreds of input-output devices that allow people to communicate with the computer itself.

It is worth the effort to examine more closely how some of these components actually work. First, we will examine an area which may appear rather complicated. However, it is necessary to understand certain basic principles to fully realize what is taking place when a human being communicates with a computer from a terminal. Computers represent information both within their memory and on storage devices by using only ones or zeroes. Thus all computers, one way or another, utilize a binary system of data representation. The binary system of representation, particularly where arithmetic is involved, is a much simpler system to understand than our own decimal system.

Within the binary system there are only two characters, a zero and a one. In the decimal system that most of us are accustomed to there are, of course, ten, zero through nine, respectively. The binary zero and one can be used to represent any number that the decimal system can. The following illustration is an example. The column on the left is in binary form, and the one on the right is in decimal form. Note that zeros and ones are the same. But when we reach two in the binary system it is represented by a one zero.

ILLUSTRATION

Binary System:	Decimal System:
0	0
1	1
10	2
11	3
100	4
101	5
110	6
111	7
1000	8
1001	9

Computers always represent characters and numbers internally in binary form. The main reason for this is that computers can recognize only two different states which are easy to think of as a one and a zero.

The principal problem that humans encounter when dealing with computers is that the computer understands one language, while it is easier for humans to work in a language that they are familiar with. In the computer field, historically, there has been a problem of devising ways by which humans can communicate easily with the computer in a familiar language.

Let me now describe this process and how it takes place so it isn't quite so mystifying. Most of the time, insofar as the user is concerned, he need have little concern over how the computer performs its functions internally.

In many respects it is possible to think of the computer as being very much like a human being, and the following analogy can be made. I should add parenthetically that it is only an analogy.

If I put the letter "A" on the board and ask you to look at it, the following takes place. Your eyes focus on the character "A" and transmit the image to your brain, where it assumes meaning. In this respect your eye is analogous to an input device. Your eyes scan the character, transmit it to your memory, and, drawing upon your experiences, it is recognized as the first letter of the alphabet, which can be used in combination with other letters to represent words.

A computer basically can perform the same type of function, except that it doesn't have eyes, and at least, insofar as the current state of technology, we couldn't roll a computer in here, put the blackboard in front of it and ask it to look at and recognize the letter "A". Because of this limitation, we have had to develop methods to get from a language form that humans use into a language that the computer can understand. This is a problem similar to that which I would encounter if I suddenly discovered when I got in here this morning that none of you in the audience understood English. I would then have the problem of trying to communicate with you in a language which none of you understand. We would have to solve the problem by using an interpreter to translate what I was actually saying into a language you could understand. It is very much the same kind of process that takes place in communicating with a computer.

One of the commonest methods of communicating with a computer is by means of punched cards. The letter "A" is recognized visually by you and me as this (writing an "A" on the blackboard). Punched cards, which I think you are familiar with, provide a capability for representing through a pattern of holes punched in the card any character that appears in our alphabet or any of the special punctuation characters or any number. Thus an "A" written on the board has meaning to you and me. An "A" to a computer on a punch card looks something like this (indicating). It is represented by two holes in known positions within the card, and the computer recognizes that it is an "A" when it reads such a combination of holes.

The computer in some ways goes through the same kind of recognition process that you do when I write the letter "A" on the blackboard. The punched card is to the computer what the printed page is to you and me, a language form that the computer or other data processing machine can understand.

The process of human–computer communication is not a complicated one. Punch cards, for example, are prepared on machines that have what resembles a typewriter keyboard. A piece of blank card stock goes into the machine, and the operator copying from a piece of paper depresses the key with the letter "A" on it. The machine automatically punches a pattern of holes in the card which correspond to what the computer will recognize as being the letter "A".

Thus the process of translation from a document such as an accident report or a crime report is very similar to the process we would go through if I had an interpreter present interpreting for you. The process involves translating from a form which you and I understand to a form which the computer can understand. To the computer those two holes in that position on a card are just as surely recognized as an "A" as the character written on the board is recognized by you as an "A".

The process I have described is called keypunching, but it is really a technique for translating information from a form read and understood by humans to a form that the computer can understand.

To understand the entire process more fully, let's follow through an entire process. We will use, as an example, my name, since one of the more interesting things that computers are doing in law enforcement is keeping track of wanted persons.

Starting with my name on a document, the translation process from the document is by means of keypunching, so that we end up with a card that has a series of punches which say to the computer just as clearly as the letters on the board that this represents the characters S-h-u-m-a-t-e.

The next step in the processing cycle after the card is punched is a reading process, by which the card is read through an input device into the computer. The computer now is able to recognize that each combination of punches represents a character. The process from that point is what we might call retention.

Finally, at the end of the process in the computer memory we have the same set of characters stored in a form that the computer can understand, and from this point on the computer can do many things with it. The process described is often misunderstood, yet it actually is nothing more than a process of translating information from a form that humans use to a form that can be entered to the computer so it can perform some function on it.

Now, once this information has been entered and is stored in the computer's memory, let's consider some of the things that a computer can do with it. One thing that has made computers particularly applicable to law enforcement is that in recent years computers have developed a vastly improved capability for storing very large amounts of information, much like we store them in traditional filing systems.

When we store information, whether it is file cards containing people's names or reports, we usually think in terms of steel file cabinets. Usually files are maintained through some system, by report number, case number, or by name. Each file drawer will contain in some form, alphabetically or otherwise, information in which there is some interest and which, when needed, can be found and transmitted to whoever requires it.

Computers have the capability of performing practically the same function, and though it is done electronically, it is done in a manner very similar to that used for manual files. The most popular media by which information is stored on a computer today is magnetic disks.

Let me start by talking about the ways that data in general is stored, and we'll compare the various methods as to usefulness. The most common way that information is stored is in punched cards. For example, the process I have described earlier, where data is keypunched into a card, is itself a storage method. It is possible, using a punched card, to compress a large amount of narrative data onto a card which can be stored in a file for later retrieval. The second way, which historically reached wide usage after cards, is magnetic tape. A computer tape looks very much like the magnetic tape that you use in a voice tape recorder. As a matter of fact, except for a slightly different manufacturing process it is exactly the same kind of tape. A reel of computer tape is usually somewhere between one thousand and four thousand feet in length and can be used to store millions of characters of information. On a strip of magnetic tape there are nine channels running laterally the length of the tape. These channels are nothing more than spaces on the tape which are used for the storage of data bits. Each character is represented on the tape like this.

Let's say we want to store the character "A" on a section of the tape. Using binary notation the character "A" can be represented as: zero zero zero one one zero one one one. The data is stored on tape as a series of 1's and 0's, and as we illustrated earlier, any character in our language structure can be represented in this fashion. Characters may be represented on tape at between five and eight hundred characters per inch of tape. In other words, one inch of magnetic tape can contain between five and eight hundred characters per inch of tape. This means in effect, that an awful lot of information can be stored on a few feet of tape and an enormous amount of information can be stored on a reel of tape, which is usually somewhere around three thousand feet in length.

Magnetic tape was one of the earlier forms of storage media, and in point of time followed the punch card. Tape has the advantage that it provides very high-speed reading and writing of information. Data can be read from a tape into a computer and examined at the rate in excess of 100,000 characters per second. Cards, on the other hand, are much slower, because they require complex mechanical devices to be read into the computer.

The interesting thing about a piece of magnetic tape, if you have never seen one, is that a visual examination of the tape does not show anything because data is represented by tiny little spots of magnetic flux that are called bits. When a bit is magnetized in one way, it is recognized by the computer as a zero, in another as a one. While it is impossible for a human to see anything on a tape, a computer recognizes the data readily, because to the computer it is like looking at a sheet of paper or a book, because this is the kind of language that it can understand and read.

Tapes have one disadvantage in that they must be treated as a continuous strip of data. Since a reel of tape is typically several thousand feet in length data items that are located in the middle of the reel pose a problem. The only way they can be reached is to unreel the tape. Consequently, tape as a storage media has the disadvantage that if you want a piece of information that is located in the middle of a reel, you must unreel the tape until you reach the section containing the data before the computer can read it and do anything with it.

The next innovation in storage devices, and, frankly, the one that really made computers applicable to many law enforcement problem areas, is the advent of the direct access or random access storage device. Direct access devices eliminate the disadvantage of having an item of information in the middle of the tape when you want it. For those of you who have not had any first-hand experience with a computer, I can best describe a direct access storage device as looking a lot like a jukebox. If you remember the old jukebox that had a stack of records and a turntable, direct access storage devices look very much like them. They consist of a series of disks which revolve at very high speed and look like very large phonograph records. Mechanical arms used to read and write data extend over the disk and resemble the pickup arm that the jukebox used to play records. Each disk consists of several hundred tracks, which individually are used very much like a strip of magnetic tape. The main difference is that the arm may be positioned to read any specific track on request.

Information is stored on direct access storage devices in pretty much the same form that is used on tapes. In fact you can think of each track as being a piece of tape. Because any track can be reached on request, the information can be extracted at the time you want it without passing hundreds of feet of tape. This has produced what the name implies, a form of random or direct access to an item of data. This means if I have a large file of names or a large file of registration numbers, I can, in response to a request coming in from the outside, go directly to that particular portion of the disk that contains the record and extract the information.

As a matter of fact, to those of you who have had or are now having experience with systems which provide remote terminal inquiry for stolen autos or wanted persons, this is the way the information is stored on magnetic disks. It is the direct access storage device that has made computers particularly applicable to law enforcement information retrieval problems by providing the capability of having a file available to the computer on which information can be retrieved in a matter of seconds.

What I have described are the basic tools through which a computer performs its functions. Considering the way in which a computer operates, let's consider how it looks externally to the person who is using it and how the parts actually fit together. To do this, let's talk about some applications which are rather specific to law enforcement problems.

When computers were first considered for use in the law enforcement field, some of the obvious areas of use were in the information storage and retrieval area. For this reason, the first applications of computers on an operating basis were for stolen car files, followed very closely by wanted person files. It will be of interest to take a look at how a computer handles this type of operation and how it utilizes the computer function which we have discussed.

We start out with a need for a method that you and I can use to talk with a computer. Incidentally, at this point I am going to introduce two new terms, "real-time" and "on-line." You will hear these terms from time to time applied to computers. The term "on-line" or "real-time" means that the computer is being used like a file cabinet. The green metal file cabinet you have in your office is an on-line filing system, on-line in the sense that any time you want an item from the file you walk over to the file, pull out a drawer and get the data. You don't have to wait for someone to come in and dig something out for you; it is right there. Computer systems which are on-line or real-time function the same way. When you want to use it, you can do so using the facilities of a terminal. Real-time really means as you need it.

The commonest way of communicating with an on-line computer today, and I think this will change in the next few years, is by means of a keyboard printer device. This may have any kind of a name or number; it may be 1050 or it may be a Model 35 teletype. They all possess the same characteristics; there is a keyboard with keys representing the letters of the alphabet, the numbers, and some set of punctuation characters. Such a device provides the tools by which human beings are able to say things to the computer.

This is the equivalent of what I am doing here and now with you. A terminal represents the means by which you communicate with the computer. In addition, the printing device is used to permit two-way communication by allowing the computer to respond to you. These terminal devices are the I/O that we discussed earlier. It provides the ability to you and me to do something with this massive amount of electronic data we have stored by the computer.

The next thing we will consider is what we called earlier the CPU. The functions performed by the CPU includes accepting information coming in from terminals, editing and comparing data, and placing it temporarily in storage. An example will help to illustrate the functions that the CPU performs.

Let's say I want to determine whether or not anybody with the name "John Smith" is in my file as a wanted person. The name itself is entered through the terminal in much the same way that I would type it on a sheet of paper. At the same time I type the information at the terminal, pulses are going out over the line, which is nothing more than the common garden variety of telephone lines. It is being received at the computer by what we would consider fairly complicated electronic gear. The characters as they are received by the central processing unit are stored in various locations in core, so that at the end of my transmission I have in the computer a set of characters which represent to the computer what I recognize as a name.

The next step in an application like this is to compare the name with those on file. Attached to the CPU is a storage device. It will be a disk which we discussed previously and which may have stored on it a hundred or a million names of people which, for some reason or another, we are interested in. The CPU must now determine whether the name I entered is in the file. Data on disk files are usually organized and stored in a fashion similar to that used in organizing and storing data in regular filing cabinets.

The most frequent approach is to employ some alphabetic method of organization, so that when the computer has a name it can determine what part of the disk it is stored in. The CPU has the capability of analyzing the name "Smith" and determining the name starts with "S," so it is in the "S" files and the "S" files are located in this portion of the disk. As in a manual filing system, it is possible to use very complicated methods of further breakdown. For example, the computer has the capability of saying not only is this in the "S" file, but actually it is in the "Sm" portion of the "S" file. What actually happens in the CPU is very similar to what happens in a manual filing system as the clerk looks for a data item. Well, the "Sm's" are in drawer 17. The computer, in effect, says the "Sm's" are in disk space 28, and then goes to this location to find the item sought.

The next thing that normally takes place is that the information in the proper section of the file is transferred name by name from the storage device by the CPU to temporary locations in core. Let's say the first name transferred to core is "Smathers." The CPU then, character by character, compares the name submitted with the one obtained from the files. Comparisons can be as complicated as you can devise. Anything that can be done by way of comparing or searching in a manual file can be duplicated on a computer through programming. The computer actually begins by making a letter-by-letter comparison. If the first name brought from storage was "Smathers," as the comparison was made it would recognize that the first letter was the same and the second letter was the same. However, when it reached the third letter it would in effect say, no, this is not the same person. Actually what it would say is this set of characters that I have here are not the same set of characters that I retrieved from the file. It may be the same person, but the set of characters are different. The computer then proceeds to bring the next name out of the "S" file and continues to do so until it has examined all the "S's" or the "Sm's" that are in the file.

The main thing is that this could be a long and tedious process in a large file if the search is performed manually, but with the kind of speeds that are measured in millionths or thousandths of a second, a computer performs this task quite rapidly. Data, for example, is transferred at rates up to three hundred thousand characters per second from disk to core. Searches and comparison usually take twenty to thirty millionths of a second.

So, to extract the information I described from a file, bring it in to core, examine the name and perhaps other identification, such as date of birth, age, sex, usually consumes a thousandth of a second or less. This means that a computer, using techniques similar to those described, can scan, search and examine hundreds and thousands of data items in what to you and me appear to be a relatively short period of time.

As the computer repeats the process I have described, the computer may at some point bring in a set of characters S-m-i-t-h. At this point the computer recognizes the fact that the set of characters from the file are the same as that contained in the name submitted from the terminal. It doesn't necessarily know whether it is the same person, but at that point it then initiates a response and begins to send a message back to the originating terminal advising that a set of characters has been matched. This may be the person's complete history, his complete description, anything that has previously been stored on the disk. The information is sent back to the terminal device and comes out as printed words. If nothing is found, of course, a message to that effect is sent to the terminal.

The main thing I want to emphasize is that the process itself is really simple. It is exactly the same process we use in retrieving items from a manual filing system, and all the computer does is to perform the function a lot faster and a lot more thoroughly. But it compares data very much the same way a clerk does, by comparing information that is brought in from a terminal through the CPU memory with data in the file to determine whether the request item does match an item in the file.

It is possible to employ very clever techniques within a computer for performing data comparisons, but then it is also possible to devise very, very clever ways of searching using a green steel filing cabinet and a clerk. There is nothing magic about the computer. It merely represents human ingenuity in being able to devise better ways of determining who is "the real John Smith."

The one important thing that I have left out that we should now discuss is how the computer actually knows how to perform these complex activities. The computer is instructed what to do by what we call programs. A program is a set of very, very detailed instructions which tell the computer step by step what to do next. A program is really detailed, far more detailed than we are used to thinking. Program steps aren't general like, "Go out and bring in a pail of water." They are specific, like, "Pick up the pail in your right hand, lift it off the floor, walk to the door," type of instructions.

Program instructions in the computer inform the computer to do things like add number "A" to number "B," subtract number "C," or more in line with what we have been discussing, compare this character with that character and tell me whether it is the same. A program is a series of instructions which, taken together, tell the computer how to perform complex activities.

The program is stored in a portion of the computing system just like data that is being used. A large program which can handle a very complicated file-searching technique may contain one to two hundred thousand individual instructions, each of which tell the computer to do some specific thing. A large and complicated program frequently makes the computer look and behave like it had an intelligence of its own. Computers, when properly programmed, are able to make decisions at a fairly complicated level. For example, there are some very complex file-searching schemes which have been programmed which carry out very complicated searches on names and are able to establish identities on fragmentary data.

The logical capabilities of the CPU, coupled with the program, make the computer seem to have this high order of intelligence because the program is able to decide at various juncture points what it will do next. For example, a typical program may compare two characters and if they are alike perform this activity, if they are not alike then do something entirely different. When you start combining this capability of deciding to do one of two things, depending upon a condition encountered, you have a capability for performing quite complicated activities internally. As more experience has been gained, particularly in applying these techniques to data storage and retrieval in the law enforcement field, more complicated programs for searching names, numbers, and identification patterns have begun to emerge.

The program is the thing that makes a computer useful. In fact, you can't really enjoy a computer without a program, and up to the time that a program is produced for a computer it is just so much electronic gear, rather colorful, very interesting, and often quite mystifying. It will not, however, solve problem number one until such time as some human beings have (1) decided what kind of problem they want it to solve, (2) determined what methods they will use to solve the problem, and (3) someone has programmed the computer to solve the problem as required.

I suspect the real mysticism surrounding computers is not that programming is complicated or that the electronic gear I have described is complicated. More to the point is that it is pretty difficult to get human beings to address themselves to problems and to break them down into how they really want them solved. What is represented by the capability of the computer is really the ingenuity of people that want to use them in the law enforcement area, people such as you. And you, applying your ingenuity, can devise new ways to use computers, and more complicated programs can be produced.

CHAPTER 20

Criminal Justice Information Systems

**President's Commission on
Law Enforcement and the
Administration of Justice**

The Need for Better Information Capabilities

The importance of having complete and timely information about crimes and offenders available at the right place and the right time has been demonstrated throughout this report and, indeed, throughout the Commission's work. With timely information, a police officer could know that he should hold an arrested shoplifter for having committed armed robbery elsewhere. With a more detailed background on how certain kinds of offenders respond to correctional treatment, a judge could sentence persons more intelligently. With better projections of next year's workload, a State budget office would know whether and where to budget for additional parole officers.

Modern information technology now permits an assault on these problems at a level never before conceivable. Computers have been used to solve related problems in such diverse fields as continental air defense, production scheduling, airline reservations, and corporate management. Modern computer and communications technology permits many users, each sitting in his own office, to have immediate remote access to large computer-based, central data banks. Each user can add information to a central file to be shared by the others. Access can be restricted so that only specified users can get certain information.

Criminal justice could benefit dramatically from computer-based information systems, and development of a network designed specifically for its operations could start immediately. Such systems can aid in the following functions:

Police patrol—Enabling a police officer to check rapidly the identification of people and property against a central "wanted" file.

Crime investigation—Providing a police officer or detective with supporting information files such as crime patterns, modus operandi, criminal associates, and perhaps in the future, the ability to match latent fingerprints from a crime scene against a central fingerprint file.

Police deployment—Altering police deployment in response to changing patterns of crime on an hourly, daily, seasonal or emergency basis.

Sentencing and correctional decisions—Providing more complete history of an offender and his reactions to prior correctional actions; statistical estimates of the effects of different kinds of treatment on different kinds of offenders.

Development of correctional programs—Analyzing complete criminal case histories to evaluate the effectiveness of different programs.

Protection of individual rights—Assuring that arrest records include court disposition, thereby presenting a fairer picture to the police and to judges; restricting access to certain criminal records after a specified period of good conduct.

Budgeting—Collecting uniform statistics on agency operations and workloads, providing a basis for estimating personnel needs and for optimum allocation of men and dollars.

Research—Providing a collection of anonymous criminal histories to find out how best to interrupt a developing criminal career and to achieve a better understanding of how to control crime.

Public education—Portraying the true magnitude of the problem of crime in the United States.

The information problem has three principal dimensions:

1. Type of information:

   Inquiry information—Facts about wanted persons or property needed on immediate recall ("on-line" in "real-time") by the police.

   Personal information—Containing relevant background facts about people with whom the system must deal.

   Management information—Needed by a criminal justice official on the operation of his agency to help him manage it better.

   Statistical information—On crime, on the nature of criminal careers, and on the operations of criminal justice agencies.

2. Component of the criminal justice system:
   Police.
   Courts.
   Corrections.

3. Government level:
Federal.
State.
Local, including county, city, and metropolitan area.

All combinations of these items must be considered in an integrated information system. At each governmental level, and in all system components, good statistical and management information are needed. Some of the statistical needs have been discussed in the previous chapter. Inquiry information is needed primarily by the police, especially at State and local levels. Personal informaion is needed for arrest, sentencing, and correctional decisions at all levels.

A major difficulty in obtaining needed inquiry or personal information today arises from the fact that it is frequently recorded in a jurisdiction other than the one in which it is needed. The mobility of offenders and narrow police jurisdictions require sharing common information banks. A stolen car or a wanted person can traverse many jurisdictions in a few hours. Criminals often leave an area where they are well known. The mobility of offenders and stolen property is evidenced by the following:

In 1965, 18.7 percent of stolen autos were recovered outside the police jurisdiction of theft.[1]

Over twenty thousand stolen autos were recovered under the Interstate Transportation of Stolen Automobiles Act (the Dyer Act) in 1965.[2]

In 1965, 8,884 fugitives sought by State and local law enforcement agencies were identified by fingerprints submitted to the FBI by agencies other than the agency wanting the person.[2]

Almost 50 percent of recent offenders in FBI files had been arrested in two or more States.[3]

These data provide important indications of the utility of information transfer, but they are only preliminary. Much more study is needed on the extent of mobility within a metropolitan area, within State, within a region, and nationally. Furthermore, the value of various kinds of files in apprehending offenders and in deterring crime must still be deter-

[1] "Uniform Crime Reports," 1965. The police jurisdictions of recovery would often be an adjacent jurisdiction.

[2] 1967 FBI appropriations hearings.

[3] "Uniform Crime Reports," 1965, based on a survey of about 135,000 offenders in the FBI "Careers in Crime" series, not a representative sample of all offenders, since it is biased in favor of Federal offenders.

mined. There must be a strong and continuing assessment of the effectiveness of information systems in criminal justice. There are now no good measures of the value of information systems, and the operating statistics on which to base such estimates are not now being systematically gathered. These data are needed to design future systems and to decide what functions they should perform. Only then can the cost of implementing various functions be weighed against their utility.

Even more fundamental is the question of the value of various information items themselves. No information system should simply put into a computer that which is now being collected. Rather, it should reexamine the information currently recorded, consider other items, and then by careful judgment, analysis, and experiment, try to ascertain what information is most important. Once a prototype installation is operating, evaluation of its performance will help highlight the critical information that should be kept and made available and the operational value in doing so.

Despite the difficulty of estimating their value or specifying their optimum information content, information systems should be developed. Experience in other applications has shown that in a new field it is more important to implement systems in a modest way to gain practical experience and understanding in operating them, using these initial installations to aid in the design of following systems.

Similarly with statistics, their precise value cannot be estimated. But understanding and analysis of other large social systems, such as the U.S. economy, developed only after good operating statistics became available for analysis.

The assessment of the value of information systems should begin immediately with ones now operating. A number of systems are now operating or being planned at each governmental level. For example:

The National Crime Information Center (NCIC) has been implemented by the FBI to provide immediate access to stolen-auto, stolen-property, and wanted-persons information nationally. It services 15 terminals initially, and will eventually be extended to all States and many large cities.

The New York State Intelligence and Identification System (NYSIIS) and the California Intelligence and Identification System plan to provide statewide services such as criminal history, fingerprint and name identification files, wanted-persons files, gun registration, modus operandi, sex and narcotics registration, and statistical information.

The California Auto-Statis and the New York State Police inquiry systems provide immediate access to stolen automobile files.

The Police Information System (PINS) of Alameda County, Calif., provides access to wanted-persons files for county and local law enforcement agencies as well as an automatic tie-in to the California Auto-Statis System for wanted vehicles.

St. Louis, Chicago, New York, and other cities have computer systems that provide information on stolen autos, stolen property, wanted persons, crimes, arrests, other management statistics, and help in police resource allocation.

Some of these systems duplicate files kept at higher governmental levels—auto files, for instance. Each agency addresses its own specific and immediate needs. To minimize this duplication and potential conflict, it would be desirable to establish some overall system structure and program of implementation. Active development to meet immediate local needs could then proceed in a more integrated way. This chapter attempts to outline such an overall program.

In developing such a program, the problems and needs for information were discussed with knowledgeable operational personnel in police, courts, and corrections agencies, and many of the organizations which have implemented some form of information system were visited. Most of the recent system studies conducted for specific agencies were reviewed.

Based on this work and with the active assistance of personnel experienced in creating information systems for this and other applications detailed information flow diagrams were developed for:

1. The operational information flow in a large municipal police department;

2. The information interchange required between police and investigating agencies on the local, State, and Federal levels;

3. Municipal courts and courts of general jurisdiction;

4. Information needed within and between correctional agencies, both juvenile and adult, at the county, State, and Federal levels;

5. The gathering of operational statistics as an analysis, evaluation, and development tool.

Examples of gross flow diagrams are presented in appendix G.[4] These can serve as starting points for many criminal justice agencies designing

---

[4] Detailed diagrams for generic operating agencies are in "Flow Diagrams for Criminal Justice Information Systems," a report now in preparation. The report will be available from the Clearinghouse for Federal Scientific and Technical Information of the National Bureau of Standards.

their own systems to meet their own needs. The flow charts are available in computer-readable form and can be used for future system function and flow analyses.

These discussions and information flow diagrams have identified a number of system functions on the basis of which the Task Force has outlined a possible system structure directed at the needs of the various levels of the criminal justice system (i.e., the local, metropolitan, and State needs), and a possible supporting national structure.

General Configuration of an Integrated Criminal Justice Information System

Since the administration of criminal justice is primarily a local and State function, a national criminal justice information system must be geared to their requirements. Fundamentally, the information system must be directly accessible to them and they must specify the information they need from other jurisdictions. This leads to a concept of a hierarchy of information interchange and information files. This approach leaves with the local implementing agencies the greatest amount of design flexibility in tailoring their own system to their unique requirements. Information to be exchanged with other jurisdictions must, however, meet minimum standards of content and format. Furthermore, reporting jurisdictions must be responsible for updating their portion of a common information pool. Only that way can the files be kept current and complete and the system not saturated with useless information.

The possible system configurations range from a highly centralized Federal system, containing all the Nation's criminal justice information with a communication link reaching every criminal justice agency, to a completely decentralized system with independent computers located at every police, court, and correctional agency. The approach recommended here relegates to the local or State levels the bulk of the information system while placing at the national level the information thought to be of significant value to a number of States and to Federal law enforcement. One version of this concept would entail several regional centers, each covering several adjacent States. A limited national system has the advantages of being easier and quicker to implement, and less costly. In addition, it could provide service to States which do not now have sufficient need for their own system, and so will not implement their own for at least several years.

Centralizing too many of the functions under Federal control has the strong danger of excessive Federal control of State operating responsibilities. Hence, the assignment of Federal functions must be done with considerable caution, perhaps under the guidance of an advisory committee sensitive to these problems and to the needs of local law enforcement.

Local and State participation in the national criminal justice information system must be optional. Those that do choose to participate, however, will have to meet minimum standards of data format and content to permit the accurate transfer and interpretation of records. The total effectiveness of this system, of course, is based on having a large segment of the criminal justice community participating.

The general form of a possible national information system is shown in Table 1. At the national level, there could be a central inquiry system.

TABLE 1
USERS OF FILES IN AN INTEGRATED NATIONAL CRIMINAL JUSTICE INFORMATION SYSTEM

| | Type of File | | | |
| | | Personal Information | | |
	Inquiry	Directory [1]	Registry [2]	Statistics
Required response time	Minutes	Hours	Days	Weeks
National	Police	All criminal justice agencies	No file kept	Criminal justice agencies, research projects, Government public information offices
State	do	do	Courts and corrections only	Do
Local	do	do	do	Do

[1] Index of record information as to formal contacts with criminal justice agencies.
[2] Collection of related background materials (probation reports, educational records, etc.) kept by some States.

It would respond within seconds or minutes to police queries from anywhere in the Nation. It would include files of stolen autos, licenses, guns, and serialized or otherwise identifiable offenses. In addition, it would list the names and identification of persons wanted for extraditable offenses. Such a system is now being operated on a trial basis by the FBI.

Personal information about adults with criminal records would be included in a *directory* which lists the formal matters of record of contact with criminal justice agencies. Dates and places of arrest for serious crimes, court disposition, sentence, correctional assignment, probation and parole would be recorded. More detailed information would be available from the local agencies. Records of persons with no recent arrests [5] could be placed in a more secure file, accessible only for investigation of the most serious crimes.

Access to the national directory will normally be by means of a set of fingerprints, using either the present manual techniques or future automated techniques that might be developed. In the future it may be possible to add latent fingerprints and a repetitive offender subfile accessible by other investigative data such as a name, personal appearance, and modus operandi.

Finally, a National Criminal Justice Statistics Center should be established in the Department of Justice. The center should be responsible for the collection, analysis, and dissemination of two kinds of data:

Those characterizing criminal careers, derived from carefully drawn samples of anonymous offenders. For specific studies, more detailed data on samples of individuals could be drawn from the States.

Those on crime and the system's response to it, as reported by the criminal justice agencies at all levels.

The Science and Technology Task Force collaborated with the Task Force on Assessment of Crime in developing a program for a National Criminal Justice Statistics Center. The proposal is detailed in full as chapter 10 of the Assessment Task Force volume.

At the State level, an inquiry file similar to the national file would be maintained. The State file would be more extensive, however. It would include other kinds of files—motor vehicle registrations and gun registrations, for example—and would have a lower threshold of seriousness—persons wanted for nonindictable offenses, less valuable stolen property, etc.

A State would also have a directory recording a person's contacts of record with the State's criminal justice agencies. Here, too, the threshold would be lowered to include offenses not serious enough for the national directory.

In addition, to support court and correctional decision-making some States could establish more detailed records on persons in their directories. This *registry* could contain such background information as education, employment, military service, and probation reports. Such files could also be used to provide basic data for assessing the effectiveness of the State's different correctional programs. Because of the sensitivity

---

[5] Decisions must be made on the minimum duration since the last contact with criminal justice agencies that warrants transferring records to the secure file. This time would depend on the types of crimes and the extent of the record.

of much of the information in the registry, its use should be restricted only to court or correctional agencies.

Much smaller and simpler information systems could be established for county courts to process court management records, to keep track of prisoners awaiting trial, to handle the probation office's information, and to provide access to State files for aid in preparing presentencing reports. This system might be integrated with local police, county sheriff, or other county management functions.

In large cities and metropolitan areas, police information systems would be established to provide access to State and national inquiry systems, to record crime and arrest reports, and for analysis of crime patterns, resource allocation, and other local management functions. In a metropolitan area, the system could be operated by a joint authority serving all the associated communities or by the core city police department offering services to the neighboring police departments on a fee basis.

Immediate Response Inquiry Systems

A police officer frequently needs to know, within a matter of minutes, whether individuals or vehicles or other property are wanted within his jurisdiction or elsewhere. This information must be available rapidly—within 1 to 5 minutes—to minimize the time he spends and the inconvenience to the detained person. Other information, which may not be needed so quickly, could similarly be made available. [6] This includes vehicle and firearm registrations, crime reports, and missing person reports.

An inquiry system could also support crime investigations. One of a small group of frequent serious offenders could be identified in response to an inquiry of name, aliases, personal appearance, modus operandi information, or other known characteristics revealed in a crime investigation. The design and use of such a file must be carefully considered to assure that the queries and the individuals' descriptors are complete enough to produce only a small number of responses to an inquiry.

Table 2 lists various files that might be maintained in inquiry systems. As indicated on the table, different information would be retained at each governmental level. The required time to respond to an inquiry would also be different for each kind of file.

---

[6] As more information is passed between the officer on the street and a central file, the need for more radio spectrum will become even more pressing.

TABLE 2
POSSIBLE INQUIRY FILES

FILE CONTENTS OR FUNCTION	CRITERIA FOR ENTRY INTO EACH GOVERNMENTAL LEVEL			REQUIRED RESPONSE TIME TO INQUIRY
	STATE	LOCAL, COUNTY, METROPOLITAN	NATIONAL	
Stolen auto [1]				
Unrecovered stolen vehicles	Immediately	Immediately (maintained if there is no State system)	After 24 hours	Less than 5 minutes
Unrecovered identifiable stolen auto parts				
Stolen auto license plates				
Vehicles wanted in connection with felonies			Immediately	
Stolen identifiable property [1]				
Individually serial numbered items	All significant items not in national system	Low valued or "special interest" items	Value greater than $1,000	Do
Multiple serial numbered items			Value greater than $5,000	
Serial numbered items related to "serious" crimes or indication of interstate movement			Discretion of reporting agency / All reported	Do
Stolen/lost guns [1]				
Serial numbered weapons				
Weapons recovered in connection with unsolved crime				
Wanted persons [1]				
Warrants and wanted-persons notices	Reporting agency not willing to extradite (does not include traffic warrants)	All warrants	Federal warrant outstanding / Reporting agency willing to extradite	Do
"Temporary felony want" (prompt action required prior to warrant (good for 48 hours only))				
Aliases				Less than 15 minutes
Warrant file administration (felony, misdemeanors, traffic, civil, record of "attempts to serve")				
Stolen auto and wanted-persons "hot sheets"	For state police or highway patrol	For local patrol officers and detectives		Once per shift

[1] These systems presently being implemented at national level by the FBI as NCIC with a nationwide teletype network.

FILE CONTENTS OR FUNCTION	STATE	LOCAL, COUNTY, METROPOLITAN	NATIONAL	REQUIRED RESPONSE TIME TO INQUIRY
Repetitive offenders Name index Personal appearance "Modus operandi" (tentative identification on basis of name, aliases, personal appearance, characteristics of crime, and other characteristics or descriptors)	Associated with serious, repetitive offenders in State directory		Associated with some serious, repetitive, mobile offenders in the national directory	Less than 15 minutes
Criminal associates (list of known criminal associates)				
Access to State motor vehicle registration (identification of owners by vehicle identifiers)	All registrations			Less than 5 minutes
Firearm registry	All registered firearms			Less than 15 minutes
Fraudulent documents, "trademarks" of fraudulent documents (checks, bonds, stocks, etc.) Names used on fraudulent documents (tentative identification of persons responsible)	All reported documents			Do
Missing persons (assist in identification and location of missing persons)	All reported persons			Do
Sex and narcotics (directory of sex and narcotics offenders)	All persistent offenders			Less than 2 hours
Crime reports (all pertinent information as source document for system files and statistics)		All recent reports		Do
Arrest reports (all pertinent information as source document for system files and statistics)		All recent arrests		Do
Ballistics (characteristics and "trademarks" of firearms and bullets on file)	All recorded characteristics			Do
Correlation of wanted persons. crime, arrest, and field interview reports (as an investigative tool for retrieving and correlating all information on presence of suspects near scene of crime, crime patterns, possible suspects, "modus operandi," checks, etc.)		All recent crimes and field interviews reported		Do

187

Separate statewide inquiry systems could provide immediate information on stolen property and persons wanted within the State. An automobile recovered with its proper license plates could be checked against the State in which it is registered. For other property and for persons, such an inquiry would theoretically have to be addressed to every State, requiring each State to implement its own system and calling for complex communications to every other State. A second alternative would be to establish a limited number of regional systems centralizing information within each region. The regions could be interconnected into a national system or could be kept separate, accepting the penalty of losing track of people or property that cross the regional boundaries. A third alternative is to establish a single national repository to which any State may address inquiries, and into which every State places information.

National Inquiry System. In operating a national inquiry system, reports of stolen automobiles, license plates, and identifiable automobile parts would be entered immediately into a State file, and then transferred to a national file 24 hours later. After transfer, the State could either clear the record from its file or retain it. Automobiles wanted in conjunction with a felony would be entered in the national file immediately. Similar high thresholds would be placed on the wanted property and people recorded in the national file.

Such a national inquiry file (the National Crime Information Center —NCIC) was established on an initially limited basis by the FBI at the beginning of 1967. This file will contain records of all cars reported stolen for more than 24 hours, all persons wanted for extraditable offenses, stolen guns, and all stolen identifiable property valued at over $1,000. It is maintained on a computer, with terminals initially connected to 15 police agencies, and with plans to include all States eventually. Any agency with a terminal can enter a record into the file or inquire whether a person or property in custody is listed in the file. It will receive an answer seconds later.

The utility of a fully interconnected national inquiry file depends on the need for interstate and interregional communications and on the need to provide an inquiry capability for those states that do not establish their own files. If such a need should be established, a cost analysis indicates that a single central computer is more economical than interconnecting separate regional computers. This result follows from the fact that computer processing and storage costs are much greater than communications costs. It is important that the States, in assessing their own needs and developing their own computer facilities, and the FBI in operating the NCIC, seek to develop information that will provide a

, basis for a sound decision on the needs for and the form of a national inquiry system.

The cost analysis is based on providing national stolen auto, stolen property, and wanted-persons files. The cost and workload estimates are based on analyses being carried out for the FBI.[7] The data rate is based on crime and arrest projections from the "Uniform Crime Reports." Inquiry rate is estimated as a function of crime and arrest rates based on operating experience with similar inquiry systems in California and St. Louis. The projected monthly crime, record entry, and interrogation rates in 1970 are shown below:

	INDEX OFFENSES	ENTRY RATES	INTERROGATION RATES
Stolen autos	60,629	57,876	254,764
Wanted persons and property	287,256	240,160	431,000
Total	347,885	298,036	685,764

These monthly average entry and interrogation rates were multiplied by a factor of four to assure sufficient capacity to handle loads at peak periods.

In operating the system, it was assumed that local jurisdictions send all their entries and interrogations to a State computer which communicates with the national file. For noncentralized inquiry systems, each national computer was assumed to update the others continuously.

Computer operation is assumed to cost $50 per hour [8] and computer storage to cost $25 per month per million characters. Communication costs are derived from GSA charges based on Telpak C and D tariffs.[9] The computer is assumed to require 1 second to process an entry or an interrogation. Communication of an entry is assumed to take 20 seconds, while the time for an interrogation (transmission and reply) is assumed to be 30 seconds.

An information processing center for each of the 48 contiguous States and Washington, D.C., was assumed located in the State capital.

[7] The data were provided by the Institute of Telecommunication Science and Aeronomy of the Environmental Science Services Administration of the Department of Commerce; National Crime Information Center Tele-Communications Study, ITSA Project Number V52362420.

[8] Based on 720 hours per month, including equipment backup and personnel costs.

[9] The value used is $262.50/month + $0.45/mile/month (for 6 100 word-per-minute duplex circuits) or $43.75/month + $0.0825/mile/month per duplex circuit (including 10-percent waste capacity).

Three separate computer configurations were considered:

1. A single centralized national inquiry system.

2. A national inquiry system divided into two locations.

3. A completely decentralized inquiry system (one in each State) in which each State retains the complete national file.

For each of these configurations, two cases were considered:

1. Each State transfers its stolen auto information to the national system after 24 hours and uses the national system to service all its interrogation.

2. Each State maintains its own stolen auto file and only interrogates the national system on out-of-State automobiles.

The results of the analysis are shown in Table 3. The most economical system for the conditions considered is the single central system in which States maintain their own records of stolen automobiles even after they are reported to the national file. The Federal cost for such a system would be about $50,000 per month. The two-location system would cost about $20,000 more per month. These results follow from the fact that computer operating costs are far more dominant than communication costs. They also depend on an assumption that any noncentralized file is updated by each entry to permit any inquirer to interrogate the entire national file. The sizable overhead costs in maintaining multiple computer installations would be additional.

Because communications costs are so low, the total cost of the centralized system is relatively insensitive to the location of the computer. The optimum location would be Springfield, Ill., but shifting it to Washington, D.C., would raise the national costs by only about $1,000 per month—less than 2 percent.

The cost of converting manual records into a computer form would be small for an inquiry file. These are active files with relatively short lifetimes, so that over a period of 6 months to a year the files could be created even without a specific data conversion program.

There are several modifications to the postulated configurations that could give rise to noncentralized systems with operating costs comparable to that of the single centralized system:

Each user could update his closest file (in his State or region) with other files updated in the slack periods, late at night. This would reduce the peak demand on each of the computers, and so reduce

TABLE 3
ESTIMATED MONTHLY OPERATING COSTS OF
NATIONAL INQUIRY SYSTEMS [1]

Cost Component	Centralized System (Springfield, Ill.) [2]		Two-location System (Harrisburg, Pa., [6] and Denver, Colo.) [2]		Decentralized System
	Case 1 [3]	Case 2 [3]	Case 1 [3]	Case 2 [3]	
National communications	[4] $7,900	[5] $6,900	$7,100	$6,300	$126,000
National computer operations	55,100	41,500	71,800	58,200	
National computer storage	3,200	3,200	6,400	6,400	
National subtotal	(66,200)	(51,600)	(85,300)	(70,900)	(126,000)
States computer operations [7]	58,300	58,300	58,300	58,300	1,251,000
States computer storage	3,500	4,700	3,500	4,700	4,700
States subtotal	(61,800)	(63,000)	(61,800)	(63,000)	(1,255,700)
National and State total	128,000	114,600	146,600	133,500	1,381,700

[1] Estimates are for 1970.
[2] Minimum Cost Locations.
[3] Case 1: States do not maintain stolen auto file beyond 24 hours. Case 2: States do maintain stolen auto file beyond 24 hours.
[4] Add $1,200 if center is in Washington, D.C.
[5] Add $840 if center is in Washington, D.C.
[6] Washington, D.C., would cost only $50 more for communications.
[7] Includes estimates of stolen-property and wanted-persons files not maintained on national level.

their required operating capacity and computer costs. In this case, the cost of storage of about $3,200 per month would be duplicated at each installation.

Each regional system would handle entries and inquiries only from its own region. This introduces the undetermined penalty of losing track of people and property that cross regional boundaries.

In either case, the economic penalties resulting from more, smaller installations and the additional fixed costs of operating the multiple installations would tend to favor the single central system.

State Inquiry Systems. Since each State has its own internal structure, legal codes, registration and reporting requirements, and crime problems, each will fashion its inquiry system to its particular needs. Many States do not have the volume of criminal information to justify an inquiry system more complex than manual records and the telephone. In some States, the primary requirement comes from one or two metropolitan areas rather than from the State at large. In some areas, several States will join together into an interstate region and create a single common inquiry system.

The accuracy of the information in the national files is the responsibility of the States since the national system is a service to the States and no means are provided for verifying the information on a national level. In general, the State systems should not duplicate information available from the national file, except perhaps for automobile information. Only items above some threshold of importance should be kept nationally. States could keep the information below that threshold, e.g., stolen property worth less than $1,000, wanted persons they would not extradite, and intrastate repeated minor offenders.

In addition, States could provide access to the motor vehicle registration files. Also, some States require gun registration, sex and narcotics offender registries, fraudulent documents registries, and missing persons files. Which of these should be made available on-line requires further examination of their utility and cost.

The States would have the further responsibility of distributing within the State access to and responses from the national inquiry system.

Whether cities, counties, or metropolitan areas establish their own inquiry systems depends on what the State implements. If the State system is complete, then access to the State and national system would normally be sufficient. Where there is no State system, major metropolitan areas would probably want to establish their own.

Even where there is a State system, certain routine functions might be implemented locally. These might include a local stolen property file, pawn-ticket records, a warrant file including "attempts to serve," and preparation of stolen-auto and wanted-person "hot sheets" for distribution to patrol officers and detectives.

Handling Personal Information

The Problems of Privacy. The most delicate part of any criminal justice information system is the record of previously arrested people and accompanying information about them. Such information is valuable in making prosecution, sentencing, and correctional decisions. But whenever government records contain derogatory personal information, they create serious public policy problems:

The record may contain incomplete or incorrect information.

The information may fall into the wrong hands and be used to intimidate or embarrass.

The information may be retained long after it has lost its usefulness and serves only to harass ex-offenders, or its mere existence may diminish an offender's belief in the possibility of redemption.

Heretofore, the inherent inefficiencies of manual files containing millions of names have provided a built-in protection. Accessibility will be greatly enhanced by putting the files in a computer, so that the protection afforded by inefficiency will diminish, and special attention must be directed at protecting privacy. However the new technology can create both more useful information and greater individual protection.

Some of these problems were reviewed in recent congressional hearings [10] on a Federal data bank. The hearings went into the problems of law enforcement information systems and the general problem of the protection of personal information files. The report stated:

> It seems evident that if the proposal to create a national data bank is adopted, we will have to rely only on the hope that benevolent people with benevolent purposes will operate the system. History, however, has already taught a terrible lesson illustrating exactly what can happen when large stores of information become available to nonbenevolent powerseekers.
>
> The risk involved now in entrusting the liberties of the American people to the men of power in the future, the names of whom we do not even know and whose benevolence we cannot presume to guarantee, is too great for us to take.[11]

However, when dealing with law enforcement data, the rights of society must be protected. Although it warned against dangers to individual rights, the American Civil Liberties Union has also recognized the value of a crime information center. John DeJ. Pemberton, Jr., the ACLU Executive Secretary, made the following observations regarding the FBI's National Crime Information Center:

> Certain valid law enforcement purposes will be served by the creation of such a data center. Police work and crime detection can

---

[10] "The Computer and Invasion of Privacy," Hearings before a Subcommittee of the Committee on Government Operations (Special Subcommittee on Invasion of Privacy), House of Representatives, 89th Congress, July 26, 27, and 28, 1966. U.S. Government Printing Office, Washington (1966).

[11] Op. cit., pp. 312–313.

be more efficiently pursued if information concerning major crimes is readily and quickly available to law enforcement officials. In addition, such a center can serve as a source of vital statistical research on crime and police practices in the United States.[12]

However, Mr. Pemberton pointed out the dangers inherent in incomplete arrest information and information not relevant to crime control purposes, particularly with regard to political expressions and beliefs. Among other recommendations, he proposes several important safeguards: [13]

Restricting the information content to matters of record.

Restricting the dissemination to criminal justice agencies.

Penalizing improper disclosure.

Providing individuals access to their records and means for correcting them.

The New York Civil Liberties Union, the Vera Foundation,[14] and Committees of the Association of the Bar of the City of New York [15] also supported the use with limitations of information systems for law enforcement purposes.

The New York State Identification and Intelligence System has addressed the problems of handling personal information in a State information system:

The system will not attempt to duplicate all of the detailed information currently stored in the individual case jacket and folder-files of participating agencies. Such information can be obtained, when it is needed, directly from the appropriate agency's files. However, the system will include adequate references to those sources, such as indications that a subject is currently on probation or parole or is confined in a particular facility.[16]

Some protection of personal files can come from technical security methods which can increase the difficulty of penetrating a system. In estimated order of increasing cost and complexity, these include:

12 Op. cit., p. 182.

13 Op. cit., p. 183.

14 Op. cit., p. 159.

15 Op. cit., pp. 180–181.

16 Op. cit., p. 163, from a NYSIIS brochure, "Information Sharing, the Hidden Challenge in Criminal Justice."

Assigning an identification code number to each user and each terminal and checking the validity of each inquiry. Codes would be changed periodically.

Transmitting the information by mail or messenger if it is not required immediately.

Keeping terminal equipment in secure locations to prevent access by unauthorized users.

Protecting the stored files themselves by "locking" them whenever unauthorized persons have access to the system such as during computer maintenance. Dummy files could be used for maintenance and program checking.

Scrambling or encoding transmitted information to minimize the danger from tapping of the lines.

No technical means, however, can guarantee that information will not be improperly used. There are many steps which can be taken, but every level of protection purchased has a possible countermeasure. Even if all the information and communications were fully encoded, some person or device must decode it, and that person or device might become accessible.

The dangers can be minimized only by insuring that the controlling organization is reliable and that the information recorded in this system is the minimum necessary. Research is needed to identify what information is useful in making correctional or investigative decisions, and the information collected and retained should be restricted to that material. The organization selected to manage and control the file must have the confidence of all agencies contributing information. The group will have to work closely with reporting agencies to assure that correct, uniform, and complete information is reported. They will be responsible for restricting the information to those authorized to receive it. In addition, some mechanism will be needed to handle the inevitable flow of requests for access to the file for purposes not anticipated when it is first established.

As a check on the users and managers of the file, all inquiries should be kept in a permanent record and that record audited regularly to verify the validity and handling of the inquiries. Unauthorized disclosure should be subject to serious penalty.

The audit should be by a different agency than the one operating the system. This group could also monitor the computer programs to insure that there are no unauthorized modes of access. They could also try by various means to penetrate the system as a running check on its security. These provisions are similar to those used to protect military information.

This problem still needs much more study, analysis, and judgment. Congressman Gallagher, chairman of the Special Subcommittee on Invasion of Privacy, in calling for such efforts, stated:

> We must call upon the scientific community, which is responsible for the development of this [computer] technology, to bear the equal responsibility for its control, in order to guarantee adequate protection of the freedoms we now enjoy.[17]

Organization of Personal Information Files.   On the basis of the limited examination it was possible to undertake, it now appears that personal criminal-record information should be organized as follows:

> There should be a national law enforcement directory that records an individual's arrest for felonies and serious misdemeanors, the disposition of each case, and all subsequent formal contacts with criminal justice agencies related to those arrests. Access should be limited to criminal justice agencies.

> There should be State law enforcement directories similar to the national directory, but including less serious offenses.

> States should consider criminal justice registries that could record some ancillary factual information (e.g., education and employment records, probation reports) of individuals listed in their State directories. This information must be protected even more carefully than the information in the directories, and would be accessible only to court or corrections officers.

The national directory would be similar to an index or telephone directory. It would contain basic identification information such as name, identification number, age, and description. In addition, it would specify, for each arrest recorded, the date and jurisdiction, the charge, the court disposition, and the assignments to correctional supervision. No further background information other than these matters of record should be maintained in the national directory. Any more detailed background information would have to come from the individual agencies noted in the directory record. This requirement may pose some added inconvenience in collecting complete histories and in conducting research on criminal careers. However, the potential dangers inherent in a massive central dossier outweigh these disadvantages.

[17] Op. cit., p. 315.

In addition to aiding criminal justice agencies directly, the directory, with names removed, represents a valuable research tool. The development of criminal careers could be studied, particularly to assess the effect of actions by the criminal justice system. More detailed background information on selected samples of offenders could be collected from the agencies identified on their records.

In establishing the criteria by which names should be entered, some lower threshold of seriousness of crime must be set. Crimes less serious than that threshold, such as minor misdemeanors, should not be recorded.

The data conversion cost to implement the national directory on a computer is large. In a study done for NYSIIS, the cost of converting the State criminal identification files averaged $4.50 per record (approximately $2,250,000 for 500,000 records). Preliminary estimates indicate than in 1970 the national identification files will contain the records of about 12.5 million persons which should be converted. This would involve, at the present state-of-the-art, a cost of $56 million. Even with the more easily read "rap sheets" and improvements in optical character readers, this cost could easily amount to $10–$20 million.

Trade-off studies must be performed to determine the optimum storage means. The low update rate (six updates in 3 months for a very active case) and the relatively slow access time required makes acceptable response times of over 2 hours. The estimated storage requirements is an average of 800 characters per record, or a total of 10 billion characters. Even at the relatively low cost of online storage in a data cell ($7.20 per million characters per month), this would involve a cost of $72,000 per month. Therefore, other means should be considered, such as offline storage and mounting or optical character storage in aperture cards.

The national directory would be similar to a current FBI service. Today, when a police department sends fingerprints to Washington, they are checked against a file of 16 million fingerprints of previously arrested and fingerprinted individuals. The police department then gets positive identification of the individual and his criminal record or "rap sheet." The process is conducted through the mail and takes about 2 weeks.

The rap sheet contains a record of all arrests that lead to the submission of fingerprints to the FBI. It is also supposed to contain the court disposition following each arrest, but this information fails to appear in 35 percent of the cases. A police department has no strong incentive for reporting dispositions after positive identification has been established. Some system of incentives should be developed to assure that the court dispositions are recorded. In addition, an individual should be able to learn the contents of his record and have access to a procedure to expunge clearly mistaken arrests, as in cases of mistaken identity or unfounded charge.

The FBI maintains a record until it learns of an individual's death, or until his 75th birthday has passed and he has not been arrested in the previous 10 years. It may be retained even longer because of the difficulty of cleaning out the files. Earlier purging—either destroying the record or putting it in a secure file to which only the most serious crimes would warrant access—would not only increase efficiency but would reduce the stigma of a stale arrest.[18]

A witness at congressional hearings claimed that "the Christian notion of the possibility of redemption is incomprehensible to the computer." Computer-stored information is easily cleaned out. By a policy of early purging of the files, computers permit restoring the notion of redemption to the existing manual files.

The primary entry into the directory would continue to be by means of fingerprints, using the present manual techniques until future automated techniques are developed. The fingerprint file would produce the individual's identification number or social security number [19] for entry to the directory. In order to permit identification and access to the secure directory in exceptional circumstances, the fingerprint file should not be destroyed when the directory record is purged. In the future, it may be possible to add latent fingerprints and repeating offender "profile" entries capable of being searched by name, personal appearance, or modus operandi.

A majority of States today maintain State identification bureaus similar to the FBI service. These States would presumably continue to maintain their bureaus until there was a more rapidly responding national directory. A number would choose to continue this service in a form modeled after the proposed national directory, particularly in order to maintain criminal records below the threshold of seriousness of the national directory.

To support decisions by courts and correctional agencies, as well as to evaluate the effectiveness of correctional programs, some States may choose to establish a more complete registry containing supplementary information such as probation reports, probation-institutional-parole history, as well as references to medical or psychiatric

---

[18] Some data indicate that 99 percent of rearrests occur within 5 years after release from the criminal justice system. Thus, only 1 percent of the people are rearrested after having gone for 5 years without an arrest.

[19] The military services are changing to the use of social security numbers as identity numbers.

opinions, schooling, or employment records. This information would aid in preparing probation reports and in selecting correctional treatment. However, because of the dangers of such a file developing into a large central dossier system, there should be no national registry. If it is to be maintained at all, it should be on a State level and accessible only to court or corrections officers.

As with directories, the criteria for the entry of new records, the purging of the file, and the retirement of records from the file, are critically important questions to be addressed in the development of State registries to protect the individuals listed therein.

Fingerprint Entry to Personal Information. Since the primary entry to personal information files will be with a set of fingerprints, the speed of response will be limited by the time to transmit a set of fingerprints. The present manual system takes about 2 weeks to respond to the transmittal of a set of fingerprints, including time in the mail. The information is often needed within a few hours. Only then can it be positively determined in time whether the man is wanted in another jurisdiction, and his previous history made available to the requesting police agencies.

The turnaround time of urgently needed requests can be reduced to several hours or less by facsimile transmission of the fingerprint card to the central fingerprint file. NYSIIS has tested such transmission and found resolution and clarity adequate for full classification 85–90 percent of the time.[20] Since the transmission time is now about 10 minutes,[21] sending all 10,000 criminal prints the FBI receives each day by facsimile would require about 70 terminals operating full time. Since only a portion of the submitted prints require rapid response, a smaller number would probably be satisfactory. There should, therefore, be some such link between the national fingerprint file and at least one terminal in each State and major metropolitan area. Similarly, State files should be connected to each major police jurisdiction within the State. New York State is installing such a statewide network. Even a large city could connect its precincts to the central identification file, as has been done in Chicago.

After identification has been made with the fingerprint, the directory record can be sent to the requesting jurisdiction, via the inquiry system communication network.

[20] "System Development Plan." New York State Identification and Intelligence System; Albany, N.Y.; 1966; p. 104.

[21] Shorter transmission time can be obtained at the expense of resolution on the copy.

Management Information

The basic criminal justice operations occur at the local level, and computers can help managers in their day-to-day decisions. Since these functions vary so widely, it is difficult to describe in complete detail specific systems that would be applicable to more than a few localities. However, it is in just this area that major direction, advice, and support should be provided to agencies desiring to implement information systems.[22]

A survey was made of about 40 agencies which now have operating information systems in order to identify the uses, costs, and other system characteristics. Based on this survey, the range of costs of off-line (non-interrogatable) police information systems was found to be $1,400 to $4,300 per month for punched card systems and $1,880 to $13,000 per month for computer systems. For online (interrogatable) computer systems, the costs were found to range from $10,000 to $30,000 per month.

A separate study was undertaken on the potential for modernizing court information systems.[24] For scheduling, case monitoring, and management statistics, the estimated total monthly costs, including personnel, for each of the 100 counties with populations of 300,000 to 1,500,000 would vary from $6,250 to $16,700. For each of the 10 counties with populations in excess of 1,500,000, the minimum cost is $18,750 per month. For smaller counties (100,000 to 300,000 population), punched card systems are appropriate with costs between $1,670 and $4,170 per month. For counties with less than 100,000 population, improved manual procedures should suffice.

Some of the uses which police departments and courts make of computer-based files are indicated below:

[22] As an initial step toward the definition, analysis, and specification of information systems to serve these functions, detailed information flow charts were developed in a computer-readable form. These are in "Criminal Justice Information System Flow Charts," now in preparation. The report will be available from the Clearinghouse for Federal Scientific and Technical Information of National Bureau of Standards.

[24] This study is contained as an appendix to the Administration of Justice Task Force report.

POLICE MANAGEMENT INFORMATION SYSTEMS

Management statistics
    Personnel
    Patrol beat workload
    Patrol performance
    Crime occurrence by beat, precinct, etc.
    Demands for service and responses
    Crimes cleared and arrests
    Inventory and maintenance
    Personnel files
    Budget
Crime pattern analysis
    Correlation of crimes by type, time, location
    Prediction, short and long range
Resource allocation
    Patrol patterns
    Beat allocation

CHAPTER 21

NCIC— A Tribute to Cooperative Spirit

Great progress has been made by NCIC since it began in January 1967. The first operations involved 15 law enforcement agencies and one FBI field office. Instead of the present 24-hour-a-day operation, NCIC pulsed to life in a pilot or testing phase of 2 hours a day and gradually increased to the current schedule.

Initially there were five computerized files: wanted persons, stolen vehicles, license plates, firearms, and stolen identifiable articles. The original data base contained 23,000 records. In 1968 a securities file was added, and the vehicle file was expanded to include aircraft and snowmobiles. In 1969 further cognizance was taken of changes in the vehicles mode by recording stolen dune buggies. Also, in 1969 a boat file was implemented.

Computer hardware needs for NCIC were not as demanding in 1967 as they are today. The beginning data base was relatively small because the NCIC Working Committee wisely restricted file entries to current and validated manual records. Initially NCIC operated with an IBM 360 Model 40 processor containing 128K bytes of core, 2311 disk storage devices, and 2702 transmission control units. In September 1968 this configuration was changed to an IBM 360/50 processor with 512K bytes of core, 2314 disk storage devices, and 2703 transmission control units.

Today the system uses an IBM 360 Model 65 multiprocessor with 2 million byte memory, a combination of IBM 2314, Telex and Cal-Comp disk storage devices, and IBM 2703 transmission control units.

The original network of 15 law enforcement control terminals and one FBI field office has expanded to 102 law enforcement control terminals and to terminals in all FBI field offices, providing NCIC service to all 50 States, the District of Columbia, and Canada. From the beginning a control terminal has been defined as a State agency or large core city operating a metropolitan area system which shares with the FBI the responsibility for overall system discipline as well as for the accuracy and validity of records entered in the system.

The first computer-to-computer interface was with the California highway patrol in April 1967. The tie-in of the St. Louis, Mo., Police Department computerized system soon followed. These events marked the first use of computer communications technology to link together local, State, and Federal Governments in an operational system for a common functional purpose.

As of January 1972, the NCIC system interfaced with 48 computers or electronic switches representing 31 State agencies and 17 metropolitan area systems and with manually operated terminal devices in the remaining control terminal locations. These links provide on-line access to NCIC for 6,000 law enforcement agencies in the United States and Canada. This immediate access makes information in the national file available within seconds of an inquiry. The original goal of NCIC to serve as a national index and network to 50 central State computerized information and communications systems is well within reach.

Whereas the original communications network was made up of a little over 5,000 miles of low-speed (150 baud) lines, the current design includes voice grade (2400 baud) lines between NCIC and nine regionally located multiplexing centers. From these centers, 150 baud lines extend to those control terminals still operating with low-speed equipment. Most control terminal computers interface directly with the NCIC through 2400 baud lines, and the remaining low-speed users are gradually converting to the faster transmission speed as they develop their own on-line systems.

Increased Usage

The communications lines are provided by the Western Union Telegraph Co. and are fully dedicated to system use; that is, there is no operational dial-up access to the NCIC computer. With regard to communications, the FBI assumes all costs up to and including the modem at the control terminal site. There is no charge made to participants for system use.

The year 1967 was one of trial, change, and growth for NCIC. By the close of that first year, however, the system was handling 15,000 transactions a day. Table 1 discloses NCIC growth in message traffic or system use for the years 1968 through 1971. Traffic is measured in

TABLE 1
NATIONAL CRIME INFORMATION CENTER, ANNUAL TRANSACTIONS, 1968–1971

	ENTRIES	INQUIRIES	CLEARS	OTHER	YEARLY TOTAL	DAILY AVERAGE
1968	923,000	3,274,688	400,036	2,427,373	7,025,097	19,194
1969	1,351,095	7,844,670	541,348	3,849,267	13,586,380	37,223
Percent increase over 1968	46.4	139.6	35.3	58.6	93.4	93.9
1970	1,632,749	11,515,851	580,416	5,901,217	19,630,233	53,781
Percent increase over 1969	20.8	46.8	7.2	53.3	44.5	44.5
1971	1,887,564	14,364,308	664,148	8,187,063	25,103,083	68,776
Percent increase over 1970	15.6	24.7	14.4	38.7	27.9	27.9

terms of computer transactions, i.e., an entry of a record, inquiry, clearance of a record, and so forth. In each transaction there are two messages, one from a terminal to the NCIC computer and the second a response from NCIC to the terminal.

Total yearly transactions from 1968 through 1971 increased from 7 million to 25.1 million; inquiries from 3.3 million to 14.4 million. This sharp increase in system usage is due to three factors: (1) the rapid development of State and metropolitan area systems which provide on-line access to thousands of police agencies; (2) user education whereby police officers and investigators increasingly make greater use of the system for routine purposes and develop new field techniques for better use of the system, i.e., checks of traffic violators, out-of-State vehicle registrations, and so forth; and (3) addition of new file applications, such as the securities file. However, the latter, although the largest file in NCIC in terms of volume of active records, has yet to approach expected system use in terms of inquiry. Optimum use of the securities file will only result from closer cooperation between the financial/securities industry and law enforcement.

Another way to measure the growth of NCIC is by its rapid buildup of active records. This is shown in Table 2 depicting growth from December 1967 to December 1971. This file growth was accomplished primarily by on-line NCIC system entries. One major exception was a batch load of stolen U.S. Treasury security issues entered by the U.S. Secret Service in 1969. File growth is, of course, influenced by periodic administrative purges, whereby records are automatically removed from the active file based on an established timespan of usefulness.

TABLE 2
NATIONAL CRIME INFORMATION CENTER, FILE GROWTH, 1967–1971 *

	Total Records	Wanted Persons	Stolen Vehicles	Stolen License Plates	Stolen Firearms	Stolen Articles	Stolen Securities	Stolen Boats
December, 1967	346,124	18,676	130,304	31,118	121,245	44,781		
December, 1968	743,950	30,082	246,640	81,800	191,371	141,107	52,950	
Percent increase over 1967	114.9	61.1	89.3	162.9	57.8	215.1		
December, 1969	1,447,148	50,913	393,156	146,819	254,085	319,763	281,554	858
Percent increase over 1968	94.5	69.2	59.4	79.5	32.8	126.6	431.7	
December, 1970	2,453,662	77,118	584,894	208,352	343,220	513,373	724,326	2,379
Percent increase over 1969	69.6	51.5	48.8	41.9	35.1	60.5	157.3	177.3
December, 1971	3,330,220	114,497	755,879	252,735	441,591	715,444	1,045,629	4,445
Percent increase over 1970	35.7	48.5	29.2	21.3	28.7	39.4	44.4	86.8

* 12-1-67 through 12-1-71

205

Maintaining Accurate Files

While on-line clearance or cancellation of records by the entering agency is the primary means of maintaining the files in an up-to-date condition, NCIC supplies users with information concerning their records for review on a continual basis. Print-outs of each agency's records are sent to the agency via the control terminal for validation. The wanted persons and stolen vehicle records are forwarded every 90 days while other property files are subject to an annual validation. During the periods between validations, FBI personnel at NCIC review records on file for completeness and accuracy. Any deficiencies noted in a record are brought to the attention of the entering agency through the control terminal. In addition to correcting the deficiency, the agency again has a chance to verify that the record should remain on file.

Off-line computer programs check each record to determine if it is in strict compliance with national standards, and the results are furnished to the entering agency. Tabulations are maintained indicating, by control terminal, the number and type of deficiencies. NCIC periodically reviews the tabulations and sends to any control terminal having a ,large number of deficiencies a letter pointing out areas wherein additional training may be needed.

Obtaining a true measurement of the cost effectiveness of the NCIC and its related systems (State and metropolitan area computer/communications networks) is difficult, as the benefits derived include a number of intangibles as well as the more obvious results. Probably the most impressive NCIC statistic is the rapidly increasing number of "hits," a term applied to those instances where a record received in response to an inquiry indicates the subject is a wanted fugitive or the item of property in question is stolen. Many of these "hits" have been set forth in the monthly NCIC Newsletter or similar monthly publications by State systems, such as those in New York, Arizona, and Pennsylvania. Many also have appeared in the news media and need no repeating here.

Successful "Hits"

In January 1968, with a year's operating experience, the system was averaging 275 interjurisdiction "hits" a day. It was obvious the "hits" obtained were inspiring increased system usage. At the time of this writing, the number of such "hits" per day averages approximately 700, a dramatic increase over the 1968 number and a figure that continues to increase month after month. In 1 week recently the NCIC provided information identifying 1,262 fugitives wanted for serious offenses, 2,333 stolen vehicles, and over 1,000 other stolen articles, securities, firearms, boats, etc.

The number of valid operational "hits" per day since the beginning of the NCIC has always been in the range of 1–2 percent of inquiries made. This "hit" rate appears to be a fairly consistent return for the money and effort put into these systems and provides solutions to more crimes, particularly auto theft, as well as a greater recovery rate for stolen property. While the apprehension of a fugitive and/or recovery of property falls in the "tangible" benefits category, the intangibles include the inestimable savings of investigative time accrued through the rapid apprehension of wanted persons who probably would have committed additional crimes. Another intangible benefit is the safety of patrol personnel when, for instance, they are able to determine, before approaching a suspect vehicle, that (1) the vehicle is stolen or, more importantly, (2) that a wanted individual known to be armed and dangerous may be driving the vehicle.

CCH File Developed

All of these examples indicate the worth of the system from an operational standpoint but do not touch on the administrative benefits. The necessity for nationwide teletype communications and for the posting of wanted notices and lists of stolen property is substantially reduced as is the need for manually maintaining thousands of local files. Also, the system has improved the quality of information exchanged and has increased the cooperation among agencies at all levels. These are but a few of the basic "management" benefits provided by NCIC and its participating computer systems. There can be no doubt but that the NCIC and its related systems have substantially improved the efficiency and effectiveness of law enforcement.

During its development the NCIC recognized a computerized criminal history (CCH) file as a logical application in the system. However, in 1966 and 1967, stress was wisely placed on implementing the more urgent and less complex file applications, such as wanted persons, stolen vehicles, and so forth.

In September 1968 NCIC staff and Working Committee members met to discuss standards, procedures, and policies for a CCH file. At this meeting a criminal history summary and a complete criminal history record were examined for the first time. By February 1969, the basic offense classification standards were established. Late in 1969 and during 1970, the Law Enforcement Assistance Administration sponsored Project SEARCH (System for Electronic Analysis and Retrieval of Criminal Histories). The purpose of this project was to demonstrate the feasibility of exchanging criminal history data interstate by means of a computerized system.

On December 10, 1970, the Attorney General authorized the FBI to proceed with its plan to develop an operational exchange of computerized criminal history with the States. After the Attorney General's decision, appropriate NCIC committees and the Advisory Policy Board and FBI representatives held national and regional meetings in January, February, and March 1971 to finalize the plans for the CCH file.

Director Hoover pointed out to the House Subcommittee on Appropriations on March 17, 1971, the desperate need to speed up the criminal justice process, especially the prosecutive and court administrations. Mr. Hoover also stressed the necessity for more realistic decisions with respect to bail, probation, sentencing, and parole. He testified that if there is to be a speedup in the criminal justic process, then there must also be a speedup in the flow of meaningful information on which vital decisions are made.

Centralized Operation

NCIC staff and members of the criminal justice community through the NCIC Advisory Policy Board, NCIC Working Committee, Technical Committee, and Security and Confidentiality Committee worked together to develop the computerized criminal history system, and in November 1971 it became operational.

Criminal history records are now available to authorized criminal justice agencies through an expanded NCIC communications network. The requests for criminal history information from Federal, State, and local police, prosecutors, courts, and correctional agencies can be met immediately.

A basic tenet of the NCIC is that it serves as a national index and network for 50 State criminal justice systems. As a developing police information system, NCIC places the responsibility for each record on the entering agency. As each State computer system was developed, all record entries, clearances, modifications, and so forth, were required to funnel through the State to fix control terminal responsibility and to provide the State with a complete and current file. The criminal history file requires that records be entered, updated, and modified only by the responsible State criminal justice agency in each State or by an appropriate Federal agency since each entry or update must be supported by a criminal fingerprint card.

Because NCIC complements the State systems of the criminal justice community, many thousands of duplicate indices in local, State, and

Federal agencies can be eliminated. All participating agencies share in centralized operational information from a minimum number of computer files.

Not all charges are considered sufficiently serious or significant for storage in the national file pursuant to the recommendations of the NCIC Working Committee and Advisory Policy Board. As a guide, the board specifically recommended excluding arrest data concerning juvenile offenders as defined by State law (unless the juvenile is tried in court as an adult); charges of drunkenness and/or vagrancy; certain public order offenses, such as disturbing the peace, curfew violations, loitering, traffic violations generally, gambling arrests involving "players" only, and so forth.

In the Last Analysis

In addition, the board noted that it is a State agency's prerogative to decide the "significance" of any offense for national file entry. In the same manner this prerogative has been historically exercised with regard to the FBI's manually operated criminal history file. In the last analysis only the contributing agencies can determine if a particular charge is significant enough to be included in the national file. The question they must ask themselves is: "Will the entry of this charge assist other users of the system or will the failure to enter this charge be detrimental to other users of the system?"

A criminal fingerprint card must be the source document for a record entry and any subsequent updating, but under the new concept the card may be retained at either the State or national level. Each record must, of course, be backed by at least one card at the national level for file integrity. Further, the concept provides that each State determine its own capability of servicing intrastate criminal fingerprint cards. Whenever a State has determined that it is ready to assume processing of all intrastate criminal fingerprint cards, the State agency will inform contributors within the State to forward all criminal fingerprint cards to the State identification bureau and will so inform the FBI through a ranking State official.

Summaries or complete criminal history records can be obtained from the NCIC's computerized criminal history file on line. The summary may be requested by any authorized criminal justice agency having either a computer interface with the NCIC computer or a low-speed manual terminal. Only an authorized criminal justice agency having computer interface with NCIC may request the online full record.

Included in the computerized criminal history summary are the personal identification and descriptive data for an arrested individual followed by the total number of times arrested. The arrest charges and convictions resulting therefrom are then shown by number of times for each offense category. Also included are the last arrest, court, and custody status.

The full record includes, in addition to the personal identification and descriptive data, complete information as to each arrest and charge within an arrest together with disposition of each charge. Also included is complete information for each prosecutive count together with disposition of each count and any appeal data. Lastly, the full record will show any custody status of an individual and any change in that status, such as parole. Every agency entering data in a record is identified with the data submitted.

The new system will change not only the flow of fingerprint cards but also the definition of felony and misdemeanor offenses. The interstate exchange of offender criminal history has required the establishment of standardized offense classifications, definitions, and data elements. Since definitions of a specific crime vary widely by State, a common understanding of terminology used to describe a criminal act and the criminal justice action is essential.

Keeping Files Confidential

The implementation of this file imposes on agencies at all governmental levels a most significant responsibility for strong and correct management control. The sensitivity of criminal history has long been recognized, and to this end the NCIC Advisory Policy Board endorsed the following statement by the Director of the FBI to the Subcommittee on Constitutional Rights on March 17, 1971: "If law enforcement or other criminal justice agencies are to be responsible for the confidentiality of the information in computerized systems, then they must have complete management control of the hardware and the people who use and operate the system. These information systems should be limited to the function of serving the criminal justice community at all levels of government—local, State, and Federal."

Specific procedures have been adopted to protect the confidentiality of criminal history data in the NCIC system. A number of these procedures have been in use in connection with the other NCIC files while others are new. These procedures include, but are not limited to: (1) the use of dedicated communications lines accessible only by terminals in criminal justice agencies, (2) assuring the physical security of participants' computer sites, as well as that of all remote terminal sites on line for criminal history data, (3) limiting the number of personnel having access to terminal devices, (4) screening all such personnel as well as all data center personnel having access to criminal history data, (5) maintaining logs and other appropriate records to identify users of the file, and (6) establishing edits to assure file accuracy.

With regard to the accuracy of records maintained in the CCH, a person's right to see and challenge the contents of his record in line with reasonable administrative procedures is an integral part of the system. Further, in operation of the CCH file, followup measures will be taken by NCIC to obtain court disposition data concerning arrest charges if such dispositions are not entered in the record within a reasonable time.

Technological Advances

Criminal justice systems throughout the country are undergoing long-needed and drastic changes. Technological advances are being adapted for use by police, prosecutors, courts, and correctional agencies. Results of efforts such as the NCIC system have been most impressive and rewarding and are forcing change. The ultimate national public safety and criminal justice system is still evolving, and much needs to be done in terms of technology, standards, information flow, organization, legislation, and so forth. The application of an efficient, acceptable, and successful criminal justice system which will best meet the needs of society is the common goal of all engaged in this endeavor. The NCIC is a most successful step in this direction and a tribute to the cooperative spirit of law enforcement nationwide which has made this system possible.

Chapter 22

Data Processing in the Criminal Justice System

Carroll R. Hormachea

Information—That's what data processing is all about.

Data processing equipment is designed to store, retrieve and correlate information. Some ultra-sophisticated equipment can take the information stored, and through a proper programming sequence, actually cause certain actions. For instance, the computers used in the space program or those used in factories. While all of this is of interest, our main concern is making an application of this method to law enforcement and the total criminal justice system.

A few years ago, some police departments were using data processing on a limited basis. But with about the same application of the credit department at the local department store. Some far-sighted administrators in planning new facilities made space available for the coming computer age. These persons were few, and consequently a real lag developed in law enforcement's application of the new science.

The first real break-through came in early 1967 with the successful inauguration of the FBI's NCIC, with which all of you are familiar. Through this system, you can check out the man you picked up on a disorderly in a local bar last night and find that he is wanted by the Richmond, Virginia police for armed robbery—all of this information will come back to you in seconds.

Additionally, NCIC stores data on all types of stolen property that could be traced by number or unusual identification that would be positive.

Eventually, the FBI will establish a similar data bank for finger prints. The machine would be able to go through the various procedures of classification and search in a matter of seconds. Of course, the introduction of this system will bring to light a host of legal questions.

212

Consider, if you will, such a case. John Smith is arrested on a misdemeanor in Austin this afternoon. He is booked and the prints sent to the FBI computer which sends back information that this man is wanted for bank robbery in Wilmington, Delaware. Along with this information on the prints, is a message to hold the suspect for extradition. What will the position of the court be when the evidence is introduced that the man was identified by a machine? Will this be sufficient proof? Or, will it be that a human expert will have to certify that he has examined this evidence? These are some real problems with which all of us will have to deal.[1]

Today, with the various court decisions and general attitudes towards crime and criminals, probable cause for arrest is a real and pressing problem, although legally defined probable cause is not always a cut and dried fact. The NCIC notification that John Smith, who is being held in the local jail, is an escapee from the Vermont State prison can serve as probable cause.

The capabilities of this system are unlimited. However, our main concern here today is the application of these sophisticated information systems to local law enforcement.

The applications are many. A few years ago, on the network news, they showed how the police in one city checked license numbers at a toll booth on a freeway. These numbers were fed to the computer and resulted in the recovery of several stolen cars.

One major city went to the computer, and using it like a crystal ball, they were able to plot the likelihood of crime and traffic incidents throughout the city. As a result, they were able to deploy personnel to those points where they would be needed.

You might laugh and say that you don't need the computer for this since you know that there will a fight at this bar by 10 P.M. Saturday night, and So and So will beat his wife, and there will be traffic problems at the shopping center on Saturday—all of this is true and you are able to do it because you are a good cop. But, think of carrying this ability further and what a help it would be to your department.

Much of this is based on probability, the mathematics of which escapes me, but using this base you can see what can be done. Of course, the first use is for the storage of information of criminal statistics. This information comes in handy in assignment of personnel, budgeting, departmental effectiveness and similar operational procedures, you can also plot the areas of crime in your city.

Another area of concern would be your criminal record files. This would contain arrest records, identification information and M.O.'s, as well as any other pertinent information. This is now stored in your files and I'm sure it goes way back to Bonnie and Clyde. Consequently, you must purge these files from time to time to make them manageable, but like any other government agency, you just find another place to store them in a dark cellar. The information from your files must be available to you quickly, and you shouldn't have to wade through the irrelevant material. The information should also be easily accessible to other departments. Another application would be the Chief's office. This would involve the storage of statistics of your operation for budget and manpower needs. Also included would be your equipment inventory, information on departmental autos and even your personnel records. Really, the use could be unlimited. This could also be used to cross-reference your departmental library as well as legal information.[2]

One projected use might be the using of the computer to assign cars to the incident scene. In other words, the cars could periodically radio their positions to the computer. Then a call comes in, the computer takes over and asigns the nearest car.[3]

Another possibility would be an automatic records facility, operated by a computer with a direct link with the NCIC. This would, in effect, expand the capabilities of your files to cover the entire FBI data bank, plus be in direct contact with any other linking computers.

I could hardly discuss the subject of police data banks, working separately and in conjunction with others, without mentioning the many proposals for, as well as the fears of, a national data bank. First, I will say I would object to such a system for non-criminal information. My reasoning is simple—I do not feel that honest and legal tax information has anything to do with a record of traffic violations or with a record of any military or government service. On the other hand, when we speak of the criminal, then I feel that we do need certain information to identify him and to find him. My other objection is to security of the information. Already, misdirected intelligence and law enforcement agents have released information to the public which has only served to create a distrust among the public. Already many government tax agencies are selling mailing lists to private businesses.

Manual files, such as most departments use, now are more secure because of their voluminous nature, as well as the misfiled information which is lost.

The American Civil Liberties Union has put forth the following proposals for safeguarding information from the proposed data banks:

1. Restricting the information content to matters of record—in other words, raw data would be excluded.

2. Restricting dissemination of law enforcement agencies.

3. Penalizing improper disclosure.

4. Providing individuals access to their records and the means of correcting incorrect information.[4]

To this point, we have discussed the use of ADP as applied to Law Enforcement. It should be realized that application of this method can be made throughout the Criminal Justice System. Take Corrections for instance. One author compares this field to that of the shipwrecked occupants of a life raft on a stormy sea. He indicates that there is a thirst for knowledge in corrections and the information is there in the form of raw data swirling around him so that Corrections is really poverty stricken in the midst of plenty.

It is said that four major information capabilities are required of the information system which would be adapted to Corrections.

1. Nationwide statistical information concerning correctional activities.

2. Selective retrieval, on a nationwide basis, of documented research and practices related to corrections.

3. Information necessary for case decisions throughout the chain of Correctional activities in each jurisdiction.

4. Information to assist management of correctional activities in each jurisdiction.[5]

These capabilities are easy enough to translate to every day use. The nation-wide information can tell Florida what Texas is doing and vice-versa. New ideas seldom communicated, except through friendships at conventions and meetings, would now be available to everyone in the field at the touch of a button. Also, the statistics of correctional activities, inmate population, average time of stay, escapes, etc. can all be recorded and available for use.

The third category is concerned with management. This would be concerned with the total picture of the individual entering the correctional scene. For instance, information on the man's social history not found in correctional records. The system could also provide other data on the individual so that a program of rehabilitation can be better planned for him. The degree of individual control necessary can also be a factor. Once programmed, the system could give correctional staff workers a comprehensive analysis and evaluation of the inmate and his progress.[6]

The needs of management would be served by such a system because just as ADP helps in the police administrative function, it would also help the Correctional Management. This would be especially true in planning, budgeting, evaluation of the program and other areas.

There can be no doubt but that we need an NCIC in Corrections to handle, coordinate and correlate all of the vast information in the field so that it may be of benefit to all rather than a few.

Even our system of courts can make good use of ADP. This is hard for us to believe at first because we think of the human elements of the court. But what about all of the behind the scenes work in a court?

I first saw this in a study my wife and I did for the state of Virginia. One court had automated the process of alimony and child support. Checks were mailed out daily and delinquent husbands and ex-husbands were noted immediately. In most courts, this listing doesn't occur until the wife complains about not receiving her check.

ADP can be used effectively in the court system in three areas:

1. Scheduling

2. Case monitoring

3. Management statistics

Through the scheduling process the system can assign judges, monitor the judge's and lawyer's case loads and schedules, as well as giving the status of the defendant at any time (out on bail, in jail, or serving another sentence.)

The system can also coordinate the activities of court by scheduling trials, keeping up to date on the status of the defendant and the charges, notification of counsel, jurors etc. It can also prepare the warrants and other documents.

The third general area would be partially administrative since this would include budgeting and other necessary data for the court operation. But it would also cover such information as the court work load, court delays, case dispositions (Think of the hours you might spend in a dusty clerk's office searching for records of a particular case.) and the probation officer's case load. And of course, it can collect and write alimony checks.[7]

Gentlemen—there is no doubt that the age of computers has arrived. Our big problem is learning the capabilities of our new toy and making it work for us. The applications I have mentioned only scratch the surface. Through imagination we could make giant strides towards winning the war we are fighting with crime and the many problems which have been spawned as a result of this activity.

Each of us remembers the tough cop days—but face it, we too have come a long way.

REFERENCES

1. VAN EMDEN, B. M., *Advanced Computer Based Fingerprint Automatic Classification Technique (FACT)*, in Yefsky, Law Enforcement Science and Technology, Thompson Book Company, 1967, p. 494.

2. ———, *Task Force Report: Science and Technology*. President's Commission on Law Enforcement and the Administration of Justice, Washington, D.C., U.S. Government Printing Office, 1967, p. 68.

3. *Ibid.*, p. 25.

4. *Ibid.*, p. 75.

5. HILL, HARLAND L., *Some Proposals for the Development of Information Systems in the Field of Corrections,"* in Yefsky, Law Enforcement Science and Technology, Thompson Book Company, 1967, p. 209.

6. *Ibid.*, p. 210.

7. ———, *Task Force Report: Science and Technology*. President's Commission on Law Enforcement and the Administration of Justice, Washington, D.C., U.S. Government Printing Office, 1967, p. 78.

Electronics and Criminal Investigation

Electronics has come of age in recent years. Through constant research by law enforcement and security personnel, as well as electronic specialists, a whole new world in scientific crime detection and prevention has been opened.

With the development of the transistor and the ability to miniaturize such instruments, the value to security minded personnel has increased. Going far beyond the elementary bugging of telephones and rooms, electronics has made it possible to maintain surveillance from thousands of miles away. Electronic homing devices, so small that they can be easily concealed, are often used in following suspects.

To many persons, electronic surveillance is Orwellian in nature, peeking into the lives of individuals with television cameras, telephone bugs, and other such devices. In order to prevent the development of a "Big Brother" type of electronic snooping, Congress enacted the Omnibus Crime Control Bill of 1968 which set forth specific guidelines for the use of electronic bugging and similar surveillance instrumentation. These sweeping guidelines were applicable to private business as well as to law enforcement agencies. Under these guidelines, all electronic surveillance is prohibited by law, except in the case of law enforcement agencies authorized by the courts to take such action in certain investigations. The law applies to actual voice communication but generally does not apply to television or other forms of electronic surveillance.

The law further forbids the sale, possession, or advertising of any electronic instrument which may be used to tap telephones or to surreptitiously record conversations. Mr. James Whitten, of the United States Department of Justice, in a speech cited instances of confiscation of such devices by the government because they violated the provisions of this act.

Electronics has an even greater value to both law enforcement and private industry as a crime prevention device. Many businesses use closed circuit television to monitor activities of employees and customers alike. The use of such devices has tended to reduce shoplifting and losses due to employee theft.

Credit cards have created many problems by their expanding use. Although a relatively young industry, the credit card companies have realized large losses by the misuse and illegal use of cards. In order to cope with the growing problem, many companies have lowered their "floor limits" (those charges which must be approved by calling the credit card office). More recently, many major department stores and credit card companies have installed imprinters connected to the central computer which instantly approve or disapprove all charges and signal the salesperson if an illegal card is being used.

Still another use of electronics is the development of a system of voice prints. Predicated on the premise that all persons have speech patterns which are as individual as fingerprints, the system can detect minute differences in speech patterns. Through such speech patterns, suspects can be identified.

This section is designed to acquaint the student with the various resources at his command in conducting an investigation. Electronics is usually neglected in basic studies because of the complexity. However, such an investigatory procedure should be placed in its proper context. With many new areas of electronics being developed and the use extended to all phases of daily life, it is important that the investigator understand and realize its many uses, as well as utilizing the knowledge as a base for the development of new methods and concepts.

Industrial security personnel have been making extensive use of such equipment in alarm systems, closed circuit television, entry-proof locks, and various communication devices. Electronic investigation equipment long has been a tool of the private detective, as well as government intelligence agencies which aided greatly in the development of these sophisticated devices.

Chapter 23

Bank Surveillance Cameras

A good photograph of a bank robber taken while the crime is being committed is perhaps the most impressive item of evidence that a prosecutor can have. This is not a new idea. The courts have long favored the admissibility of such evidence on the grounds that the identification of persons by photographic means is more accurate than by eyewitness verbal description. [*Considine* v. *United States,* 112 F. 342 (6th Cir.), cert. denied, 184 U.S. 699 (1902).] However, it should be pointed out that the photograph of the suspect at the time of the robbery is not conclusive evidence of guilt. It is only a means of identifying the person on trial with the suspect at the crime scene. [*Madden* v. *United States,* 20 F. 2d 289 (9th Cir.), cert. denied, 275 U.S. 554 (1927).]

The regulations issued in accordance with the Bank Protection Act of 1968 do not require but encourage all banks to have camera systems and contain the following minimum specifications:

(1) Surveillance systems—(i) General. Surveillance systems should be:

(A) Equipped with one or more photographic, recording, monitoring, or like devices capable of reproducing images of persons in the banking office with sufficient clarity to facilitate (through photographs capable of being enlarged to produce a 1-inch vertical head-size of persons whose images have been reproduced) the identification and apprehension of robbers or other suspicious persons;

(B) Reasonably silent in operation;

(C) So designed and constructed that necessary services, repairs, or inspections can readily be made.

Any camera used in such a system should be capable of taking at least one picture every 2 seconds and, if it uses film, should contain enough unexposed film at all times to be capable of operating for not less than 3 minutes, and the film should be at least 16 mm.

The FBI cannot make specific recommendations concerning the installation of surveillance equipment in banks nor survey a bank's security needs or deficiencies. However, some basic photographic principles can be used in evaluating certain types (not makes) of cameras, and the following facts are presented for consideration.

Two types of cameras may be used: motion picture and sequence, both of which are available in many sizes. Movie cameras, generally 8 mm. or 16 mm., take pictures at 16 to 24 frames per second. The sequence cameras are 16 mm., 35 mm., and 70 mm. and take still pictures at regular intervals, such as every second or every few seconds.

For Best Results

Some bank surveillance systems require a bank employee to activate the cameras while other systems operate automatically—taking pictures every second or more during banking hours or in some cases at all times, day and night. Also employed as surveillance apparatus are closed-circuit television cameras, in constant operation, storing pictures on tape which can be erased and reused if there are no bank robberies. In the case of a robbery, the tape is replayed and pictures taken of the monitor.

On the basis of the many bank robbery photographs reviewed, it has been found that the 35 mm. and 70 mm. sequence cameras generally produce the best pictures for use in identifying the subject, although the 16 mm. and 8 mm. cameras produce good photographs when properly installed. The size of the image on the film determines, to a large degree, the quality of the picture, provided of course that the lenses and other components are of equal quality and lighting and focus are properly adjusted. If an 8 mm. or 16 mm. camera is used, the image of the bank robber's face is small and the lens and film cannot resolve sufficient detail to show those facial contours and characteristics that distinguish one person from another with a generally similar appearance. A 35 mm. camera covering the same area will record the bank robber's face on the film in a size approximately two and a half to three times that of the image on the 16 mm. film. Therefore, if the 16 mm. camera is set to photograph a proportionately smaller area, the bank robber's face on the film will be approximately the same size as it would be on the 35 mm. film.

Two millimeters of lens focal length for each foot of distance from camera to subject is sufficient to produce recognizable pictures of individuals. For example, a 35 mm. sequence camera with a 50 mm. lens would take identifiable pictures up to 25 feet from the camera, while a 16 mm. camera with a 25 mm. lens would be effective up to 12.5 feet. Usually, if pictures are taken beyond one foot of camera-to-subject distance for each millimeter of lens focal length, recognizable photographs will not result. A camera placed over exit areas will probably gain a larger size image of the subject on the film because, leaving the bank, he gets closer to the camera. Also, this location is advantageous if the victim employee does not activate the camera until the subject has left the counter.

Since lighting in the bank is important to good pictures, the cameras should be positioned to take advantage of the best lighting on the subject, or it may be desirable to revise the lighting. In placing the cameras, remember that a picture taken against the bright sunlight outside will provide a very unclear picture of facial features.

Equipment, control devices, condition of the film, and aim and focus of the system should be periodically tested to insure good results in the event of a robbery. Such tests should take into account any variance in light available at different times of the day due to the presence or absence of sunlight from the outside. If test photographs are unsatisfactory, bank officials should be advised.

Identifying the Suspect

When a bank robbery occurs and surveillance camera pictures are of good quality, wide publicity of the photographs may result in the robber's giving himself up or a relative or friend's furnishing information about the identity of the subject.

In the absence of such assistance, it may be necessary to compare the bank pictures with the photographs of a suspect. In comparing these photographs, FBI Laboratory experts study all the facial characteristics and contours. Unless these general characteristics are of an unusual nature, there must also be some scars or marks or other features that will support a positive identification. Mug shots are usually full-face or profile views and are generally not useful in comparison with the bank pictures unless they also are full-face or profile views. Facial features do not appear the same in a three-quarter view as in a full-face view. If the suspect is available to be photographed, his picture should be taken at the same angle and distance as the pictures of the robber. The possibility of identifying other items in the picture, such as details of the subject's clothing with that of the suspect, should not be overlooked.

Bank robbery photographs may be useful in determining the height of the subject. Many times the height can be calculated by ascertaining where the subject was standing when the picture was taken. By relating the subject in the photograph to objects around him, such as floor design, teller's station, or tables, the investigating officer can make a close estimate of his exact position. A large scale like the one in Figure 1 should be mounted on a vertical support and placed in the spot where the robber was standing. A hall tree, collapsible light stand, or camera tripod can be used as the vertical support. The scale should be mounted facing the camera lens and with the height measurements the correct distance from the floor. Pictures are then taken with the surveillance camera in the same position as when the bank robbery photographs were taken.

Reference Points

If the subject's foot position does not correspond to a pattern on the floor, his position can be calculated as follows: (1) suppose an imaginary line from the camera to a designated reference point on the wall behind subject; (2) place the height scale along this line; (3) moving the scale about 6 inches for each picture, take photographs in the approximate area of those taken during the robbery. The Laboratory examiner can determine the subject's height by superimposing the bank robbery picture over the photographs of the height scale and matching similar background objects. The film may be processed locally and the prints submitted to the FBI Laboratory, or the undeveloped film may be submitted to the FBI Laboratory. Pertinent photographs of the bank robber or robbers and the original bank robbery film, if available, should also be submitted to the Laboratory.

An alternate method to determine the suspect's height involves locating some point on the wall or other fixed object in the robbery photograph in juxtaposition to the top of the robber's head. From this reference point a length of light string or fishing line should be stretched to the center of the camera lens. Subsequently, the unknown subject's height can be determined by measuring the distance of the string from the floor at that point where the photographed suspect was standing. (It is important that the string be stretched tightly.)

Reference points are necessary for effective use of the two methods described; some photographs will not adapt to either procedure. For example, the posture of the unknown subject (if he is leaning on a counter, walking, or running) may make the process of determining height most difficult. On the other hand, the Laboratory reports that in those instances where favorable conditions exist, that is, where reference points are employed, the calculation varies less than an inch from actual measurements.

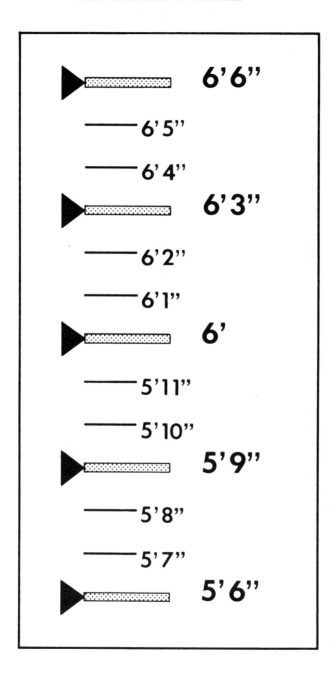

Figure 1. By using this scale (left) and the surveillance camera used at the time of the robbery, authorities can determine the height of the suspect.

Legal Evidence

If the camera system is in good working order, the photographs of the robbery should be acceptable as legal evidence of the crime scene, subject to verification by the photographer, that is, the bank employee who activated the camera, or any witness having sufficient knowledge of the crime scene to say the photograph is a true representation of it.

Both still pictures and motion pictures of the bank robbery along with individual frames and enlargements of them may be used as evidence (29 Am. Jur. 2d, Evidence, sec. 785–801). Regarding the use of sound-tracks in connection with motion pictures, the Second Circuit Court of Appeals has ruled that ". . . in this day and age of photographic and recording devices, there is no reason why relevant conversations and scenes should not be brought before the jury by these means." [*United States* v. *Birnbaum*, 337 F. 2d 490 (2nd Cir. 1964).]

The bank camera photographs may be shown to the eyewitnesses to the crime for the purpose of having them identify the robber. Such viewing will not jeopardize the admissibility of their testimony at trial on the identification issue as this ". . . would not be a circumstance tending to cause misidentification." [*United States* v. *Parhms*, 424 F. 2d 152 at 157, cert. denied, 400 U.S. 846 (1970).]

If, by comparison of the bank picture and an available photograph of a suspect, the U.S. Commissioner or other magistrate determines that the person in the two photographs is one and the same, sufficient cause for the issuance of an arrest warrant exists. The descriptions of weapons, items of clothing, or disguises observed in the photograph may be used for purposes of an affidavit for a search warrant.

An illustration of the use of bank camera photographs resulting in conviction for bank robbery may be found in *United States* v. *Hobbs*, 403 F. 2d 977 (6th Cir. 1968). A teller saw a man wearing a stocking mask run into the bank with a gun in his hand. She activated an automatic camera which took sixty pictures. The photographs, assembled in a looseleaf notebook and offered in evidence, were authenticated by the trial testimony of the teller that they clearly represented what she personally witnessed and that she had examined each of the photographs and found each to be a fair and accurate representation of what occurred. The court was solely concerned with whether the scene photographed was an accurate representation of the robbery and did not require evidence of how the surveillance system operated.

CHAPTER 24

Identification of Suspects by the Voiceprint Technique

**Ernest W. Nash and
Oscar I. Tosi, Ph.D.**

The voice as a tool of the criminal is used more frequently than a gun and car combined. Because of this, identification of a person by the voice is often a critical part of a trial. The courts for many years have allowed the layman to testify in court to his opinion with reference to the voice of the offender and the defendant being the same, basing such an opinion just on listening. However, scientific experiments have shown that speaker recognition by ear is not reliable; in fact, when the speaker is unfamiliar to the listener his accuracy in identifying is not much better than chance. Considering also the possible incidence of mimics, voices of twins and similarities of voices of unrelated persons, the problem of speaker recognition purely by listening becomes almost unsolvable, especially if the witness is not a trained professional in speech sciences or phonetics.

Experimentation to determine if it were possible to identify a speaker by visually scanning spectrograms of his voice started during World War II. This technique of speaker identification later became known as the "voiceprint" technique. Lawrence Kersta, a researcher from Bell Telephone Laboratories, believed he had found the affirmative answer to such a possibility after he performed some experiments. He retired from Bell and formed his own company, Voiceprint Laboratories, Inc., for the purpose of commercializing voiceprint. In 1966, Kersta attempted to establish voiceprints in the courts as scientifically reliable evidence. However, he encountered a great deal of opposition from both the legal and scientific communities, possibly because Kersta's experiments did not include forensic models and he failed to answer questions during cross-examinations. By 1968, voiceprints were not allowed as evidence in the courts and totally rejected by the scientific community. However, the courts, in their refusals, namely in *California v. King* and *New Jersey v. Carey*, indicated that if the scientific community would accept this technique after further experimentation was performed, it might possibly be used as evidence at that later time.

Technology Development

In an attempt to gain support, first from the scientific community and eventually from the courts, reliable, scientific experimentation on the voiceprint technique then became absolutely necessary.

To achieve this goal a two-year comprehensive experiment was planned through cooperative efforts of Michigan State University (MSU) and the Michigan State Police. Dr. Tosi, MSU, was appointed director of this research project, responsible for the scientific design and performance of the experiment.

In addition, during the period of time Dr. Tosi was experimenting, Detective Sergeant Nash was using the voiceprint technique as an investigative aid in the crime laboratory of the Michigan State Police to determine the necessary conditions and requirements for the use of this technique in practical field work. This experience involved several hundred field cases and over 40,000 spectrograms. The categories of crimes related to these investigations ranged from murder, attempted murder, rape, extortion, abortion, bribery, burglary, conspiracy, larceny, bomb threat, false fire alarm, impersonating a police officer, false report of crime, obscene calls, to nuisance phone calls.

These tasks concerning identification in field cases allowed for the establishing of standards covering all aspects of voiceprint identification as applied to police work and established, through practical application, the high degree of reliability connected with this method of identification when applied by a trained examiner.

These scientific and field studies were funded by the U.S. Department of Justice. Their complete description, results, and data are offered in the *Final Report on Voice Identification* submitted to the LEAA by the Michigan Department of State Police (December 1970).

To briefly review the MSU scientific experiment, a total of 34,996 experimental tasks of identification were performed by 29 trained examiners. Each task involved up to 40 known voices and various experimental conditions: closed and open trials, contemporary and noncontemporary spectrograms, 6 or 9 clue words spoken in isolation or in a fixed or in a random content, recorded through a telephone line with or without background noise, etc. The speakers used in this experiment—a total of 250— were a statistical, representative sample of a homogeneous population of 25,000 male students.

The results of this experiment confirmed Kersta's experimental data (which involved only closed trials of contemporary spectrograms of clue words spoken in isolation by a heterogeneous population). The more realistic forensic models (open trials, noncontemporary spectrograms of fixed and random contents) tested in Tosi's experiment yielded data that, after being statistically analyzed through a CDC 3600 computer, demonstrated that the voiceprint technique is highly reliable when applied by trained examiners who follow the standards set by the authors.

After the results of both the scientific and field studies were publicized, the scientific community reacted most favorably to voiceprint as modified and standardized by the authors.

Very well-known adversaries of voiceprint, one of whom was Dr. Ladefoged, stated in court that this new experimentation had changed their minds with respect to the present feasibility of using voiceprint as legal evidence. The authors presented voiceprint evidence in three trials, and this evidence was accepted by the courts in the three cases.

Description of Innovation

The voiceprint technique as improved by the authors through their studies and experiments is a method of personal identification. This technique requires recordings of the speaker's voice that is to be identified. In the forensic application, a recording is obtained of an offender's voice which in some way connects him to a criminal act. For example, most police agencies record all incoming phone calls, which allows them to automatically collect a recording of a bomb-threat caller's voice. Then, as suspects are developed, recordings of their known voices can be compared with the voice of the unknown caller. The recordings collected as evidence may be recorded on any tape recorder and then these recordings are analyzed through the sound spectrograph. The output of this instrument, called a spectrogram, is recorded on a special paper and displays the patterns of the individual's acoustic energy, using three parameters: time, frequency and relative intensity. The expert examiner then listens to the sounds of both the questioned and the exemplary voices, and at the same time he visually scans the spectrograms. By this method a properly trained examiner will be able to decide whether the unknown and the known voices are the same or different.

General Application

The voiceprint method of speaker recognition is the most objective, reliable technique presently available for this purpose. Its application to law enforcement is vast and limited only by lack of imagination. As has been previously stated, the authors have assisted investigators in nearly every major crime category by using this technique. There are other crimes that lend themselves to the technique; however, lack of knowledge and experience could cause some limitation. Take bogus checks for example. It would be less expensive, more reliable and more practical to make recordings of the check passer's voice than to take a picture. The recording could be used to positively identify the passer and the employee who accepted the defective instrument. In addition, the recording could be used to refresh a witness's memory as to what did happen and to better recall what was said.

The voiceprint technique insofar as the investigator is concerned is relatively simple. The only equipment necessary is a tape recorder and in most cases a device to record telephone conversations. The identification task properly requires the sound spectrograph, and it is expensive and it must be operated by a trained person. However, law enforcement agencies in general should consider voiceprints as they consider other scientific investigative techniques: that the spectrograph and the examiner will be a service available at the crime laboratory. With this in mind the voiceprint technique is available to every police unit, from the smallest department to the largest, provided that they are able to supply a crime laboratory with the proper voice samples. The type of crime does not limit the use of voiceprints and, as information is disseminated to all law enforcement agencies, the use of this method of identification will become as routine as fingerprints.

In summary, the authors believe that through their studies, experimentation and concern, the voiceprint technique of speaker identification has presently become a reliable tool for the crime laboratory. They recognize, however, that its reliability depends heavily on the professional qualifications of the examiner. To insure that proper requirements for these qualifications are met by candidates, the authors have incorporated the nonprofit International Association of Voice Identification with the main goal of testing and certifying these candidates. In addition, they are planning the creation of an Institute of Voice Identification, sponsored by the Michigan State University and the Michigan Department of State Police. This Institute will provide police officers with proper training in the field of voice identification.

CHAPTER 25

Privacy of Voice Communication

Robert L. Carlson,
J. M. Tellez,
W. L. Schreiber

Law enforcement agencies today are looking for means of ensuring the privacy of their communications links, particularly two-way mobile radio channels. Numerous voice privacy devices presently on the market can minimize casual eavesdropping and deter sophisticated listeners intent on anticipating police tactics during civil disturbances. A cursory description of the principles of operation of voice privacy systems is presented here in order to provide police officials with a basis for evaluating the relative effectiveness and applicability of the various types.

Listening in on police broadcasts, long a favorite amusement, has become an important tactic for today's lawbreaker. He listens for inside information on police dispatches and status of incidents in order to counter possible police moves.[1] He may even seek to confuse and misdirect police activity by transmitting false commands and information, a stratagem known as "spoofing." A notorious example is the reported misdirection of patrol cars immediately following Martin Luther King's assassination.

We can undoubtedly expect this interference and "electronic warfare" to increase greatly in the near future as it accompanies the growing threat of revolutionary activity in this country. Participants are not illiterate hoodlums, but increasingly are well-organized and directed individuals whose ranks contain personnel familiar with modern communications equipment and techniques. While they may be deterred temporarily by a very simple speech privacy device, it should be expected that the sophisticated revolutionary will work on a means to decode the device.

[1] See, for example, "Transistor Radio—The Criminal's Monitor for Police Dispatches," Thomas A. McParland, *Police*, Nov.–Dec., 1970.

Law enforcement agencies may achieve a level of secure communications by installing in patrol cars nonvoice communications devices such as miniature teletype units, which print out dispatches and other data and encode queries back to headquarters. However, voice communications among patrolmen, dispatchers and their commanders will always be needed. Therefore, consideration should be given to selecting an appropriate electronic coding (voice privacy) system. Such systems will make police calls unintelligible to unauthorized listeners and will also prevent false messages being sent unless the lawbreaker possesses identically coded transmitting equipment.

As the basis for an understanding of the devices, it is necessary to have some insight into the physiology of speech and the physics of its interactions. Human speech is a complex phenomenon. It is propagated by vibrations in the air; the relative rapidity with which sound vibrations follow one another is known as frequency, measured in Hertz (formerly cycles per second). Human speech contains frequencies from about 70 Hertz (low tones) to around 10,000 Hertz (very high pitch), but most of the sound energy is concentrated in the frequency range of 300 to 3000 Hertz. Thus, a normal telephone line is designed to pass only that range of frequencies. While the telephone voice may sound different from face-to-face conversation, intelligibility does not suffer significantly.

Many different frequencies are present simultaneously in a speech signal, each with a different intensity. However, individual frequencies are not identifiable as such in the composite signal that is the sum of all the frequency components. If the signal intensity is plotted against time, the result is a single, continuously varying, "squiggly" line (Figure 1).

Normal speech has many identifiable characteristics and patterns. These characteristics must be altered by electronic processing to gain voice privacy. Voice privacy systems are classified into two broad categories: analog devices and digital devices. They are defined as follows:

Analog devices produce an output with continuously varying levels, similar to a light bulb controlled by a dimmer to provide light varying in intensity from maximum to zero. Typical analog privacy systems employ alternating inversion, spectrum shifting, bandsplitting and bandsplitting inversion techniques to distort the continuously varying voice signal.

Digital devices produce only *discrete* level outputs, with no values between these levels; an example is a light bulb controlled by a switch to be either on or off. A simple type of digital communications is transmission of Morse Code by Navy signal men flashing lights on and off. At present there are two basic digital voice privacy systems—which transmit a synthetic signal to be reconstructed by the receiver.

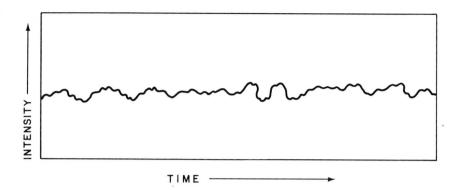

Figure 1. Typical Speech Signal.

Analog Voice Privacy System

All analog voice privacy systems, generally known as "scramblers," are based on the principle of distorting the normal voice pattern before transmission in such a way that it cannot be understood unless the listener has the equipment to restore it to its original form. In the simplest form of "scrambler," the lower tones (around 300 Hertz) are converted to about 3000 Hertz and vice versa. Thus, the entire band is turned upside down, a technique known as frequency *inversion*. The result is a queer sounding signal which is more or less unintelligible to the untrained listener. However, with a little practice, almost anyone can understand this signal without any decoding equipment, so inversion alone is inadequate for voice privacy.

Alternating Inversion. Frequency inversion can be improved as a voice privacy technique by also distorting the normal syllable patterns. Whether the speaker talks rapidly or drawls, the normal syllabic rate ranges from 0.1 to 0.4 second. This rate is an important factor in understanding speech; when it is distorted, intelligibility is reduced significantly. The principle involved in degrading syllable recognition is called *alternating inversion;* to achieve it, short intervals of speech are transmitted alternately in normal frequency and inverted frequency. Syllable distortion occurs when the alteration between normal and inversion occurs at a much faster rate than the normal syllabic rate.

While alternating inversion provides greater voice privacy, if the alteration is performed in a regular and predictable way (producing alternate segments of normal and inverted speech of equal duration) a sophisticated opponent can devise a decoder fairly easily. Therefore, the alternation must be based on a pattern that appears to be random and unpredictable. This requires a *pseudo-random generator*,[2] which transmits a pattern known only to authorized listeners, who are equipped with receivers containing the pseudo-random codes needed to restore the signal to intelligible speech. Even this series of segments of normal and inverted speech, with each segment of apparently random duration, can be decoded in time by a determined listener. Therefore, the detailed pattern of the pseudo-random generator should be changed frequently, such as once per shift or once per day, when it is the "code of the day."

Considering the temper of national affairs today, alternating inversion probably would provide sufficient voice privacy for police communications. If, however, the dissident elements in America were to make greater use of technology to disrupt law enforcement activities, a more sophisticated device would be required. The techniques described below are currently available, but require considerably more equipment and cost more than the inversion techniques.

Spectrum Shifting. With this technique, the voice signal is inverted (300 Hertz to 3000 Hertz and vice versa) and also offset in frequency by a given number of cycles. For example, the low frequency (300 Hertz) would be inverted to 3100 Hertz (3000 + 100) and to 2900 Hertz (3000 − 100) when the spectrum shift is 100 Hertz. By alternating the frequency inversion to the plus or minus number at a rate faster than normal syllabic speech, good voice privacy can be achieved. Needless to say, a pseudo-random generator would be used to establish the alternation rate and coding.

Bandsplitting. A rather sophisticated analog device for scrambling speech, *bandsplitting* provides a high degree of voice privacy. In this system, the 2700 Hertz transmitted band (300 to 3000 Hertz) is divided into distinct groups, or sub-bands. In a typical system, eight sub-bands would be used, each being one-eighth of the total band of 2700 Hertz, or 337.5 Hertz. As shown in Figure 2, the bands are numbered consecutively from lowest to highest. These sub-bands can then be translated in frequency in such a way as to "shuffle" their transmitted order in numerous sequences, *e.g.*, 2, 7, 4, 1, 3, 8, 5, 6 or 6, 4, 1, 3, 7, 5, 8, 2, etc. The unauthorized listener finds this signal extremely bewildering, but the authorized listener will hear a normal voice communication as it is reconstructed by his receiver.

---

[2] For a description of pseudo-random generators, see "Modern Cryptology," *Scientific American*, July, 1966.

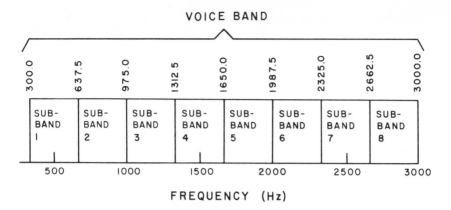

Figure 2. Sub-Band Division.

Bandsplitting Inversion. Finally, by combining the alternating inversion technique with bandsplitting, the signal will be transmitted with the sub-bands randomly changing in order of occurrence and also randomly normal or inverted. This is known as *bandsplitting inversion.*

Digital Voice Privacy Systems

Vocoder. The *vocoder* is a complex device that produces synthetic speech. At present the cost is too high for most law enforcement agencies, but the principle is described here with the aim of completeness. The vocoder measures several key parameters of the voice signal (frequency, amplitude, syllabic rate, harmonics, *etc.*) and transmits the measured values in binary form to the receiving unit. (The binary system, which uses only 1 and 0 symbols rather than the digits from 0 through 9, can be represented electrically by many forms, such as current flow (1) and no current flow (0), positive voltage (1) and negative voltage (0), *etc.*) The receiver synthesizes a replica of the original voice signal from the transmitted binary information.

Delta Coder. The *delta coder,* a relatively simple digital device, has good potential for law enforcement usage. It creates at the receiver a straight-line segment replica of the continuously varying true voice signal (Figure 3A) based on transmitted voltage samples taken at very short intervals. This synthetic signal forms a reasonably accurate facsimile of true speech when reproduced through an amplifier, as can be seen in Figure 3B.

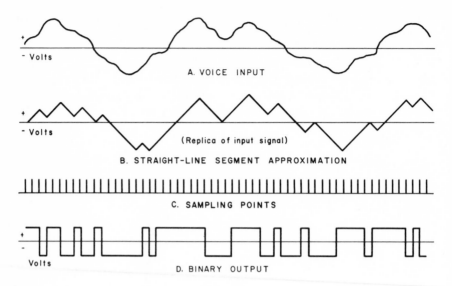

Figure 3. Delta Coder Waveforms.

Type of System	Principle	Comments
ANALOG		
Inversion	Turns speech band "upside down."	Inadequate Security.
Alternate Inversion	Speech band is alternately upside down and right side up in random pattern.	Adequate Security.
Spectrum Shifting	Alternately displaces frequency of entire speech band from one shift to another.	Adequate Security.
Bandsplitting	Divides voice band into a number of sub-bands and shifts frequency of each sub-band and inverts sub-bands in a random fashion.	Good security.
DIGITAL		
Vocoder	Measures key voice parameters. Transmits measured values in digital form, and reconstructs voice signal at receiving end.	Too expensive for law enforcement use.
Delta Coder	Approximates complex voice signal waveform with a series of straight line segments using digital transmission to carry information on selection of straight line segments for reconstitution at receiver.	Has promise for future all-digital systems.

Speech, through the microphone, produces an electrical voltage similar to the "squiggly" line of Figure 3A. A timing signal input to the transmitter (Figure 3C), determines the rate at which the voltage of the speech signal is sampled. The output, since it is in binary form, is either off or on, positive or negative, producing a transmitted code that looks like Figure 3D. Note that when the sampled voice signal is positive, the binary signal is "+"; several positive voice samples result in a long sequence of positive samples.

At the receiver, these positive or negative impulses are translated to a series of straight-line segments which are of two types, upward sloping and downward sloping. The degree of the slope is the same in every case, and the time duration is equal in every case. Each timing interval during which a positive voltage is transmitted signifies to the delta coder receiver that an upward sloping straight-line segment is to be generated. A long, upward sloping line is composed of several consecutive upward sloping straight-line segments. The receiver, in this manner, generates the signal shown in Figure 3B, which is a reasonable approximation of the original voice signal. To achieve a satisfactory degree of intelligibility, sampling must take place at a rate of 14,000 to 15,000 times per second, and better performance can be obtained at a rate of 20,000 samples per second. Figure 4 depicts the delta coder system with the waveforms of Figure 3 shown at the appropriate points in the circuit.

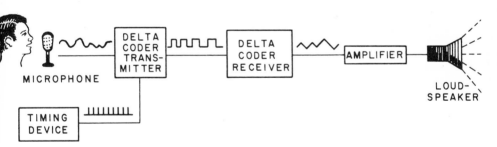

Figure 4.   Delta Coder Voice Privacy System.

Because the decoding mechanism for a delta coder is so simple, a pseudo-random generator must be added to prevent unauthorized listening. The generator must be synchronized to the timing device, and its output combined with the delta coder output by simple circuitry. At the receiver end, the pseudo-random stream is stripped off prior to decoding, using an identical pseudo-random generator.

The compound binary signal is not suitable for direct input into a normal police radio, however, and an intermediary device, known as a *modem*, is required to 'condition' the signal. This is a simple device, but present police ratios will require modification to accept the modem signal. The greatest advantage of the delta coder is that, when digital communications devices (such as patrol car teletype units) are implemented, all police communications can be digital—even voice. The patrol car communications equipment can be integrated and the entire system made smaller and more economical.

The Promise
of the Future

Appropriately, the final section is devoted to contemplating the future of scientific methods of investigation and crime prevention. As the technology advances, so then will the technology of law enforcement and security advance.

Heretofore unthought of applications of scientific methods are presently being devised. Devices tested in war often find their way into crime fighting. A good example is the sniperscope which employs the use of infra-red rays to sight a target in the darkness. Such devices now can be applied to security and police work in surveillance, as well as the protection of life and property.

A growing scientific technology will someday make the science fiction of today the truth of the future. Devices will utilize heat transfer to determine the presence of a person after he has left the scene.

Neutron Activation Analysis is already a reality in testing various substances. Such a device can be used to track down criminals and bring them to justice.

Research serves as the key to the future development of criminalistics and its expanded use. One of the most pressing needs is for an understanding of the evaluation of physical evidence by scientific technique. The call for an automated fingerprint process is being answered by the FBI as they are conducting research with the assistance of several private firms on methods and techniques of such a process.

Space technology and other scientific advances are constantly opening new vistas to the alliance between the scientist and law enforcement. It is hoped that the expanding technology will give rise to an expanded dimension for the field of criminalistics.

CHAPTER 26

Security Needs Science

Jon Hawington

As society has become more advanced technologically, law enforcement has become more technologically and scientifically oriented. The law enforcement specialist in these areas gained the title of criminalist due to the adaptation of scientific techniques to crime investigation. Meanwhile, security, both proprietary and governmental, has relied upon classic methods except in certain areas such as electronics, alarms, etc.

Esoteric developments in the realm of violations in security are creating a need for a new breed. The newness of many improper and illegal activities that cause losses and damage to property under security control require correspondingly new investigative techniques and tactics. The same situations were encountered in law enforcement during the recent past. Criminal investigations were assisted by the tools and facilities discovered in physical sciences.

While security organizations operated in these modes, law enforcement utilized the criminalist in many varied fields of investigation. The criminalist dealt with investigations ranging from examination of crime scenes to lipstick marks on a white collared shirt. These wide utilizations enhanced the knowledge and abilities of the general investigator in law enforcement.

Educational programs were developed to meet the demands of investigative administrators. These programs reflected on the status of the relatively new type investigator. The institutions utilized educational courses that provided the necessary new information to the student.

To adequately cope with investigative situations, the modern security officer must have access to personnel with specialized training, experience and formal education. The security organization must develop an adjunct for his investigations similar to criminalistics. This adjunct might well be entitled "Securalistics." Studies could be conducted to develop in depth training programs for the securalist.

Securalistics would need properly supervised training in security as well as the specialized scientific techniques modified to fit security needs.

Investigative processes could be improved in security areas as: 1. Detecting falsification of reports and records. 2. Deliberate misuse of property. 3. Solving internal larceny. 4. Fraudulent applications. 5. Public criminal activities against the organization and employees. 6. Criminal activities by employees. 7. Surreptitious entries and industrial espionage. These, and many others, require new assists for successful solvation. Scientific techniques could, in many cases, reduce the number of man hours currently devoted to these investigations.

As an example, scientific sleuthing would greatly assist an examiner of suspected false records. Personnel trained in handwriting examination might exclude many suspects thereby narrowing the field of investigation. Further examination of the records by forensic techniques such as a document examination for erasures or obliteration might yield very crucial information. Analysis of the ink used in the falsification of the document could yield further investigative leads towards the perpetrator. The presence of fingerprints, when properly developed, must be considered as an important tool for the examiner. Instrumental scrutiny should be available for further in-depth penetration by the searchers.

Probably the arena in the security world where the securalist would devote a major part of his time would be in the investigation of internal larcenies. The cost attributed to employee larcenies is impossible to determine exactly, however the problem is well known. As mentioned by Raymond Momiosse in "Industrial Security for Strikes, Riots and Disasters" with respect to theft investigation, "It may be advantageous to institute an undercover operation and surveillance. At other times, because of the nature of the theft, ultraviolet powders, crayons, pastes or inks might be used to identify the culprit."

These statements reflect the need for existing techniques as well as properly trained personnel for implementation. Utilization of powders, crayons and the like would be more effective in the hands of an expert. Selection of the type of powder or technique to be used is extremely critical. Incorrect choice of a powder might reveal to the culprit that an investigation is ensuing. Improperly chosen or used powders would yield erroneous or no information.

Similar examples can be cited for other objects or things involved in a security investigation but not in this short paper. However, a recent court decision has placed a further burden upon the security investigator. The case relates directly to non-law enforcement use of the fingerprint files belonging to the Federal Bureau of Investigation.

In Menard vs. Mitchell, 430 F. 2d 486 (1970), U.S. District Judge Gerhard A. Gesell, handed down an opinion that prohibits the FBI from releasing fingerprint records for non-law enforcement purposes. From this, we find that the FBI can not accept fingerprints for processing if connected with local employment, licensing or other non-criminal activities related to these areas. "Thus the court finds that the bureau is without authority to disseminate arrest records outside the Federal Government for employment, licensing or related purposes."

In essence, there appears to be no exceptions to this new guideline, thereby creating a further need for trained specialists who can operate in these fields. But, where will, or how will these technicians evolve?

The critical lack of educational programs in this area forces a possible suggestive format for study. Prior to, or after, entrance into security work, the prospective student (or administrator) might consider the following course selection:

Fingerprints—Classification and Identification

Arson and Fire Investigation

Chemistry—Basic and Forensic

Biology—Basic Courses

Criminal Investigation

Security Investigation

Securalistics (or Criminalistics)—Selected Courses covering document examination, glass examinations, crime scene examinations, polygraph techniques, detection equipment, and the like.

Other related, particularly relevant to the specialization, courses might be added while deleting the extraneous or unapplicable courses. Courses that would enhance the native ability of the student should be included to form a well-rounded securalist.

Realizing that there are many administrative and economic drawbacks present in this suggestion, the concept must receive some exploration or thought. Industrial, private and public security programs need dependable, reliable, and available facilities for their own self preservation. Each organization would not require a separate functioning securalistic operation, but several organizations might consolidate their efforts to formulate a breakthrough in the area.

CHAPTER 27

A National Criminalistics Research Program

Charles R. Kingston, D.Crim.

Introduction

A large portion of the research funds in the criminal justice area is now administered by the National Institute of Law Enforcement and Criminal Justice under the authority of the Omnibus Crime Control and Safe Streets Act of 1968. A stated purpose of Title I of that act is to "encourage research and development directed toward the improvement of law enforcement and the development of new methods for the prevention and reduction of crime and the detection and apprehension of criminals." Title I authorized the establishment within the Department of Justice of the National Institute of Law Enforcement and Criminal Justice, which has the broad mandate to "encourage research and development to improve and strengthen law enforcement." Criminalistics is among the many facets of law enforcement to which the Institute has directed its attention. This paper presents the first phase of a recommended national criminalistics research program geared to the goals of the Institute as defined by the above named act.

The operational framework to which the research program is directed is shown in Fig. 1. The primary emphasis of the program is on improving the effectiveness of the criminalistics operation, the overall function of which is to "provide scientific support in the overall administration of justice" (1). Since the most active role of the criminalist within present operational settings in the criminal justice system is to provide scientific support for criminal investigations, the first phase of the research program addresses itself to that specific role. In order to maintain a reasonable balance, attention is also given to the related areas of research, education, adjudication, and general criminal investigation insofar as they interact with the criminalistics operation.

244

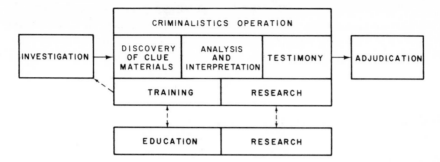

Figure 1. Functional setting of a criminalistics operation.

In its supporting role to the general investigative process, the criminalistics operation provides a means for examining and interpreting physical clue materials when they are present. It makes specific contributions to four major functions of the investigative process, as described here.

1. *Discovery of clue materials:* Some clues obtained in an investigation are physical materials that require expert examination. The criminalistics operation may assist in the finding of physical clue materials by either sending criminalistics personnel out to search for such materials or by training the investigative personnel so that they can recognize and submit those materials that may be potentially useful to the investigation.

2. *Reconstruction of events:* The key to reconstructing the events of an unlawful act (which generally includes demonstrating the elements of the act) may lie often in the examination of clue materials. The criminalist, with his understanding of the physical and chemical properties of such materials, is often in a position to interpret their significance far better than the general investigator.

3. *Development of suspects:* In rare instances, clue materials may be the most direct means of naming one or more particular suspects. More often, the criminalist can provide information based upon these materials that will point the investigator in a general direction or will limit the area or number of persons to which the investigator must give detailed attention.

4. *Demonstration of a positive or negative relationship of a specific suspect to an unlawful act:* Physical materials transferred from the perpetrator of an unlawful act to the victim or the area within which the act occurred, and vice versa, frequently offer the most convincing means of relating a suspect to the act or scene, or of

showing that a person has been incorrectly suspected. The examination and interpretation of these materials, which may be present only in trace amounts, requires the specialized training and equipment associated with the criminalistics operation.

The relationship of criminalistics to the adjudication process is primarily one of providing expert testimony when required. Its relationship to the education process is one of obtaining properly educated personnel and of a constant exchange of ideas and research results. Both relationships have a bearing on the ability of the criminalistics operation to contribute to the investigative process. If the expert's examinations and evaluations are not properly presented at hearings, in court, etc., when this is required, the results of the total investigation are diminished in value. If too much time is required of criminalistics personnel in court, they will have less time for active assistance in ongoing investigations.

The fundamental education a person receives at the university level has a bearing on how he will function in the law–science setting of the criminalistics operation. Research done in universities and research organizations can be of significant value to the criminalistics operation if the university and other research personnel are kept aware of the real problems in the field and if the operating personnel are receptive to new ideas and procedures.

With the overall orientation and the various relationships in mind, the general goals of the proposed research program can be formulated.

General Goals of the Research Program

The research program has two general goals:

1. Provide research results that can be used to make significant improvements in the criminalistics operation's effectiveness in the four investigative functions listed above.

2. Develop a means for measuring the overall contribution of the criminalistics operation to the four investigative functions.

The first goal is general enough to allow for considerable flexibility, yet is keyed to specific functions which can provide guidelines for the selection of research projects. Any aspect of the criminalistics operation that has significance in terms of the four investigative functions is open for consideration. This would include administrative and operational organization, education and training of personnel, technical methods, and so on. The potential benefit of any project can be estimated by considering the potential benefits to each of the four functions.

The second goal will provide an objective basis for determining the role of criminalistics in the investigative process. Feedback information from a record and reporting system that might be developed will be very useful in evaluating and monitoring the research program, and in guiding the selection of future research projects. This information will, in all probability, consist of numbers, perhaps in the form of ratios of the number of cases in which the criminalistics operation produced positive results within each investigative function to the total number of cases investigated or reported. In that case, the trap of relying too heavily on numbers and not enough on common sense (one into which too many systems analysts have fallen) must be avoided. The numbers must serve only as guides, not as directors.

With the guidelines suggested, the next task is to examine briefly the "state of the art" of the role of the criminalistics operation in the four investigative functions.

State of the Art

Each of the four investigative functions will be considered separately and in the same order as presented in the introduction.

1. Discovery of clue materials: There can be little doubt that potential physical evidence goes undiscovered in a large number of criminal investigations. Some reasons for this state of affairs are:

a. The investigators or units assigned to the collection of clue materials may be inadequately trained to know what to search for or how to go about the search for such materials.

b. There may be a general belief among the investigators or evidence technician units that the criminalistics operation cannot provide much help to the investigation even if all physical clue materials were found and brought in for examination. This will cause them to direct their attention to other tasks where they expect to get more positive results. Only the most obvious of the clue materials will usually be collected under these circumstances.

c. The administration of the investigating unit may assign a higher priority to general investigative activities than to the utilization of physical evidence, even though it may realize the value of the latter. Under conditions of a high case load per investigator, time will not be allocated for locating and collecting clue materials other than those that are patently obvious.

For the reasons given above, and occasionally others, a search for clue materials is often made only as a last resort when all else fails to produce any results. At that time many of the materials that were originally present are likely to have been removed or destroyed. It is perhaps fortunate, however, that all available materials are not brought in for examination at the present time. As expressed by Lucas, "If it were, already overloaded criminalists would disappear beneath piles of evidence material never to surface again" (2).

The primary needs in this function appear to be those of: (a) establishing the actual value of the criminalistics operation to an investigation, which may provide better motivation for the collection of physical clue materials; (b) organizing criminalistics operations so that they can handle increasing case loads; and (c) providing for better discovery and collection of clue materials at the time of the original investigation. This would include better training of investigative personnel in that aspect, consideration of increased use of special technical units, and so on. As with any situation where multiple needs are identified, care must be taken not to leap ahead with solutions to one need without adequately considering the others, or an undesirable imbalance in the overall system may be created. For instance, it will be folly to create suddenly a situation where a significant increase in the collection of physical clue materials becomes a reality without a corresponding increase in the capability of the criminalistics laboratory or other units in the criminalistics operations to handle adequately the greater load.

2. Reconstruction of events: This function generally involves the active participation of the criminalist in the investigation, particularly at the scene of a crime or in connection with objects associated with the crime. An example of this is reported by Hoover in a case history of the investigation of an airline crash (3). In the article he states

> . . . scientists were dispatched from the FBI Laboratory to supervise the collection and preservation of evidence and to provide guidance and assistance in other technical aspects of the investigation. . . . The men on the scene coordinated their search with the scientists working around the clock in Washington and with investigators performing other phases of the broad-scale inquiry to reconstruct the series of events leading to the tragedy.

The state of the art here is fairly well tied in with the availability of qualified criminalists who are given the time for such activities. Although such persons are available for local work from federal and state agencies, experience shows that local agencies are not likely to take advantage of this in most instances. A continuous interaction between the criminalists and the investigators seems to provide the setting for the best results.

Thus, the requirements appear to be twofold: (a) an educational process that produces the required number of criminalists (that is, a scientist—who may specialize in analytical chemistry, serology, etc.—who has also been educated in the philosophy and techniques of criminal and general investigation and in the interactions between law and science); and (b) an organizational arrangement that provides the best balance between local availability of criminalists and overall costs for adequate criminalistics services.

3. Development of suspects: This is probably the one area where the contribution of criminalistics to an overall investigation is exceedingly poor compared to what it possibly could be. In part this is due to the frequent procrastination on the part of the investigator in collecting clue materials until after other leads fail to produce results. The most important reason, however, is the lack of adequate methods and data for tracing clue materials back to a limited number of suspects.

It is difficult to pinpoint specific needs with respect to this function since the general philosophy of how one goes about developing suspects from physical clue materials has not been put together in any organized form. Cases where the examination of such materials has been instrumental in identifying or locating a suspect give testimony to the ingenuity of the individual investigators or criminalists rather than to an organized or systematic approach to the problem.

The one possible exception to this is in the case of latent fingerprints, which have been responsible for identifying many suspects that probably would have remained undiscovered otherwise. The basic approach with latent fingerprints is, of course, to search a base file of fingerprints of known persons to see if any compare to the latent, although this process is extremely inefficient with current techniques. A possible direction of research in this general area is to determine whether or not files can be built up from data extracted from a variety of materials that will permit the selection of a limited group of persons or objects through a searching process. Such data files would be complementary to (and not competitive with) organized collections of the materials themselves such as those maintained by the FBI Laboratory in Washington, D. C.

4. Demonstration of a positive or negative relationship of a specific suspect to an unlawful act: This function historically has been the one in which the strongest contribution of criminalistics to the investigative process has been made. The criminalist is able to demonstrate convincing relationships between materials, objects, and persons when certain kinds of pattern configurations are present. Fingerprints and bullet striation comparisons are well-known examples of this. Many other kinds of materials where patterns do not exist can still permit firm negative relationships to be demonstrated but only possible positive relationships. An example of this is a comparison of the blood groups of a dried blood stain with those of a suspect's blood. A primary need here is the ability to draw more definite conclusions from positive comparisons of materials that do not exhibit morphological patterns. That need is a high priority subset of the general need to obtain better knowledge and methods for making both positive and negative comparisons with respect to a large variety of materials that come into the criminalistics operation for examination.

The requirements for satisfying this need are:

a. Research to find out what data can be extracted for comparison purposes from various materials of interest and how to best obtain these data in the operational setting. Those materials that appear most frequently as physical evidence would be given top priority.

b. Research to understand the statistical nature of individualizations and to develop good experimental designs for collecting and analyzing data for that purpose.

c. The development of "data bases of characteristics of materials most often involved in crimes," as suggested in a major report prepared under contract to the Office of Law Enforcement Assistance in 1968 (4.) Although this data base is not the same one envisioned in connection with the previous investigative function, there will probably be many similarities. For many materials, the files may simply contain the same data organized differently for each purpose.

Current Project Areas

The following is a summary of pertinent current and recent project areas for which funds were made available from the National Institute of Law Enforcement and Criminal Justice.

1. Analysis of the criminalistics operation: Two projects were funded in this area. In one project (NI–032, University of California at Berkeley) attention was directed at the kinds and amounts of potential physical evidence that occur at crime scenes. The project is thus directed at the first investigative function of discovering clue materials. By examining the scenes of a large number of crimes, the project participants expect to draw some conclusions about the frequency with which clue materials could be found at crime scenes if they were searched for, and some idea about the distribution of the kinds of materials that would be found. The other project (NI–044, Midwest Research Institute) is directed at a systems analysis of the criminalists operation. One goal is to provide management with the kind of information that is needed to make rational decisions about setting up or expanding criminalisics facilities and oper- atons. The approach taken by MRI is to devise an objective description of the individual tasks performed by a criminalistics operation and form this into a model that can be handled by a computer. The input to the operation that would be necessary for a given locality (e.g., the kinds of materials examined), the output desired by management, and the amount of the funds available for the operation would be fed to the computer as constraints. The computer would then provide calculations from which the best criminalistics operation that fits the constraints could be designed.

2. The analysis of blood traces: Three projects were funded in this area. One project (NH–051, Herbert L. MacDonell and Associates) was directed at the determination of prior events by the interpretation of blood splatters and stain patterns. The second project (NI–042, John Jay College of Criminal Justice) is designed to bring the details of the methods used by Scotland Yard for the identification of subgroups in dried blood by microelectrophoresis over to the United States and to teach these methods to interested and qualified persons in this country. The third project (NI–053, Pittsburgh-Allegheny County Crime Labo- ratory) will develop routine techniques for indentifying numerous spe- cific factors in dried blood beyond the A–B–O groupings.

3. Determination of major and trace elements: Two projects were funded in this area. One project (NI–020 Atomic Energy Commission– Gulf General Atomic) is directed at the collection of adequate data to evaluate the significance of element quantitation by neutron activation analysis for origin determinations. The problem of gunshot residues was given careful attention; further attention is being given to paint chips, paper, and bullet lead. Emphasis is being given to the statistical basis for any conclusions reached. The other project (NI–017, University of Virginia) will compare and evaluate the relative advantages of spark- source mass spectrometry and neutron activation analysis in forensic work.

Proposed Project Areas

A few individuals have reported on the research needs in criminalistics and have suggested a number of projects (2, 4, 5, 6, 7, 8, 9). Each of these reports has been carefully studied for guidance in the selection of the proposed project areas. The criterion for the selection of projects is that a reasonable probability exists that the results of the project will significantly improve the contribution of criminalistics to one or more of the four investigative functions. The areas discussed here are the ones that are initially recommended; a broader scope should, of course, be considered as the overall research program progresses.

Area 1: Development of a management reporting system that will permit the measurement of the involvement and effectiveness of criminalistics in the investigative process.

A management reporting system will provide information needed by management and budget personnel for rational decisions relative to budget allocations, and directions relative to the various components of criminalistics operations. It will also provide feedback information that will be of value in monitoring and evaluating the research program, and in the selection of future research projects.

The first step in the project will be to define exactly what measures of performance and effectiveness are necessary. A minimum requirement for this would be the numbers derived from reportable items indicated in Fig. 2. It is clear that these numbers cannot be obtained through the criminalistics operation alone, and cooperation among all organizations and units involved will be necessary. This suggests that the necessary funds be drawn jointly from those available for criminalistics and those available for general law enforcement improvement, with joint direction and monitoring.

One point should be noted here. Most criminalists recognize their responsibility to determine the true significance of physical clue materials, whether it leads to the conviction of a guilty person or to the release of an innocent person. The criminalistics operation must be neutral; thus, the contributions to demonstrating both guilt and innocence must be considered in any evaluation of the operation. It is somewhat surprising that systems analysts, who would presumably be neutral, seem to become prosecution oriented when examining the contributions of criminalistics and tend to think in terms of the number of convictions only. Rather, it would seem that one innocent person whom the criminalist gets out of the criminal justice system is worth many more points than one guilty person whom the criminalist helps to convict. This must

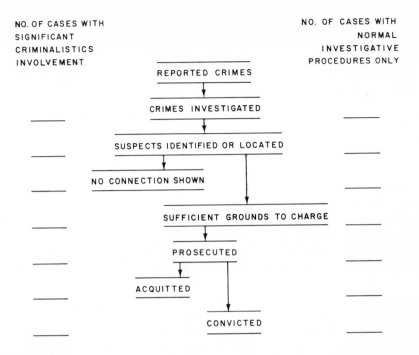

NO. OF CASES WITH
SIGNIFICANT
CRIMINALISTICS
INVOLVEMENT

NO. OF CASES WITH
NORMAL
INVESTIGATIVE
PROCEDURES ONLY

REPORTED CRIMES

CRIMES INVESTIGATED

SUSPECTS IDENTIFIED OR LOCATED

NO CONNECTION SHOWN

SUFFICIENT GROUNDS TO CHARGE

PROSECUTED

ACQUITTED

CONVICTED

Figure 2. Flow chart showing the reporting stages in a record system during an investigation and prosecution.

be taken into account in any evaluation of the criminalistics operation.

The next step is to develop a record system that will accurately provide the desired data and information. Any forms that are designed must be simple and easy to fill out. The entire record system should ideally cut down on the overall record-keeping time while still providing for all management information (e.g., annual report data, etc.). The records should be designed so that they can be used in any jurisdiction in order to obtain consistent data from the various agencies.

In order to have maximum value, the project should involve a commitment on the part of one or more law enforcement agencies to install and use the new record system on a trial basis if a satisfactory one is developed. After a period of use, the records can be analyzed to provide an effectiveness (and possibly a cost) baseline against which improvements in the criminalistics operation can be measured.

Area 2: Testing of candidate criminalistics operations structures that appear to offer the greatest effectiveness within reasonable cost limits.

There are a large number of candidate systems for a criminalistics operation that can be structured from the various kinds of operational units. Seven such operational units can be identified.

Type A—The individual investigator. The investigator's function in this respect is to find the clue materials and transmit them to the criminalistics operation.

Type B—The evidence technician unit. Such a unit would be composed of investigators who have been specifically trained to locate clue materials and transmit them to the laboratory. They may also make simple examinations and interpretations.

Type C—The mobile laboratory. This is a laboratory on wheels that is capable of performing a variety of functions. The mobile personnel may be scientist-investigators who search the crime scene, collect potential evidence materials, and make those examinations that are possible with portable equipment.

Type D—The screening laboratory. This is a laboratory that performs routine functions on high volume materials. Most of this work can be done by well-qualified, trained technicians, and does not require the specialized education and knowledge of the criminalist or scientific specialist, except in a supervisory capacity.

Type E—The crime laboratory. This is a full scale laboratory that is equipped to handle all but the most specialized phases of examining physical materials in criminal investigations. The size will depend on the region to be serviced.

Type F—The public safety laboratory. This is a full scale laboratory that can perform all of the functions of the type E unit, but which also handles similar types of cases in the general area of public safety. One example might be an alleged violation of antipollution laws where physical materials must be examined to determine whether or not the suspected origin of the pollution is the true one.

Type G—The individual specialist. Such individuals would be used on a consulting basis, but are not part of the formal organization of the criminalistics operation.

The range of combinations that are possible go from the large central laboratory to which all investigators send all physical clue materials, to the localized structure where each city, county, etc., has its own crime or public safety laboratory. The major elements to be balanced seem to be the overall costs and the extent of use. The central laboratory would seem to be the least costly, but would probably not be very effective in terms of immediately procuring the materials sent to them. The localized structure would be prohibitively expensive if all services were to be available in the laboratory, but would be the most effective in getting the materials in, provided the laboratory is properly directed. These two extremes represent the "local A–national E" and "local A–local E" configurations. The proper structure probably lies somewhere between these two extremes.

The first task in the project is to identify those configurations that appear to be the most promising from all points of view. Some have been suggested in the literature (10, 11, 12). This is a task in which a systems approach can be extremely useful. The next task is to identify those areas in the United States which have criminalistics operations corresponding to each of the promising configurations. The third task is to encourage the agencies within the selected areas to use the record keeping system that will hopefully be developed in the first program area. The fourth task is to evaluate the effectiveness of the various candidate structures after a period of time using all available information in addition to the data from the record system.

This systematic approach is somewhat idealized and may not be realized in practice due to a number of factors. It should, however, be used as a guide for whatever approach is proposed. It is only through a systematic study of the better structures for criminalistics operations that a logical basis can be made available for rational action in expanding old, or in developing new criminalistics operations. A pure systems study cannot provide the answers at the present time, since such a study requires real data if it is to be anything more than an academic exercise, and the data simply are not available now. A systems study must be combined with the intermediate tasks of implementing and maintaining the necessary record system for getting the required data.

Area 3: Development of an automated single fingerprint processing system.

The development of a system to search a single fingerprint (which includes latent prints) through a large base file of fingerprints would be a major contribution of science and technology to the investigative process. Such a system could be utilized in a number of ways. It has been estimated that latent fingerprints could provide the name of a suspect in about 3% of the reported burglaries (13). This should be compared to the somewhat less than 0.1% of the burglaries for which latent searches provide the names of suspects at present. Three percent may not seem like much, but it would be a significant jump ahead. In 1950, Tamm (then Chief of the Identification Division of the FBI) said:

The setting up and installation of a single fingerprint file is an expensive proposition. We feel that our file paid off in the course of fifteen years. We made fifteen identifications. . . Fifteen identifications in fifteen years and yet the file definitely paid for itself. We solved three of our biggest kidnapping cases by latent fingerprints searched in the file and identified (14).

The searching of scene prints is certainly not the only benefit to be derived from an automated system. With a little thought, many ways of removing the anonymity of the criminal can be devised. Might not a single print be used to make the risk of detection so high in check forgeries that it would become an unprofitable pursuit? What about hitting at the sales end of the burglary business by requiring that persons pawning items leave a single print on the form the pawnbroker keeps, or better, for him to send to the identification unit? In 1948, Dwyer (then an inspector in the Detroit Police Department) reported on such a process. One of the tasks of the Detroit Identification Bureau was:

> Receiving from every pawnshop in the city the descriptive data and right thumb print of every person who pawns property, and checking these prints against prints of suspects in all cases where such items of property prove to be, or we believe may have been stolen. . . . This pawnshop work was added to our other duties in January 1946. That year we made 299 pawnticket identifications; in 1947, 679; and during the first eight months of this year, 518. I think that you will agree that those of you gentlemen present who are engaged in police work in localities where printing of pawnshop customers is not compulsory are indeed working under a handicap (15).

Many benefits of an automated single fingerprint processing system (ASFPS) that are hidden now will undoubtedly come to light once the system is a reality. A plan to bring it to reality has been suggested in a previous publication (16). Two firms (Cornell Aeronautical Laboratory and the Autonetics Division of North American Aviation Inc.) have completed the development of a laboratory device for reading fingerprint minutiae under contract to the Federal Bureau of Investigation. A semiautomated latent fingerprint system that uses minutiae data is being tested by the New York State Identification and Intelligence System (NYSIIS) in Albany, New York.

Ideally the agencies working on the automated fingerprint problem, whether it is the 10-print or latent system, should be working on a formally cooperative basis. Until that happens, an informal exchange of information to avoid duplication of effort is the next best approach. Perhaps each agency can build parts that will eventually fit together to form the whole. In this light the National Institute of Law Enforcement and Criminal Justice should proceed with a project to develop a working semiautomated fingerprint coding station; the design for this station (except for some recent modifications) has been previously described (17). Two or three of these stations would be built and made available for experimentation and operational testing. A primary use of the stations should be to gather data for testing various fingerprint coding schemes; this could be done in conjunction with small operational files similar to that being tested at NYSIIS, and funds should be made available for that purpose.

Consideration should also be given to small projects aimed at devising coding schemes and at developing a better method of taking fingerprints which is economically competitive with the regular inking process.

Area 4: Developing improved methods and procedures for identifying narcotics and dangerous drugs.

The identification of narcotics and dangerous drugs is rapidly becoming one of the most frequent tasks required of crime laboratories. Already many laboratories find themselves falling further and further behind as the case load piles up. There is definitely a need for better and more rapid analytical methods and for better systematic procedures for handling the large case loads. The possibility of automating the identification process to whatever extent is possible needs to be explored. Care must be taken that any automated process is designed to maintain full continuity of the evidence.

Separate projects should be funded to develop improved methods for identifying narcotics and dangerous drugs in whatever form they are seized prior to their use, and for identifying the users of the various drugs, preferably through the analysis of urine samples.

Area 5: Developing data bases of characteristics of materials most often involved in crimes.

This is a project area that is quite broad and will span a period of many years. Specific projects that should be considered initially in this area are listed here.

a. A survey to determine which materials should be given first attention. Once the materials are agreed upon among criminalists as being those that should receive attention, subsequent projects should be considered to find out what data can be extracted for comparison purposes from those materials and whether or not it is worthwhile to set up files based on those data.

b. Research on the statistical nature of individualizations, including the development of appropriate experimental designs for collecting and analyzing data that will be used in the files.

c. Development of a literature reference service that will provide upon request, references of forensic value relative to a given material involved in a case. This service would presumably be computerized, and would probably be maintained by the National Institute.

d. Attention should be given to the development of standard methods of analysis for the purpose of collecting data for the files once specific types of materials have been selected.

Area 6: Evaluating procedures that will cut down on the time spent relative to testimony in court by criminalists. Two projects can be identified in this connection.

a. A study of the use of written depositions in lieu of personal testimony in those situations where thoroughly tested routine analyses are used.

b. A study of the use of closed circuit television for personal testimony in selected situations. This would cut down the travel and waiting time that cuts deeply into the effective time of criminalists.

Conclusions

The specific project areas and projects that have been recommended are, of course, only a few of the many worthwhile ones that could be mentioned. The ones selected for this initial phase of the program are those that hit at the pressing problems that exist now and for which solutions are needed at the earliest possible time. This should not preclude other projects from being considered, including those that search for knowledge (i.e., basic research) as well as those that provide a basis for action (i.e., applied research). A good research program depends upon the quality and interests of the people involved as well as upon the selection of projects. Thus, projects other than those that are specifically mentioned should be funded if they aim at the same general goals and will serve to bring creative individuals into the research program.

The overall direction of this first phase is toward the investigative aspects of law enforcement. Assistance in investigations has historically been the role of the crime laboratory, and it is here that specific goals can be identified. As the research program progresses, however, the goals must be examined more critically in terms of their overall impact upon the public needs as they relate to the criminal justice process. A national criminalistics program must be fully responsive to public needs and policies. This is possible only if criminalists themselves become responsive to those needs and policies. The future of any national research program rests largely in their hands.

REFERENCES

1. KIRK, P. L. and BRADFORD, L. W., *The Crime Laboratory*, p. 6, Charles C Thomas, Springfield, Illinois, 1965.

2. LUCAS, D. M., *Criminalistics—The State of the Art*. Paper presented at the 22nd Annual Meeting of the American Academy of Forensic Sciences, Chicago, Illinois, Feb. 25–28, 1970.

3. HOOVER, J. E., *Science and Technology in Law Enforcement*. Anal. Chem. 34, 23A–32A, 1962.

4. BLUMSTEIN, A., *A National Program of Research, Development, Test, and Evaluation on Law Enforcement and Criminal Justice*, p. 171. Institute for Defense Analyses, Arlington, Virginia, 1968.

5. BRADFORD, L. W., *Criminalistics Looks Forward*. J. Crim. Law, Criminol. and Pol. Sci. 60, 127–130, 1969.

6. NICOL, J. D. and OSTERBURG, J. W., *Working Group Report: Crime Laboratories, Fingerprints, and Physical Evidence*. National Symposium on Science and Criminal Justice, Washington, D.C., June 22–23, 1966, pp. 151–155. (United States Government Printing Office, Washington, D.C., 1966.)

7. NICOL, J. D., *Present Status of Criminalistics*. Law Enforcement Science and Technology I, 245–246. Academic Press, New York, N.Y., 1967.

8. OSTERBURG, J. W., *What Problems Must Criminalistics Solve?* Ibid., pp. 297–303.

9. JOSEPH, A., *A Study of Needs and the Development of Curricula in the Field of Forensic Science*. Law Enforcement Science and Technology II, pp. 349–352. (Port City Press, Inc., 1969).

10. DUBOWSKI, K. M., *Organization of Forensic Chemical Laboratories in Nonmetropolitan Areas*. J. Crim. Law, Criminol. and Pol. Sci. 51, 575–580, 1961.

11. KIRK, P. L. and BRADFORD, L. W., Op. cit., Chap. 4, pp. 22–25.

12. BORKENSTEIN, R. F., *The Administration of a Forensic Science Laboratory*. Curry, A. S. (Ed.). Methods of Forensic Science III, 155–156. Interscience Publishers, New York, N.Y., 1964.

13. Latent Value Study. An unpublished study by the New York State Identification and Intelligence System, Albany, N.Y., 1969.

14. TAMM, Q., Talk reported in the Proceedings of the 35th Annual Conven-

tion of the International Association for Identification, pp. 149–150. July, 1950.

15. DWYER, T. A., Talk reported in the Proceedings of the 33rd Annual Convention of the International Association for Identification, pp. 99–102. Sept., 1948.

16. KINGSTON, C. R., *Research Plan for an Automated Fingerprint Processing System*. New York State Identification and Intelligence System, Albany, N.Y., June, 1968.

17. An Evaluation of Representative Equipment Configurations for Encoding Fingerprints, Semiautomatically. Report submitted to the New York State Identification and Intelligence System by the Electronics Division of General Dynamics, Rochester, New York, 1967.

CHAPTER 28

X-Ray Standards
for Law Enforcement

Charles N. Smith

The National Bureau of Standards (NBS), through its Law Enforcement Standards Laboratory (LESL), is producing voluntary performance standards for purposes of assisting law enforcement agencies in their selection of equipment. The effort by LESL is being funded by the National Institute of Law Enforcement and Criminal Justice of the Law Enforcement Assistance Administration, Department of Justice.

This brief article discusses the performance standards effort in the area of x-ray systems which is being carried out by the Applied Radiation Division of NBS. The standards discussed below apply only to x-ray systems used in investigating inanimate objects which may conceal illegal or dangerous contents. A standard applicable to the scanning of human beings for concealed items is a future possibility.

The user of an x-ray system can obtain information about the contents of a given subject in a nondestructive manner; that is, by using an x-ray system, most containers do not need to be physically opened in order to see what is inside. From a law enforcement point of view, the operator of the x-ray system must be able to recognize illegal and explosive contents from a two-dimensional image.

Subjects

The subjects or items of interest to law enforcement agencies include narcotics, weapons and explosive and incendiary devices. Of these three types, the narcotics are the least detectable by an x-ray system in a given situation because of the low density and variety of shapes. The majority of the weapons, which include knives and firearms, are made from medium- to high-density materials and have recognizable shapes. The

261

explosive and incendiary devices, on the whole, are not as recognizable as are weapons, although this is not the case for the individual components of an explosive device.

Use Modes

There are at least two different use modes for x-ray equipment. One use is on discrete items—that is, where a given item is highly suspected of containing explosive and/or incendiary contents. Requirements for an x-ray system used in this case include high degree of portability and fast, informative results. Users of such equipment are "bomb squad" personnel responsible for handling and disposing of such devices.

Another use mode for x-ray equipment is in screening operations. Such operations can be either routine or emergency in nature. Activities falling into this type of work include the inspection of briefcases and handbags in critical areas of public buildings, e.g., courtrooms, large numbers of packages in a post office, in a transportation system or on a common carrier such as an airline, etc. The low-intensity x-ray equipment in a screening operation is really used as a culling tool. Items which are suspected by the x-ray system operator are weeded out for further inspection. Requirements for such an x-ray system include low exposure to screening operation personnel and no radiation damage to to the items or contents. Development of x-ray systems during the last few years has concentrated heavily on these two aspects.

Because the specifications for the two use modes differ, two separate voluntary performance standards are being produced: X-ray Systems for Discrete Item Applications" and "X-ray Systems for Screening Operations."

Contents of the Standards

Each standard will contain specifications that relate only to the performance of the x-ray system, not to design. Specifications will be included for radiation and general safety, image quality and dependable operation in various environmental conditions. The standard will contain test procedures which are designed to provide guidance in determining if the x-ray system meets the specifications. These test procedures are considered a very necessary part of the standard.

Closing Comment

In determining the users' needs in the field of x-ray systems, one finds many instances where there has been a mismatch between the job to be done and the tools being used. Several years ago only x-ray systems suitable for discrete item work were available; no low-exposure systems for screening operations existed. That is not the case today. The bomb squad personnel have prime responsibility for dealing with explosive devices and have discrete item type x-ray equipment to undertake such work. However, this same group is often called upon to lend assistance on a screening operation. At this point, the mismatch between tool and job occurs. Hopefully, the two standards described above will assist law enforcement officials in selecting the most appropriate x-ray equipment for their particular needs.

CHAPTER 29

Modern Methods Solve Crimes, Foil Crooks

Hair and ballpoint ink evidence remains the nemesis of crime laboratories around the world despite the success of isolated cases, according to Joseph English, director of the Forensic Sciences Laboratories, Georgetown University, Washington, D.C. The university's crime laboratories, along with many others, are the scenes of extensive research in both hair and ballpoint ink analyses. Many of the new advances exciting criminologists are coming from studies on neutron activation analysis of hair and spectrophotometry of ballpoint inks.

Ink investigations, says Mr. English, are handicapped by the proliferation of ballpoint ink pens and inks since 1945. Because ballpoint pens have been used to sign or even write many legal documents, examiners of questioned documents are often called upon to discriminate between visually indistinguishable specimens of ballpoint pen writing. Lawyers, criminologists, and scientists at a recent GU surface analysis symposium heard how document examiners can non-destructively distinguish ballpoint inks on questioned documents, such as fraudulent checks, extortion notes, and wills by using multipurpose spectrophotometers. The symposium, chaired by Mr. English, a former FBI documents expert, was co-sponsored by the American Society for Testing and Materials and the American Bar Association.

Fingerprints. Spectrophotometric analysis of ballpoint ink is supplanting older methods, explains Mr. English. "Until recently, most ballpoint inks were analyzed by paper chromatography, which destroys a section of the document and often does not give adequate resolution of inks in difficult cases." About two years ago, Bette Hamman, a chemist (and blue-belt karate expert), hit upon the idea of applying visible spectrophotometry directly to the ballpoint inks on the documents while working at GU. Using an Aminco-Bowman spectrophotofluorometer to examine 238 ballpoint ink samples on paper, Ms. Hamman obtained a "fingerprint" of the dye components of each sample. She also used thin-layer chromatography (TLC) to separate ink components. (Although a destructive technique, TLC needs less than a centimeter of line from a document to give good resolution of components, whereas paper chromatography requires a larger sample—5 or 6 cm. and even then resolution is usually poor.) TLC plates are automatically scanned spectrophotometrically to determine the proportion of dyes in the ink sample. In addition, chemical tests are frequently applied to the spots to further establish component identity.

Multiple. Ms. Hamman's multiple technique method of analyzing ballpoint inks was quickly snapped up by crime labs and government agencies, which had been stymied by attempts at ink analysis.

The method is not without difficulties since the data from a single-beam instrument could include spectral characteristics of the lamp and background due to the paper (aging or yellowing) which must be subtracted from the total spectrum to reveal the spectrum of the ink. The required spectrum recalculation and replotting may introduce errors.

To eliminate some of these problems, Ms. Hamman uses a Shimadzu MSP-50L multipurpose recording spectrometer distributed by American Instrument Co., Silver Spring, Md. This instrument automatically subtracts the background.

Although Ms. Hamman has already analyzed 76 blue ballpoint inks using both TLC and the Shimadzu, she and Mr. English stress that much more research remains to be done before a data bank of ballpoint ink can be made available to crime laboratories. Future studies include establishing the date of earliest manufacture of inks and determining the effects of aging on inks.

Whereas some progress has been made in nondestructive analysis of inks, forensic scientists complain about the paucity of nondestructive techniques which give statistically meaningful identification of a single hair or hair bundles found at a crime scene. Neutron activation analysis (NAA), a nondestructive technique in that the hair sample remains intact and readings can be repeated, has been applied to studies of soil, drug, and surface evidence in forensics. But it is only recently that statistical methods of reporting NAA data have made NAA hair evidence valuable in crime solving.

Microcosm. Unlike fingerprints, which never change, an individual's hair is a changing microcosm of his total metabolic processes. Although hair contains amino acids, minerals, and biochemical transformations of dietary constituents, measurements of these components are not uniquely individual. The value of NAA hair identification techniques depends on trace element analysis.

Microscopic comparisons of hair, such as those performed in more than 9000 cases this year at the FBI laboratories, reveal only a limited amount of information about the suspect or victim because visual comparisons with the best of microscopes (except for the scanning electron microscope) are somewhat subjective.

"For example," explains an FBI spokesman, "in a hit-and-run accident hair, blood, and paint may be found on the suspect's automobile. These are analyzed and one of our experts might testify in court that the hair morphologically was very similar to that of the victim. This piece of evidence alone is not very convincing but the chain of evidence could be quite strong."

ATOMIC SUPERSLEUTH HELP SOLVE HIT-AND-RUN CASE

In one difficult case, neutron activation analysis was performed on hair bundles taken from the victim's head and from the windshield wiper of a car suspected in a hit-and-run accident:

SAMPLE	TRACE ELEMENTS IN HAIR (PARTS PER MILLION)									
	Na	Cr	Mn	Cu	Zn	Br	Ag	Hg	As	La
A [a]	4340	3.57	0.627	80.7	53.2	2.03	0.107	12.68	none	none
B [b]	4110	4.50	0.583	77.8	37.5	2.06	0.039	11.08	none	none
C [c]	1370	0.31	1.700	132.8	733.0	0.08	0.058	5.34	2.14	0.505

[a] Hair from victim.
[b] Hair from suspect's car.
[c] Hair from randomly selected individual.
Eight elements are present in similar amounts in hair samples A and B. The probability of a random match of two unrelated samples with the characteristics of A and B is less than 1 in 3,710,000. This small probability removed the question of "reasonable doubt" from the jury's mind on the identity of the hair.

With the help of NAA, a hit-and-run case can be handled quite differently, as noted by Dr. Robert E. Jervis (University of Toronto, Canada), a pioneer in the field of NAA:

"Hair found on the suspect's car is divided into two samples. One half of the sample is washed with ether to remove external contaminants, which are also analyzed. We send the washed and unwashed samples to the nuclear reactor with standards where they are continuously bombarded with neutrons for two days.

"After bombardment has stopped, we take gamma ray spectra of the strands at various time intervals. We feed the spectral data into a computer and out comes our list of elements in the hair. The computer program also computes the absolute concentration of elements in the hair by reference to a library of standard spectra."

Probabilities.   Testimony in court, Dr. Jervis continues, might then consist of the probability of a chance coincidence between the concentration values of the victim's hair and the hair from the suspect's car being present in two different individuals (see Table).

This simplistic scenario belies the years of research it took to make hair NAA a working proposition for criminologists, lawyers, and judges. The general acceptance of NAA evidence in the courtroom is largely a consequence of the detailed studies on human hair carried out by Dr. Jervis and a former student of his, Dr. Auseklis K. Perkons, now a research scientist at the Center of Forensic Sciences, Toronto. More recently, new and confirmatory work has come from Ronald Coleman, of the United Kingdom Atomic Weapons Research Establishment, Aldermaston, England.

Dr. Perkons and Dr. Jervis have irradiated more than 1500 hair samples collected from some 1000 people distributed randomly in Canada, the United States, Europe, and Asia. Using a thermal neutron flux of 1.2 to 1.8×10^{13} neutrons per sq. cm.-second at the MacMaster University nuclear reactor in Hamilton, they analyzed bundles of hairs (10 to 20 strands) for 20 trace elements. Most of the gamma ray spectra were taken using a thallium-activated sodium iodide crystal with a Victoreen 400-channel pulse height analyzer (PHA). In recent work, Dr. Perkons has used a high-resolution germanium lithium detector and a 4096-channel PHA to measure 25 elements in hair bundles and up to 15 elements in single hairs.

Complex.   But the analyses are plagued with many problems. For example, Mr. Coleman found that hairs from different parts of the same head differ slightly in composition and with time. The complexity of gamma ray spectra may lead some investigators to wrongly identify and mislabel peaks. "A perfect example of this," says Dr. Perkons, "is the confusion of a backscatter peak in the spectrum with an isotope of germanium occurring in our own early work."

The misrepresentation and misuse of the NAA technique resulting from some of these problems is responsible for the lack of confidence in the technique expressed by many crime labs. An FBI spokesman says that NAA has tremendous potential, but many "so-called experts offer identification of a single hair sample based on qualitative comparison of a few peaks or even the mere presence or absence of a particular element in the hair."

In spite of these occasional problems, NAA hair evidence has been offered and accepted in 12 cases in Canada, 10 in England, and five in the United States. Coupled with miscroscopic examination and more sensitive detectors, NAA offers enormous potential for the characterization of a single hair.

Index